John C. O'Neill

John C. O'Neill

*The Irish Nationalist
and U.S. Army Officer
Who Invaded Canada*

THOMAS FOX

Foreword by Michael P. Ruddy

McFarland & Company, Inc., Publishers
Jefferson, North Carolina

ISBN (print) 978-0-7864-9793-5
ISBN (ebook) 978-1-4766-3675-7

LIBRARY OF CONGRESS AND BRITISH LIBRARY
CATALOGUING DATA ARE AVAILABLE

Front cover image: desperate charge of the Fenians (left side),
under Colonel O'Neill, near Ridgeway Station, June 2, 1866,
and total rout of the British troops (right side), including the Queen's
Own Regiment under command of Col. Booker (Library of Congress)

Printed in the United States of America

McFarland & Company, Inc., Publishers
Box 611, Jefferson, North Carolina 28640
www.mcfarlandpub.com

In memory of Patrick and Jennie (McGregor) O'Connor,
my great-grandparents—natives of Dunglady,
County Derry, and like John O'Neill,
Ulster emigrants to Elizabeth, New Jersey.

Table of Contents

Foreword
by Michael P. Ruddy

Driven by poverty and famine, a flood of mostly poor Roman Catholic Irish emigrants arrived in America in the mid–1800s. These emigrants provided the embryo of a process from which emerged the present-day Republic of Ireland. In the 1850s and the decades that followed, among these new Irish Americans, some of whom were exiled by Great Britain for their nationalist connections or activities, leaders appeared. Men of strong nationalistic will who began to organize clubs and societies among the Irish American immigrant communities, signing up members who wanted to bring about an end to British rule in Ireland. Some of these clubs had their members enlist in state militias to gain military training in hopes of returning to Ireland to join their brethren in a fight for Irish freedom. These often secret societies began to merge with each other into loosely-run organizations. The plan was to wait for an opportunity to catch Britain at a time when she was involved in a foreign war. They reasoned that such an event would place the British Army in a weak military position, unable to respond with force in the event of an Irish rebellion. Into this vacuum came one such man, County Monaghan—born John O'Neill.

The largest of these military societies was the Fenian Brotherhood. The Brotherhood, with each member paying a small monthly subscription, spread out across America. Many of the Fenian Brotherhood torchbearers were exiles forced to leave Ireland after an unsuccessful rebellion that had occurred in Ireland in 1848. The Fenian Brotherhood clubs sent delegates to yearly assemblies throughout the United States. In the first of these conventions a constitution was adopted that governed the activities of affiliated clubs called "circles" that were multiplying in many urban centers across the country and Canada where there were large Irish American communities. The funds they collected from members allowed them to begin to accumulate the arms and provisions with which to outfit an armada to sail to Ireland. The Fenian

Brotherhood began to train members for that moment. At peak tens of thousands of members were involved in this process.

The Fenian Brotherhood initially made an ineffective attempt to foment a rebellion in Ireland in 1865. This uncoordinated attempt failed and those involved were locked up in British prisons. When the American Civil War ended, thousands of armed Irishmen were released, many of whom were members of the Fenian Brotherhood and had taken part on both the North and South sides. At this point the Fenian Brotherhood split into two factions. One faction, under Fenian Brotherhood president John O'Mahony, wanted to follow the original plan to build an army of liberation, sail to Ireland, and begin an island-wide rebellion. Because of the failure of their first venture, it was obvious that it would take time to rebuild the infrastructure in Ireland for such an event. The other faction, the so-called "Men of Action," wanted to put to immediate use the arms already accumulated in a plan to force the United States into an annexation of Canada. They believed that a successful attack by the Fenian Brotherhood into Canada would cause the United States to lend them support. Once a Fenian Brotherhood outpost in Canada was established the Brotherhood's hope was that the United States would annex Canada. It was expected by the Fenians that the annexation of Canada would cause the United States government to take up the cause of Irish America and demand an end to British rule in Ireland.

The turmoil resulting from the Fenian Brotherhood breaking up into factions was a series of disjointed attacks against the British in Canada. The Canadian annexation faction, the "Men of Action," of which John O'Neill was one, gained a major portion of the membership thereby draining many dues paid by members of the O'Mahony faction. The O'Mahony faction, losing its status as the spokesperson for Irish American nationalism and facing its dwindling membership rolls, felt the only solution was to make their own move on Canada.

The Canadian annexation group, encouraged by some mixed signals from Washington, D.C., including the president and several of his cabinet, were convinced the U.S. government would allow them the time to cross into Canada. On June 2, 1866, the Fenians made a more formidable attack across the Canadian border near Buffalo, New York.

The leader of the only actual crossing from Buffalo to Fort Erie in Canada was John Charles O'Neill, an Irish-born Civil War hero stationed in Nashville, Tennessee. O'Neill defeated a British contingent at the Battle of Ridgeway. O'Neill was forced to retreat back across the border after a glorious two days when the United States cut off his supplies and arrested his reinforcements, but the defeat of the British at Ridgeway made O'Neill a hero. He was called the first Irishman to lead an Irish defeat of the British and soon was promoted first to the military general of the Fenian Brotherhood forces and then the president of the entire organization. Later O'Neill led two more small attacks in 1870 and 1871 across the border, both without the Fenian Brotherhood's approval and both failures. From his sudden rise in June of 1866 until his death twelve years later, John O'Neill was an Irish American celebrity, both loved and loathed.

So far very little has been written about John O'Neill and most of the information on hand was written by those who read reports based on what O'Neill told reporters or by those who knew him as a Fenian general. The present book is unique in that it provides the reader with a detailed and thoroughly researched account of the life of this man who played such an important role in United States and Canadian history.

John C. O'Neill: Union Army Officer, Irish Republican Raider of Canada by Tom Fox is an examination of the life of John Charles O'Neill that brings us an in-depth look at the man who personified the Fenian Brotherhood attacks on Canada in the 1860s and 1870s. In too many instances biographies of famous men spend a lot of time on published information available on their subject, effectively only publishing a recapitulation of what is already known. Readers of Tom Fox's biography of John Charles O'Neill, on the contrary, will find that while Fox provides an excellent account of General O'Neill's actions on behalf of Irish American nationalism, most of the book is dedicated to providing information hitherto unknown about the character and personal life of O'Neill.

Without this book, those interested in O'Neill's life are only likely to encounter what O'Neill told reporters at various times during his life in the public eye during the period of Fenian activity in the years 1850–1880. Fox has done a remarkable job going beyond the public pronouncements of his subject, ferreting out information which allows us to perceive John Charles O'Neill as the man he was, not the image that O'Neill wanted us to see.

From his childhood and family ancestry in County Monaghan to his death in Omaha, the book follows in detail the life of John O'Neill who, with the possible exception of John O'Mahony, typifies the essence of the Fenian Brotherhood movement. Uncovered are the extant records available in County Monaghan added to extensive interviews of O'Neill's living ancestors. Fox lays before us a treasure trove of documents discovered across three continents in addition to O'Neill family papers previously unavailable that flesh out the early life of O'Neill and later the intimate parts of his personal life until his lonely death in Omaha, Nebraska. With this information in our hands we are able to gain an insight into what the man behind the larger-than-life general of the Fenian Brotherhood was like in reality.

O'Neill is a major figure in Irish American history, but the general also played an important part in actions that altered the paths of both United States and Canadian history. Where the politics of those times might have taken the British Colonies on our northern border without the Fenian raids is anyone's guess, but what is sure is that Fenian General John Charles O'Neill at the head of three Canadian invasions was a deciding factor in the actions that led to the formation of the modern nation of Canada.

Three short years after his Fenian career seemingly ended, O'Neill switched course and made a second celebratory career as a colonizer of the Irish in Nebraska before dying at the early age of thirty-nine. Anyone interested in the rise and fall of General John O'Neill's life in the Fenian Brotherhood movement or in John O'Neill the land developer, who played an important part in the formation of Irish American farming communities in Nebraska, will find Fox fills in what has been to this point missing in the published articles and accounts—and the answer to why there is a town named O'Neill in Holt County, Nebraska.

Michael P. Ruddy specializes in the history of the American Fenian movement of the mid–1800s. He has a degree in history from the University of California Santa Barbara.

Preface

Historians, no matter their training, never work alone, and collaboration is never to be underestimated, always to be appreciated. Thus it was with the story of John O'Neill. The genesis began as a simple genealogical search. After decades of studying U.S. Federal census records, I came across the 1870 census for Laurence Fox, my great-great grandfather, in Elizabeth, New Jersey. I was shocked to see an asterisk next to his neighbor, Catherine O'Neill. In years of such early searches I had never seen such a mark, and at the bottom of the page the asterisk defined her as "General O'Neill's mother."

I was stunned, having never heard of a General O'Neill, much less realized his mother lived next door to emigrant Foxes. That moment in 2009 began the search for the mind and heart of Irish revolutionary John Charles O'Neill. Cursory studies showed minor biographical mentions, but no major studies, despite the fact that the Fenian had been a formidable historical force in mid–nineteenth century nationalist Irish America. Speaking to dozens of Irish American audiences throughout the East showed the overwhelming majority had never heard of John O'Neill or any invasion attempts from U.S. soil into Canada. It would no doubt surprise, if not shock, most Americans to discover that an American-based military force numbering in the tens of thousands prepared to invade Canada not once but twice! Added to the shock is the commander of these two "invasions" was an American Civil War hero who for almost a decade was the most famous Irish American personality in the country.

O'Neill was a Famine emigrant of eleven years, a dissociative personality whose early life was a panoramic study of American success, failure, and redemption. Following a proud career as a Civil War officer in Indiana and beyond, O'Neill unwittingly but energetically stepped into history as the man who led 1,000 or so Irish and Irish Americans on an invasion of Canada from Buffalo in 1866. Returning a national hero, local praise soon became nationwide and O'Neill was raised to the presidency of the 50,000-member secret organization known as the Fenian Brotherhood at the incredibly early age of thirty.

General John Charles O'Neill was a friend of President Andrew Johnson; a U.S. Army deserter who became a courageous and respected officer in the Civil War; and the commander and president of a secret organization allowed by the United States government to legally raise funds, train, and arm. His charisma, despite meager education, could dazzle large crowds with eloquence in two languages and his meteoric rise was equaled only by his sudden fall from grace, yet O'Neill has become a forlorn and forgotten man in American history. Even after his personal plummet, O'Neill remained a most popular national figure as a leader in the vanguard of Irish settlement in the Midwest, and the town he founded, O'Neill, is still considered the Irish capital of Nebraska.

Ego, pride, Irish nationalistic fervor, and a love of America but long-burning desire for a free Ireland all combined to a precipitous downfall, often orchestrated by a scurrilous British spy, and ended with imprisonment in Vermont. Pardoned by President Ulysses Grant, O'Neill soon reinvented himself as an early Irish proponent of colonizing Nebraska before dying at the early age of thirty-nine. The O'Neill story, never before fleshed out in detail, shows Irish America in all its glory, a tale to be told.

All of this and more was accomplished before dying in 1878 of complications from a stroke at age 39, alone in an Omaha hospital. A prime player in late nineteenth-century American and Canadian life, his death was reported nationally and his funeral was a dignified farewell to a fallen prince. O'Neill was, however, soon forgotten as Americans moved on emotionally from the throes of war and reconstruction and then physically moved westward even further than O'Neill himself ever envisaged. It would be almost a half-century before the exploits of this fallen American immigrant would be resuscitated, albeit briefly, when the future president of Ireland, Éamon de Valera, would unveil a monument in Omaha to General John C. O'Neill in 1919. But O'Neill would remain buried in Omaha, one of the few places in America he never lived.

There has been no definitive biography of the nineteenth century John Charles O'Neill, though numerous newspaper and periodicals, especially in the mid–nineteenth century, portrayed the general's career piecemeal. The early articles were often written with direct assistance from O'Neill himself, thus allowing for inaccuracies that have never been challenged.

After the general's death in 1878, scant further information appeared until the unveiling of his monument in a cemetery in Omaha in 1919, and then only from a published speech anointing the County Monaghan-born O'Neill but filled with inaccuracies. As time has gone on, O'Neill has passed into legend, much like the gunfighters of the old West, whose histories are filled with exaggeration and untruths.

Though the arrival of the Internet has allowed the story of John O'Neill to remain alive, inaccuracies and misinformation have often been repeated and are now accepted as fact. In 1937, Sister Mary M. Langan wrote the first dissertation on O'Neill and, though leaning toward a very Catholic public relations view of the man, was helped by input from the O'Neill grandchildren, who provided some valuable yet incomplete information on O'Neill and his family.

Many articles have reported on specific aspects of this Irishman's life, in particular his time with the Fenians from 1866 until 1868 (this is the best history of the general thus published); others have focused on the Nebraskan era of his life (1874–78) while some more recent views have been put forth by Irish nationalists claiming O'Neill was one of the greatest Irish freedom fighters since the Famine of the mid-nineteenth century—an exaggerated view at best.

In 2011 I was fortunate to meet an American whose interests matched my own. Kate McKenna of Washington, D.C., had once driven cross-country to Nebraska and California with the idea of telling the unknown story of General John O'Neill. She had it right, but life, as it often does, got in the way, and O'Neill was placed on Kate's back burner. Picking the story up again in 2011 Kate and I crisscrossed through Fenian websites led by the wonderful Fenian expert Mike Ruddy of Tennessee. Two years of sporadic lunches with Kate saw us pursuing the dream of introducing the forgotten story of John O'Neill to both America and Ireland. Kate soon became the Editorial and Multimedia Director of the Special Olympics and pushed the project to me.

With Mike Ruddy as a mentor to the Fenian world, I began searching for the early O'Neill. Brief biographies in America, Canada, and Ireland often seemed contradictory, but a search from Ireland soon led to research in New Jersey, Canada, Australia, Nebraska, Washington, D.C., and California, with results confirming a much more complex individual than simply a minor figure in Irish American nationalism. The O'Neill family, sequestered permanently in the San Diego area since 1885, was vigilant in their protection of the general's reputation, and eventually placed their trust with all O'Neill papers and correspondence in the study. My gratitude for allowing me this access has only made the unfolding of John O'Neill's life more honest.

The history books have not been especially kind to either the Fenians or Irish American nationalists of the nineteenth century, and much of their disdain has been shown in the life of John O'Neill. The anti–Fenian bias has extended even into twentieth-century Ireland. On the government-sponsored television network, RTE, a history of the Brotherhood movement shown in 1967 portrayed O'Neill as "dying in the gutter," a grossly untrue statement.

Nonetheless, the cult-like study of the Fenian attack at Ridgeway across the Niagara River in June 1866 has developed its own following, despite the

fact that little has been unearthed about the life of O'Neill, its main protag-
onist. Work at the National Archives in Washington, D.C., revealed the early
O'Neill as a young dragoon and later a Civil War stalwart. The Mormon War
and his desertion and life in San Francisco prior to the Civil War was
enhanced with the assistance of Tom Carey of the San Francisco History Center Public Library and Christine Doane, the archivist of the Sisters of Pres-
entation, also in San Francisco. Both were invaluable resources as to the early
life of O'Neill and his Australian-born wife, Mary Ann Crow.

Working further westward, Anne Copeland, librarian at the State Library
of Victoria, Nina Gosford and David Berg of the New South Wales library
system, and Emma Stockburn of the Parramatta Heritage Center in New South
Wales were all particularly helpful to the life and times of the Crow family
in Australia.

In Ireland, Anna McHugh of Headford, County Galway, who has always
been generous with Irish sources, facilitated me especially in the transportation of Irish convicts in the early nineteenth century. The study of the Fenians
in the Irish Biographical Dictionary and interviews with the renowned Derek
Warfield of the Wolf Tones added to the mystique of John O'Neill. Unveiling
the O'Neill story during and after the Civil War, the Milstein Division of U.S.
History at the New York Public Library is any historian's dream, and for the
Fenians in particular, the Fahey Memorial Library at Villanova is a treasure.
O'Neill's important stay in Nashville was helped by the Nashville Public
Library.

In Canada, Peter Vronsky and David A. Wilson of Toronto provided
much guidance from the Canadian perspective; Vronsky a leader on the isolated Battle of Ridgeway and Wilson the preeminent expert of Fenianism in
Canada and beyond. The University of Toronto Library provided a gem with
the long-forgotten handwritten notes on a planned biography of O'Neill by
the esteemed late Canadian historian C.P. Stacey. Stacey died before he was
able to establish his work, but had planned on titling it "A Fenian Paladin—
The Life of John O'Neill."

Back in New Jersey, Bette Epstein of the New Jersey State Archives
remains a researcher's best friend; further work was found in the Rutgers
University Library in New Brunswick, in addition to local information in
Elizabeth, New Jersey, at the Hall of Records and at St. Mary R.C. Church
Records. Special thanks to Jude Digidio, Vince Perella of Sparta, and Joe Bilby
of Wall, New Jersey, each of whom provided constant encouragement.

The most maligned and least understood period of O'Neill's life was his
time as a Nebraska colonizer, perhaps his greatest legacy. Assistance was
found everywhere in the Midwest, starting with Michele Reicks of the St.
Boniface Parish in Elgin, Nebraska; Becky Cemper at the O'Neill Public
Library; Andrea Faling of the Nebraska State Historical Society; Justin Davis

of the Indiana State Library; the Allen County librarians in Fort Wayne, Indiana; and especially Kathy Manoucheri of Holt County Historical Society.

David Emmons and Kirby Miller, whose studies of the emigrant Irish in America are standard works, provided guidance known and unknown, and Emmons especially perused the work on O'Neill with keen insight. With dogged pursuit, Linda and Virgil Berney of Nebraska flushed out the complex O'Neill finances, traversing for months the labyrinth records as accountant sleuths throughout small towns in northwest Nebraska relating to O'Neill, digging out information beyond the norm with their pleasant personalities. The guidance of David Emmons and Linda Berney in particular enabled me to gain a final and full examination of the Irish revolutionary, with proof of O'Neill's legacy as a committed colonizer of downtrodden Irish. Though he may be remembered fondly as an often misguided, perplexing personality with revolutionary aims, the totality of his life shows great character.

The O'Neill family in America no longer exists under that name, but the blood of John O'Neill remains strong in San Diego with the Martin family, its matriarch Sister Kathleen Martin, CSJ, and Meyling Eliash-Daneshfar, CSJ Director of Communications. Their kindness and sharing of papers collected over more than 125 years has given me a much more balanced view of John O'Neill of Drumgallan, County Monaghan. O'Neill, like all leaders, left behind scars, but there remains little doubt of his passionate love of two countries. May all writers be blessed with the support I have received from three continents and a home hearth centered in New Jersey. All mistakes, of course, are my own.

The prolonged search for the life of John O'Neill owes a central debt and love to my wife, Nancy Fox, whose loyalty and compassion equals that of the heroine of this story, Mary Ann Crow. As with Mary Ann, a debt that can never be repaid.

Introduction

Between 1845 and 1851 Ireland experienced the last major famine in Western Europe. This cataclysm reduced a population from eight million to approximately five million, and more than a million found their way to the shores of America. This exodus helped propel hundreds of thousands with a hatred of English rule toward freedom at home.

Organizations calling for change had been a permanent staple of Irish life since 1798, but all insurgencies were crushed before becoming major factors. Emigrant nationalists forced by hunger to flee to the United States soon formed a secret society known as the Fenian Brotherhood with the aim of freeing the homeland by military means. With the American Civil War providing ample opportunities for such a plan, the Fenian organization grew rapidly. American politicians, grateful for the burgeoning Irish vote, in addition to the needed manpower during the war, gave great latitude of movement.

Recruiting occurred throughout the Confederate and Union armies, sometimes with a wink, and often openly. It has been estimated that by war's end the Fenian Brotherhood membership numbered more than 50,000, and could be found in every state. The aim—freedom for Ireland—saw its momentum in the United States accelerated by three simultaneous factors— the mass migration of a clannish and outcast population, the effect of the newly created Irish vote, and the training and experience of more than 100,000 Irish and first-generation Irish Americans during the Civil War. Once the war concluded, relations between the U.S. and England became so strained by English assistance with the Confederate effort, the Fenians believed the time had come to begin a revolution.

As money poured in from 1864 to 1866, two factions of action developed. The first failed when money and trained military men were sent to Ireland. Military movement and logistics were hampered by distance, and the native population was still reeling from the effects of the Famine. Soon the majority of the Brotherhood became convinced that an attack on Canada would be the best opportunity, forcing Britain to defend the Dominion with small forces and opening the way for armed action back home. Though difficult to imagine today, it was indeed opportune for the Irish. Within a year of Abraham Lincoln's death, the Fenians had, with government consent, established a headquarters in New York City that flew their own flag, purchased thousands of arms and ammunition from federal depots, and openly trained men in uniform.

Following a national and not very secretive convention, the Brotherhood announced plans for a three-pronged attack against Canada in the spring of 1866. Led by famed Union General Tom Sweeny and with a staff of three dozen highly ranked ex–Union and Confederate officers, the plan called for almost 25,000 men to cross into Canada from Chicago/Detroit, Cleveland/ Buffalo, and, on the east, Vermont. From a military viewpoint the plan was feasible, but it soon became a fiasco as men were late or failed to show, logistics were mishandled, and presumed American government approval proved false.

Into this quagmire stepped one man, a former Union Cavalry leader, John Charles O'Neill. Born in County Monaghan, Ireland, O'Neill eventually found his way at eleven years old, in the midst of the Famine, to Elizabeth, New Jersey, joining his mother and sister. A restless spirit, he ran a bookstore in Richmond at age seventeen; joined the U.S. Army as an underage teenager in Baltimore, finding his way to Utah as a member of the government forces contending with the Mormon uprising; deserted the Army and fled to San Francisco; rejoined the Army just prior to the Civil War; and became a heralded leader of the 5th Indiana Cavalry.

In 1865, following the war, the popular O'Neill was living in Nashville with a young wife and baby son, running a successful claims agency with a fervent hatred of England and its hold on Ireland. Joining the Fenians, O'Neill was named a colonel of the Nashville regiment and found himself in Buffalo. As the planned invasion seemed to fall apart, O'Neill led 800 men into Canada under cover of darkness on June 1, where his forces for two days startled the entire Dominion of Canada, winning a minor engagement known as the Battle of Ridgeway before retreating and being arrested by U.S. naval forces. Though the invasion was a failure, Ridgeway and O'Neill's leadership were an inspiration to all Irish American nationalists, and the young O'Neill, not yet thirty, soon became the face of the Fenian Brotherhood, and a heralded and prominent figure across the land.

With all Fenians involved granted a pardon for their involvement, John O'Neill, now recognized as General O'Neill, rose rapidly in the Brotherhood's administration, becoming president in 1868 and promising to continue the fight against England with another invasion of Canada. O'Neill's Fenian career was nothing short of meteoric. Though believed to be thirty-three while in command at Ridgeway, he had just turned twenty-eight, and was thirty when elevated to the Fenian presidency.

While in office for just two years, his brief term was marked by brashness tending to arrogance and a demand for total loyalty from fellow Irish nationalists. In 1870, as promised, he led a second attempt against Canada in Vermont, but was arrested, tried, convicted, and sentenced to two years in prison before being granted a pardon by President Grant after six months. After 1870, and with many Irish Americans losing their taste for revenge against England and settling into life as Americans, the Fenian Brotherhood faded away as just another Irish attempt at freedom falling along the wayside. O'Neill, now broken with the Brotherhood, would not accept this softening philosophy and embarked on one more attempt on Canada. He led three dozen men in North Dakota in a bizarre attack before being arrested again by U.S. forces. Not a shot was fired, and General O'Neill was eventually released when it was discovered he and his men never actually reached Canadian territory.

Forced by circumstance, the still-honored hero of Ridgeway turned the corner and began a second career as a proponent of Irish colonization in Nebraska. His sound argument for the Irish to abandon the mines and ghettos of the cities for a better life on the prairie was echoed by many, including Bishop John Ireland of Minnesota, but the national depression of the mid 1870s made it difficult despite his well-traveled urging. The ever-optimistic O'Neill worked feverishly for five years, abandoning publicly his urge to fight the British, and finally established an Irish enclave in what is now O'Neill, Nebraska, before dying of a stroke at age thirty-nine in Omaha.

O'Neill was a friend of two American presidents, Andrew Johnson and Grover Cleveland, and well known by a third, Ulysses S. Grant. A devout Catholic in an organization condemned by the Church, John O'Neill could never let go of his hatred of English rule in Ireland. After he died in 1878, he was remembered as one of the leading Irish nationalists in the country. Even though the invasions led by the strident O'Neill were considered a failure, Irish American nationalism showed resiliency and less than forty-five years later would be one of the progenitors of Irish freedom in the 1916 Uprising.

Like many Irish nationalist leaders, O'Neill was flawed but accomplished, though his story has never been told until now. In 2016 a major conference on the 150th anniversary of the Battle of Ridgeway convened in Buffalo. Canadian, American, and Irish historians met for two days, but not one topic discussed covered the life of Colonel—later General—John Charles O'Neill, the most important player in the attack.

1

Maimed from the Start

Born to the harsh uncertainties of Ulster, where a spade's a bloody shovel and you need to know what foot to put to it.—Victor Price

He was born in Ireland and died in Nebraska, but John Charles O'Neill was perhaps the most famous Irishman ever to call New Jersey home. O'Neill was a celebrity, a pop star whose different careers over two decades are reason to be studied, but today is largely forgotten, misunderstood, or, most often, unknown.

Dying tragically young of a stroke, O'Neill served in the Union Army during the Civil War, rising from an enlisted cavalryman to captain; from an Army deserter to a man beloved as an Irish hero; a military opportunist who would lead not one but three invasions into Canada for the cause of Irish freedom; and ultimately as a proselytizer of colonization of Irish downtrodden immigrants to Nebraska, where the town of O'Neill, Nebraska, would be named in his honor.

John O'Neill possessed all the qualities of a modern star. Strong, darkly handsome, and charming, he captivated people with a rich, sonorous voice. This adopted son of New Jersey was compulsive and ambitious, yet inspired loyalty in thousands. One newspaper said O'Neill "was of calm temperament, but with a firm will, and when excited was stern."[1] As with many celebrities, however, he sometimes appeared arrogant, unbending, and even manipulative. At the end he let alcohol get in the way. But the O'Neill story is compelling, and like William Grace and John MacKay, other nineteenth-century immigrants whose American success occurred after very improbable beginnings in rural Ireland, John O'Neill's story is a novelist's dream.

Conventional history lists John, never "Jack," as being born March 8, 1834, to a grieving widow in Drumgallan townland, near Clontibret in County Monaghan, and named after his dead father. Catherine (née Macklin) O'Neill's husband John had gone to assist some neighbors on the Monaghan/Armagh border, with cholera once again rampant in the Northern Ireland province of Ulster, only to succumb himself just weeks before Catherine gave birth to her fourth child at age thirty-three. Cholera and typhus were twin disasters and caused panic in Ireland, especially in rural areas.

The French sociologist Gustave de Beaumont visited Ireland the very year John O'Neill Senior died, and commented that the Indians in the American hinterlands and the African Americans in their chains may be better off than the entire nation of Irish paupers under English domination.

William Carleton, born and raised in nearby Tyrone, and the most famous Irish historical fiction writer of the early nineteenth century, described the rural effects in his book, *The Black Prophet.*

> The dreadful typhus, was now abroad in all its deadly power, accompanied, as it always is among the Irish, by a panic, which invested it with tenfold terrors. The moment fever was ascertained, or even supposed, to visit a family, that moment the infected persons were avoided by their neighbors and friends as if they carried death, as they often did, about them, so that its presence occasioned all the usual interchanges of civility and good neighborhood to be discontinued.[2]

There was no good time in Ireland to be a young widow with three children. Catherine moved four-year-old Bernard, two-year-old Mary, and baby John O'Neill to her parents', George and Mary Macklin, house in nearby Fintully townland, five miles away from the O'Neill home in Drumgallan, though still within the boundary of Clontibret Parish.

Townlands were the smallest and most ancient divisions of land in Ireland; many had names of Gaelic origins dating back centuries, even to pagan times. In the entire island of Ireland, there remain some 60,000 townlands, some as small as an acre, others approaching 8,000 acres. Both Fintully (*Fionn tulaigh,* "the fair hill") and Drumgallan (*Droim Gallain,* "the ridge of the standing stones") were less than two hundred acres and lay within minutes of the western border of County Armagh. Then and now, the country is out in the countryside, far from a city or tourist area.[3]

Catherine, who had lost a son, Eugene, in infancy, would lean on her family and remain near them the rest of her widowed life, both in Ireland and America, with one notable exception.

By 1840, when she was thirty-five, Catherine and her younger brother John Macklin left this exceedingly tense land and settled in Elizabeth, New Jersey, five years before famine would strike the island and decimate its 8.5 million people by half; war, starvation, and emigration would all contribute.

In 1843, according to John O'Neill later in life, his brother Bernard and sister Mary joined their mother and settled into life in Elizabeth. O'Neill told his biographers that he stayed with his paternal grandfather who educated him in the Irish nationalist tradition, hating England and emphasizing the wrongs done to the Irish for centuries. In 1848 he said he arrived in Elizabeth at fourteen, went to school for one year, worked three years at the family grocery store, then struck out on his own at eighteen. This personal history, once printed, has been perpetuated as dogma for more than 150 years. The truth, as is often the case, is much more revealing of the character of John O'Neill.[4]

Recent research has found that John C. O'Neill was indeed born in tiny Drumgallan on the eastern border of County Monaghan abutting South Armagh. The townland is small even for Ireland, just a scant 187 acres and only a quarter-mile long. The Catholic families had been residents for hundreds of years, and the names Hughes, O'Neill, Macklin, and McKenna still can be found throughout the area today. John and Catherine (Macklin) O'Neill had son Bernard in 1830 and daughter Mary in 1832. Bernard was named in the Irish tradition after his paternal grandfather, Bernard O'Neill, and Mary after her maternal grandmother, Mary Macklin. A son Eugene came next, but died in infancy. Baby John was born in 1838, not 1834. He was indeed named after his father, who had passed away of cholera, which struck in 1838 during the cholera epidemic five weeks before young John was born on March 8.[5]

When Catherine O'Neill and her younger brother John Macklin made the decision to emigrate to America, they left the three living O'Neill children with their grandparents, though we are unsure which grandparents—George and Mary Macklin or Bernard O'Neill and his wife. Both lived in the same small parish of Clontibret. Soon, the Macklin grocery store that Catherine and John established was doing well on Elizabeth Avenue, then and now the main street in Elizabeth, the oldest street in New Jersey. Though Catholics were not welcomed for almost two hundred years in Elizabeth, the advent of the railroads and the soon-to-be mass exodus of Irish running from hunger during the Famine would convert the Macklin store into a staple of the new immigrant community. How and why John Macklin and Catherine O'Neill settled in Elizabeth is unknown, and there is little history of any Monaghan people settling in the area, but they were successful from the beginning.

The historic town, ripped apart by intense internecine fighting during the Revolutionary War between Loyalists and Patriots, had a population of approximately 3,000 in 1830, reveling in its unbending conservative short history of a staunch new "American" town, richly deserved. It was the original home of the now renowned Princeton University and was, for a short time, the home of both Aaron Burr and Alexander Hamilton. But the railroads changed Elizabeth, like so many other Eastern Seaboard localities. The Irish, the first foreign emigrants, were not welcome, but were eventually accepted. In 1840 the population had grown to 4,000, and by 1850, 5,500. By the start of the Civil War, it was 12,000, and the German and Irish Catholics had changed the city.[6]

Within just a few years, St. Mary's, the first Catholic Church in the two-hundred-year-old history of Elizabeth, would be erected, and John Macklin would be a major benefactor. Indeed, both John and Catherine O'Neill would never leave Elizabeth, and would be buried in the now forgotten St. Mary's Cemetery on South Washington Avenue, just blocks from the church.

With business gaining acceleration in the busy Elizabeth of 1843, Catherine sent for her children. Bernard was now thirteen and Mary eleven, unknowingly escaping the impending famine. Both began working with Uncle John Macklin, Bernard as a clerk and Mary, along with her mother Catherine O'Neill, keeping house above the store. Baby John Charles was left at home in Monaghan. There is no reason to doubt O'Neill's later statements that his grandparents wished to hold onto this last grandchild, easing their hearts as they watched the others leave, but it is more likely that John's young age was the primary factor. If he were born in 1834, he would have been old enough to travel—his sister Mary was only two years older. But if he was born in 1838, as research now shows, he was only two when his mother left, and five when his sister and brother emigrated. It is completely understandable that the Macklin/O'Neill clans remaining in Monaghan would never let a five-year-old travel with two barely older siblings across an ocean.[7] So the youngest stayed, and as he later told anyone who would listen, John was educated to be a nationalist with hatred of England emphasized and veneration of Irish heroes foremost in his mind. Whether he was living with Bernard O'Neill or George Macklin, the result was the same. Hatred of England and love of ancient Ireland became ingrained and the youngster was not sent to the local school for fear of being raised as an anglophile. Despite this most oppressive atmosphere, O'Neill was well schooled, and he may even have had a tutor, at least according to interviews given by O'Neill years later.

Though all of Ireland has been a birthplace of rebels for centuries, the East Monaghan and South Armagh areas of young John's early upbringing has long been linked with a raised level of virulent ancient hatreds, centuries-old vendettas, and is even today often referred to as "bandit country." Drumgallan sits right on the border of South Armagh, still today a place tourists avoid. During the first decade of O'Neill's life, the British military was called out to break popular local resistance and secret societies abounded on both Catholic and Protestant sides. Modern Irish novelist Benedict Kiely said pre-famine County Monaghan "was a land infested with disorder and injustice, a place where men were bitterly discontented, a land where slavery and oppression were real."

This sectarian violence has been present in Monaghan for centuries. The county has always been a borderland, contested in both landscape and mindset from the sixteenth century to the present. Unlike many sections of the country, the goal of British conquest was eventually Ulster, and all roads to Gaelic Ulster had to go through Monaghan, a gateway from the English Pale and Dublin. In 1595, the Irish struck first, handing the British their most severe defeat ever in Ireland in the Battle of Clontibret, with a thousand English troops killed, a shock to all of Elizabethan England. Fifty years later the English retaliated, with Cromwell's soldiers displacing ancient Gaelic families, many named O'Neill and Macklin. Adding to this displacement, in the 1690s famine in Scotland drove thousands of Presbyterians into Monaghan. Gaelic Catholic displacement left resentment, sectarian violence, and hatred on every ridge and hill. None of this was or has been forgotten, and all of it was passed on orally and in hedge schools.

Monaghan, even in modern times, can find disorder and injustice, whether bitterly perceived or real. Rural Monaghan suffered in particular because of two factors leading up to the Famine. It had the most absentee landlords in the country and some of the most severe overcrowding, with 1,000 people per square mile; in tiny Drumgallan, there were upwards of ninety people per acre in 1846, when John O'Neill was eight years old. Forty percent of the homes around the Monaghan/Armagh border—one-roomed, frequently windowless abodes, not necessarily the home of the O'Neills, but neighbors and friends—were held by landless laborers and certainly enough to shape the mind of a young boy.[8]

The English attitude even prior to the Famine might shock people today, but it was clear and prevalent to both races at the time. The English magazine *Punch* declared the Irish to be, "by their very nature, the laziest and dirtiest people in all of Europe, if not the world. Irishmen were the sons and daughters of generations of beggars. You can trace the descent in their blighted, stunted forms—in their brassy, cunning, brutalized features. They are indeed the missing link between the gorilla and the Negro."[9] It would not be difficult to raise a young boy to hate the nation that considered him a gorilla.

Discontent, rivalries, and viciousness did not end with the Famine or the emigration of John O'Neill, and the O'Neill hatred of England can still be found in the present day. From 1972 until 1997, the South Armagh/Monaghan border was as vicious as any area found during the civil rights "troubles." Landmines, car bombs, kidnappings, assassinations, and cross-border attacks maimed and killed dozens of young and old in this bandit country within the ten miles of Drumgallan. In 1980, fifty-year-old Catholic farmer Frank McGrory sat down on a bench in Carrickduff townland to rest. Just a hundred yards from O'Neill's birthplace, he picked up a newspaper and was blown to bits, the bomb intended for British soldiers. In 1974 a UVF British loyalist force placed a car bomb in Monaghan townland, killing seven and wounding thirty, a case that to this day remains unsolved.

In 1983 at Darkley, County Armagh, just six miles from Drumgallan, sixty local Protestant farmers worshipping in church on a Sunday morning opened the door for latecomers and were ambushed by the local IRA, with three men holding bibles killed inside the church, and another seven wounded. No one was ever charged. In Clontibret Parish, a large arms cache was found in a local farm. In 1986, five hundred loyalists crossed the border from Armagh and vandalized Clontibret in opposition to the Anglo-Irish Agreement signed in 1985. In truth, the borderland John O'Neill was born into was still considered in the 1980s "the most dangerous posting in the world" for British soldiers.[10] Irish author Sam McAughtry has said, "The history of Monaghan is a dark, violent, murderous one. The tumbled, hilly countryside still has a whisper of it. It has a Balkan look about it, the feel of a border country."[11]

As an adult in America, O'Neill was adamant that "as a young boy I attentively read the history of my native land and her public men. I wept over the speeches of her orators, and asked myself whom of the Irish patriots I would seek to emulate. I decided that that eloquence would not do unless it be that which follows from the cannon's mouth."[12] Even allowing for hyperbole, it is obvious O'Neill's grandparents did their job well in creating a warrior mentality in the young boy. It would be clear very soon that a settled, comfortable family life as a grocery clerk was not to be the destiny of John Charles O'Neill.

Of course, after arriving safely in New York harbor, the boy who had not seen his mother since he was two, nor his sister and brother for six years, would have problems acclimating. The poor luck of being an eight-year-old child as the worst famine in history struck Ireland might be a difficult acculturation to any family life. The Famine hit northeastern County Monaghan in 1845 with ferocity more than most, if that is imaginable. In Ireland, a country which saw a population of 8.5 million in 1844 bottomed out in 1855 at 4.5 million. In next-door Castleblayney Parish, which was economically slightly better off than Clontibret, British soldiers were called in to assist with collecting rents and much of the population simply sold up where they could and emigrated—or died.

In 1841, County Monaghan's population was just over 200,000. Ten years later it was under 140,000, and some districts like Drumgallan suffered at a forty percent decrease. Rural areas in the county, including all of Clontibret Parish, lost more than 50,000 people and 3,700 homes in that shocking decade. Thus it would be no surprise when, in 1901, O'Neill's son John Hugh visited Monaghan searching for his ancestral home and not one local person could say exactly where the O'Neill homestead was in Drumgallan. In postfamine Ireland, a great many houses simply disappeared, like ghosts, from the local scene. When John left for New Jersey in 1848 some people in Monaghan were homeless, subsisting on green cabbage and wild herbs.

In Drumgallan hunger struck first in 1845 when young John O'Neill was seven. Catherine, like all Irish both home and abroad, always believed the one-year potato failure would be temporary. There had, after all, been seasonal failures of the potato crop many times, so Catherine left the youngest at home never dreaming what would occur. But of course it soon became calamitous, and the next four years brought famine, typhus, fever, and finally emigration, thus reducing the Irish population to numbers unimaginable. By the time John O'Neill left for Elizabeth, New Jersey, more than 5,500 natives of County Monaghan, most of them women and children, had died in the county workhouses.[13]

The disastrous effect on the minds of the Irish has been studied and debated for over a century, never completely understood, but to a young boy without a father and missing a mother, it was simple—the English had to get out of Ireland. O'Neill would spend his entire life trying to make it happen.

We have no idea what happened to the Macklin and O'Neill grandparents, but there are no records that they survived or emigrated. John Charles O'Neill left on the ship *Gertrude* out of Liverpool with a Bernard O'Neill, most likely a Monaghan/Armagh relation. John was then ten or eleven, not the fourteen he later claimed to be after they landed in New York in late June 1848. He would be just one number in what was not an exodus, but a headlong flight from death. Emigrants, as historian Kirby Miller remarks, "leave their home but may not want to. Exiles feel driven out of their home places by treachery."[14] O'Neill would never be an emigrant but an exile looking to exact pain on England. But that would have to wait.

The future boy warrior, now armed with hatred and memories few youngsters would know, much less understand, arrived in Elizabeth to see a mother and uncle he didn't recognize at all, and a brother and sister he barely remembered. John was sent to the new St. Mary's Church grade school for a year, and then spent two difficult years as a clerk at the family grocery. Further proof of the O'Neill family history as misleading—if O'Neill was indeed fourteen upon arrival he would undoubtedly be placed immediately as a clerk with his brother Bernard. Fourteen would have meant work, not school, and there was no high school for the Irish in Elizabeth. But by 1854 he was sixteen and knew one thing—he wanted out of Elizabeth, out of the grocery business, and would not be held at home by his own crowd.

One has to wonder at the price paid on the break-up of a family, and there is always a price. In effect, John O'Neill, who never knew a father, was also left motherless from age two to eleven. Despite being educated locally and raised by loving grandparents, Monaghan was a tough locale in those formative years, and John was exposed to life in a dark and secluded side of rural Ireland.

The dark haired, good-looking teenager's arrival must have been a stark study in contrasts. Fluent in both Irish and English, he may have rejoiced in being reunited with his mother, brother, and sister, but it couldn't have been easy. Additionally he now shared a home with his uncle, John Macklin, Macklin's wife Sarah, and two new young cousins, George and Mary Macklin. Comfort in a new home with a loving family and no fear of hunger was definitely an improvement. But John O'Neill had not seen his mother since he was two, and the grandparents who raised him were now gone overnight either to death or distance. That he might be independent and detached, or both, would be an understatement. His very popular brother Bernard was now twenty, and had a seven-year head start on American life, but Bernard and O'Neill would walk two very different paths.

There is no record of the remnants of any other Macklin or O'Neill relatives elsewhere in the United States related to the Elizabeth family. No one appears in any baptism, census, marriage, burial, or obituary records. In the mid- to late nineteenth century, this was very unusual among Irish diaspora families. Though one branch might live in New Jersey, cousins, siblings, and in-laws found each other, no matter where they settled. This lack of outreach makes one believe that this particular Macklin/O'Neill family group lived as they had in Monaghan, exclusively staying in Elizabeth for fifty years before branching out even a little, and then, only one strayed permanently more than twenty miles from the original home base of Elizabeth. The one glaring exception would be the last arrival, John Charles O'Neill, the future Irish American nationalist leader.[15]

So in 1854, after almost three years working with groceries in Elizabeth, John quit and went to work as a book salesman for a New York Catholic publisher, traveling throughout New Jersey, Pennsylvania, Maryland, and Virginia. It was a sudden move, and against his mother's wishes, but it is hardly surprising given his background. O'Neill was only sixteen, but he had been alone and independent for more years than is normal for a boy that age. It would be the first in a lifelong pattern of sudden and rash decisions with little or no thought of consequences.

The headstrong youngster, born into internecine hate, raised to despise the anti–Catholicism found in rural Monaghan, and witness to the Famine without a mother or father, may have also felt a need to leave Elizabeth when he observed firsthand similar anti–Catholic hatred in his new hometown.

Life in Elizabeth was a vast improvement on Monaghan in the Famine, but it was no Garden of Eden for the Irish. Founded in 1664, it was a bastion of colonial English life. During the American Revolution, the town was deeply divided among families, joining both Loyalist and Patriot sides. Skirmishes took place frequently from British bases in Manhattan and Staten Island, culminating with an attack on the town in 1780. Local loyalists aided a British attack that saw half the buildings burned, including the First Presbyterian Church and the courthouse. The Rev. James Caldwell, pastor of the church and the son of Scottish-Irish parents from Ulster, often conducted services on Sundays with two pistols at the pulpit, and was himself murdered by a

British trooper in 1781 in Elizabethport after his home and church were burned to the ground.[16]

Elizabeth was, like Monaghan in Ireland, a center of revolutionary activity, and saw Hannah Caldwell, the pastor's wife, struck and killed by a British bullet in 1780 while holding her infant in her arms. In the seventy years following the Revolution, Elizabeth remained staunchly American but solidly Protestant, finally accepting that immigrants—both Catholic and Irish—were needed to build the railroads if Elizabeth was to remain strong economically. Accepted if not embraced, these early Irish performed the dirty and difficult work in a semi-hostile culture.

When John turned sixteen, just before he left for Virginia, native Americans, alarmed at the massive influx of Irish and German Catholic immigrants, began a movement to promote homegrown Protestants in the political arena, and after some success took to the streets to terrify local populations along the entire Eastern Seaboard. This nativist party, forever after known as "Know Nothings," whose extremist popularity lasted only from 1854–57, burned churches, convents, and orphanages along the East Coast from Maine to Maryland. The Know-Nothings were convinced that immigrants, especially Catholics, led by the Pope would take over the government with the huge European surge of the 1850s. Membership, limited to Protestant men, spread as far as California, where their aim was to exclude Chinese, who certainly were not Catholics from Europe. It was a bizarre short period of American life, but the violence was very real. The Know-Nothings were defended and protected by mob rule and nativist American newspapers, and for a short time was very strong politically in New Jersey. One Newark, New Jersey, newspaper, just five miles from Elizabeth, declared the Know-Nothings "a friend of order."[17]

In April of 1854, hundreds of anti–Catholic Orangemen and Know Nothings from New York City attacked St. Mary's Church in Newark, the first Catholic church in the city. They broke windows, smashed statuary, and murdered an innocent Irish bystander. Weeks later, emboldened with the success in Newark, another Protestant group made plans to destroy St. Mary's Church in Elizabeth, the Irish parish of the Macklins and O'Neills, the new and only Catholic church in town. Father Isaac Howell, the church's first pastor and himself a native American, convinced the Catholic men to stay away, hopefully avoiding open confrontation. Father Howell grouped the women of the parish together at the steps of the church and as the mob of local men arrived armed with weapons, prepared to burn down the church, they encountered dozens of Irish women and children, some with babies in their arms. Mrs. Mary Whelan has gone down in history as the woman who faced down the mob, telling the leader, "Sam, you'll have to kill me and my baby before you can pass."[18] Humiliated, the mob dispersed. There can be little doubt that

Catherine O'Neill, her daughter Mary, and her sister-in-law, Sarah Macklin, were present. All three were leading women and founders of the fledgling parish.

Though violence was averted and the Know Nothings were never again a physical threat in Elizabeth, oral history remains that some parish men, all Irish, felt embarrassed and angered by their own lack of involvement. Though they bowed down to the astute judgment of Father Howell, it is possible that the sixteen-year-old O'Neill, a lifelong devout Catholic with a temper and anger to match, felt the need to leave a place that did not allow him to physically confront what he had grown to despise. The local Elizabeth paper, *The Jersey Journal,* avoided the entire incident, treating it with veiled reference so as not to offend its nativist population or incite the Irish. "The Know Nothings have, of a sudden, become a state power. What they are—what they want—where they come from—what they do, not knowing, we cannot say. Their meetings we stated the other day are called by posting sheets of blank paper against walls—but when we send our reporters, they bring back the old story, 'Nobody knows nothing' and there is nothing to print." The Know Nothings thankfully disappeared politically as suddenly as they arrived, but the memory of the attack on St. Mary's remained alive among Elizabeth Irish for more than a hundred years.[19]

By year's end, young John O'Neill, whether tired of working in a grocery store, resentful of his uncle, or just an adventurous young man in a new country, left his family and headed south to form his own future. It would be ten years before he would return to Elizabeth.

Ever the optimist, in 1856 the ambitious veteran teenager opened a Catholic bookstore and news depot in, of all places, Richmond, Virginia. Why Richmond we will never know, and how the brash eighteen-year-old was financially able to open the business is a mystery. The store was located downtown on Broad and Eighth streets, but soon failed. Richmond had then a sizable population of 27,000 but the only Catholics were poor German and Irish immigrants trying to eke out an existence working on a canal, and there was only one Catholic church in the whole city. The store closed within eighteen months in the spring of 1857, when O'Neill had just turned nineteen. But it was in Richmond that O'Neill literally ran into his true calling, one he said he always wished for but was rebuffed for by his mother and relatives.[20]

During his sojourn in Virginia the Irish-born bookseller joined the Emmet Monument Association, which by most Irish standards was a very secret militia organization named after Robert Emmet. Emmet was just twenty-five when executed for treason against the King in 1803, and his famous speech from the dock has resonated with every Irish patriot since: "When my country takes her place among the nations of the earth, then, and not till then, let my epitaph be written."[21] The EMA's purpose was to train young Irish and Irish Americans to attack Britain and free Ireland by any means necessary, and the association claimed to have more than 25,000 members nationwide. Found throughout all the larger cities in the country, but especially in New York, the EMA was an early progenitor of the Fenians, founded in the early 1850s on the notion that England would soon be at war with Russia, thus opening the way for all Irish freedom fighters.[22]

The Irish in the South have always been given a short shrift historically when it comes to their involvement prior to the Civil War. Yet the Emmet Club in New Orleans gave more than $1,000 to William Smith O'Brien to foment Irish rebellion after the failed 1848 Young Irelander Rebellion. During O'Neill's brief sojourn in Richmond Irish clubs like the EMA were found in every Southern state with the stated intention of creating Irish self-determination. Irish newspapers like the *Southern Cross* in Knoxville sold throughout the South, where both Irish Protestants and Catholics received it with approbation, and became known as the "voice of Irish Southerners."

It would therefore be no surprise when John O'Mahony and Michael Doheny, Irish refugees of the failed 1848 uprising known as the Young Irelander Rebellion, approached Russian officials in Washington with the age-old adage, "the enemy of my enemy is my friend." It was the perfect outlet for the hazel-eyed O'Neill. John trained on weekends with the EMA but when the Crimean War ended and English war with Russia no longer seemed plausible, O'Neill, his bookstore failing financially, headed back north at nineteen.

With the prospect of returning to his family a failure, or thoughts of having to work once again with groceries, it must have been a dejected 150-mile steamship trip on the first leg north to Baltimore, then the nation's second largest city. But while the strident and rash O'Neill waited for a train home to New Jersey, he literally strolled into his future. The U.S. Army had just begun active searches for recruits to quash what would be called the Utah War against the Mormons, and the nineteen-year-old O'Neill made a sudden decision, signing on in May 1857 with the U.S. Army 2nd Dragoons, Company G. He would not see his family for seven more years, but that would be nothing new.

Unlike Russia and England, the United States was faced with its own dilemma, a political game of chicken between Washington and Salt Lake City. Brigham Young's Mormons had been ensconced in Utah territory for a decade, ruling it almost by default as a medieval fiefdom. No one really cared about the state now called Utah, exactly the reason the Mormons settled the area. But when gold was discovered in California, thousands of migrants moved west in a human tsunami through Mormon territory, threatening the Mormons' determined isolation, thus simultaneously worrying Washington about the perceived Mormon tendency to run Utah as a private entity.

A political standoff between newly-elected President William Buchanan and Mormon leader Brigham Young escalated to the point the Army was sent to "protect" the government's interests and political appointees—and replace Young, known to his flock as the "American Moses." Brigham Young forced the issue by trying to set up Mormon land as an independent nation and, when rejected in Washington, forced the president to establish federal law in the territory or cave in to Young's demands. President Buchanan quickly ordered 2,500 men to build a post in Utah. The Mormons, victims of conflict in their trek across the country, saw this as a threat, and planned for the worst—war. But the U.S. Army did not have 2,500 men, especially not cavalry, so a hurried recruitment began nationwide.

O'Neill said later in life he had no wish to return to New Jersey and that his mother and relatives were always against him joining the Army, but the chance encounter with Army recruiters was kismet for both.[23] The teenager was smart, able-bodied, trained, and anxious to fight somebody. There was only one impediment. John Charles O'Neill was nineteen, old enough to enlist but only with parental consent, which was neither readily available nor forthcoming in any case. Pre–Civil War rules required soldiers to be twenty-one, so on May 30, 1857, two months after his birthday, O'Neill enlisted in the Army for five years, telling his recruiter, Captain John Adams, he was twenty-three.

O'Neill's paperwork showed the youngster to be 5'7" with hazel eyes, black hair, and a dark complexion. Captain Adams was a Nashville, Tennessee, native and first-generation son of Irish immigrants from County Tyrone in Northern Ireland, just a long walk from O'Neill's birthplace in Monaghan. It is not a large leap of faith to believe the two men hit it off, as their lives would intersect years later.[24] The future General John O'Neill recalled writing his mother about his decision, but as Private John O'Neill of the U.S. 2nd Dragoons, Company G, headed west, the O'Neills and Macklins were left to wonder just what kind of boy they had brought into the world. In truth, they and the rest of the country would learn John O'Neill was shaped more by his early upbringing in ravaged Monaghan and hatred of England than by any family in America.

If O'Neill was looking for adventure, he soon got it. After six weeks training in Carlisle, Pennsylvania, Company G, with their all-black horses, began the long 1,000-mile summer journey to Fort Leavenworth, arriving in late August. On September 17, O'Neill and his fellow cavalrymen made an arduous six-hundred-mile trip to Fort Laramie, Wyoming, after being given just a week to prepare for the expedition, fighting off early heavy snow and blizzards and arriving on October 26. The Dragoons, under their able commander, General Philip St. George Cooke, were granted permission to stay and winter at Laramie. They had lost 134 horses out of 278 on the hard journey and could use the respite. Less than two weeks later Cooke, often called the "Father of the U.S. Cavalry," was ordered by Commander Albert Sydney Johnston to winter at Henry's Fork on the Green River, 240 miles away. Cooke objected but followed orders and pushed his unit, including O'Neill, to Wyoming, with temperatures reaching -16 degrees along the way. Their winter job was to safeguard both the politicos who made the trip from Washington and some seven thousand cattle. The 2nd Dragoons were now within a hundred miles of Mormon country, and two hundred of Salt Lake City itself. It had been six months since O'Neill enlisted in Baltimore, and he was a long way from Elizabeth, New Jersey, not that he cared. One report said that "privations of the winter of 1857/58 in Green River were no less than those endeared at Valley Forge 81 years before," while another said the men were "confident and even cheerful." O'Neill and the others in the army had great commanders which no doubt allowed for the latter comment. Johnston, Cooke, and Captain Adams (still with the 2nd Dragoons) were then and later judged superior leaders of men, and proved it repeatedly in the Civil War to follow. It was surely a heady time for any young American, Irish or not.

But the West in the 1850s was a different world, and after six months of

U.S. Dragoons en route to Utah from Wyoming, winter 1857 (Library of Congress).

traveling cross country, the Army command under General Johnston would be forced to wait six additional winter months before heading to Mormon land. By June 28 the entire U.S. force left winter encampments, arriving July 8 at what would be called Camp Floyd, forty miles south of Salt Lake City.

But if the Utah War began as a national show of force by President Buchanan and the politicos in Washington, it ended a total farce. Camp Floyd epitomized the rest of the "war." Soldiers and officers agreed it "was one of the most miserable, disagreeable and uninteresting places ever placed on earth." It was built on a dry plain with no grass or vegetation except sage. In addition to the 2,500 troops, there were said to be 1,000 camp followers. There was no water except a dirty little stream. The only wood besides light cedar was twelve miles away and the closest deep stream was fifteen miles away. The Mormons simply waited the army out, burned supply trains, and destroyed forage. The wonderful dream of the teenage O'Neill and his fellow young enlistees became a tedious assignment. It was, of course, the Army.

Bad became worse. The men loved Johnston and Cooke, but monotony and mismanagement found men deserting on a regular, almost nightly basis. They were supposed to be paid twice a year, but the pay never arrived. There were often fifteen men in a tent with saddles, valises, coats, blankets, sabers,

AN ARMY TRAIN CROSSING THE PLAINS

U.S. Army forces settling in at the new open air Camp Floyd, forty miles south of Salt Lake, 1858. It would be abandoned in 1861 (Library of Congress).

and rifles. Soon the Mormon civilians were spreading circulars promising $50 and protected passage through Indian country to California for any soldier willing. Desertions became more frequent and the officers admitted that these were often some of their best men. Though some left the Army and stayed in Utah territory, most deserters went west towards California, many becoming guards for wagon trains with no pursuit by the U.S. forces.[25]

The political boondoggle lasted from May 1857 until late August 1858, and there was not a single armed fatality or one pitched battle. The Mormons' chief success was burning three wagons loaded with 50,000 pounds of supplies, while the 2,500 U.S. soldiers showed their national might simply with their presence. It wasn't enough. Small Army units remained for two more years before being recalled for service in the Civil War. The entire episode was characterized by a *New York Herald* reporter, "Thus was peace made—killed, none; wounded, none; fooled, everybody." Though President Buchanan took bad press for the fiasco, it was the right move and federal law, not Brigham Young law, began to be established in Utah for the first time.

Whether O'Neill was bored at the non-action or just simply impulsive, two attributes he would possess until his death, there is no doubt the Irishman from Jersey departed, as did four hundred others—a total of sixteen percent of the force sent to Utah. Army pay records show O'Neill rode out at the very end of this sloppy affair on August 2, 1858. The year-and-a-half-long experience of training and traveling in the Army would help O'Neill immeasurably in his future life as a soldier, but it would be a lesson he buried in his public life as an adult. Desertion, however, is desertion, and it would haunt O'Neill and some of his favorite biographers, who downplayed or ignored it, when O'Neill's career became national news.[26] He later said it took him six weeks to travel the seven hundred and fifty miles to San Francisco. Whether he simply rode off into the sunset or took the Mormon bait is unknown, but there is no record that any of the Utah defectors were ever actively sought. Arriving on the West Coast, O'Neill had now been in the United States for nine unsettled years, and was barely twenty years old, twenty-four by military record. Three thousand miles away, the Fenian Brotherhood, an organization he had never heard of, was founded in New York by Irishmen John O'Mahony and Michael Doheny. Ten years later runaway John O'Neill of the 2nd Dragoons, Company G, would be called General John O'Neill, become one of the most revered Irish American nationalists in the country, and elected president of the Fenian Brotherhood. It would be a remarkable journey for a remarkable man—as has been said so many times—only in America.

2

West Meets East

Until, on Vinegar Hill ... the fatal conclave.
Terraced thousands died, shaking scythes at cannon.
The hillside blushed, soaked in our broken wave.
—Seamus Heaney, *Requiem for the Croppies*

At twenty years of age, O'Neill, not technically an orphan, may have felt like one. A son of an Irish emigrant family and a deserter, he was alone again, this time of his own volition, and again because of a rash decision. It seems fitting John would meet, bond, and fall in love with someone more alone than himself. Within a decade O'Neill would be known throughout North America, and though his wife went virtually unknown, her story is just as compelling and heroic.

An Gorta Mor ("The Great Hunger") was the seminal event of the 19th century in Ireland, but it was far from the only specter facing the island in that century. A terribly planned and executed uprising in 1798 culminated in County Wexford, when perhaps 1,500 people, mostly peasants, were slaughtered at Vinegar Hill, their bodies thrown into the Slaney River or discarded as they lay. For decades after, children of these massacred common folk roamed the countryside trying to survive. They begged, stole bread, illegally fished, trespassed, or stole rabbits. Between 1791 and 1853, 26,500 Irish people were transported to New South Wales, Australia, for these trivial offenses by the government sitting in London. More serious crimes, such as rape or murder, were not transportable offenses.

In 1828, twelve-year-old Patrick Crow, an errand boy from County Wexford, not far from Vinegar Hill, was sentenced to life imprisonment for housebreaking a second time. A Roman Catholic, he was referred to at trial as simply "an Irish Rebel." He was 4'11" with a small scar on his left thumb, and convicted on March 15, 1828. Patrick had brown hair, and after being convicted, waited almost a year in jail before being transported on the ship *Ferguson*, arriving in Sydney, New South Wales, on March 26, 1829.[1] For ten years the little Irish rebel worked before being granted parole at age twenty-three and meeting the daughter of another Irish convict, Bridget Walsh, who arrived on the *Albatross* at age 20 in 1841.[2] The couple was married in St. Patrick's Church, Parramatta, a suburb of Sydney in New South Wales, by the Rev. Nicholas Coffey on October 26, 1843. Six months later, on April 16, 1844, Bridget gave birth to a daughter they named Mary Ann in Melbourne, a town then of fewer than five thousand inhabitants.[3]

Melbourne was not the magnificent city of today, and the Australian economy was reeling. Most of the population lived in two-room shingle-roofed cottages, with open hearths in brick-floored kitchens. From the center of tiny Melbourne, sheep centers radiated for hundreds of miles. For a few years the Crows survived in Melbourne, but everything changed worldwide when gold was discovered in California in late January 1849. Within eight months, 80,000 immigrants arrived in the San Francisco area trying to strike it rich. Australians were among the very first, and Patrick and Bridget Crow got the gold fever faster than almost anyone. What, after all, did they have to lose? On June 27, 1849, less than five months after gold was discovered at Sutter's Mill, the Crow family, with five-year-old Mary Ann, boarded the first ship from Australia to San Francisco.[4] The *William Watson* was a 480-ton barque, and carried 161 passengers. None of the California-based vessels preceding her had booked that many. Eighty-two days later she arrived in San Francisco with 157 on board. Prior to leaving, the editor of the *Melbourne Morning Herald* expressed the hope that the vessel "carried arms to ward off the pirates on her return trip with gold."[5] Gold had victimized the whole world, but there would be no need in the end to ward off pirates, and certainly not for the Crows.

This exodus from Australia was so immense, and so shockingly sudden, it reminded some later observers of the Irish migration to America during the Famine. Indeed, Australia was the closest English-speaking destination to California. It was only 7,000 miles away compared to the 16,000 miles from New York. One can only surmise that Patrick Crow was enterprising enough to be among the very first to recognize a great opportunity for his family, but it was not to be—in fact, it was disastrous. But the Crows were not alone. Ships from more than fifteen countries landed in San Francisco in 1849 alone, and one year later in the 1850 census, a quarter of the city's population was from foreign lands. In January of 1848 the population of the city hovered around 1,000. By December 1849, it was at 25,000 and as a result all of California became dangerous almost overnight.

Accidents, disease, and violence led to a high mortality rate. One estimate is that one in every five miners who arrived on the West Coast in 1849 died within six months. Alcoholism was rampant, suicide rates soared, gunfights and stabbings occurred daily, and racism was everywhere. Frenchmen were hunted down, whites attacked Mexican and Chileans, Australians formed gangs to protect themselves, the Chinese were hated, and everybody tried to exterminate the Indians. Within months, runaway debtors, rogue gamblers, ruthless adventurers, and criminal outcasts enveloped the city.[6]

Into this often-hostile environment Patrick moved into a tent house with his family on Market Street in San Francisco, but he didn't stay long. At some point after arrival, Patrick, a coward at the very least, abandoned his wife and daughter and returned to Australia alone. Bridget and Mary Ann lived together on Jones Street near Greenwich until Bridget died at home of a tetanus infection at age thirty-seven on July 13, 1855. Bridget was buried at the Mission cemetery, Mission Delores, extant in San Francisco, in an unmarked grave.[7] She left her eleven-year-old daughter in a tumultuous city. At her mother's death, young Mary Ann Crow was the same age as John O'Neill when he left County Monaghan for America.

If a young girl 7,000 miles from home can be considered somewhat lucky, Mary Ann Crow fit the bill, thanks to five incredible women from the East Coast. In 1852, seven nuns were chosen to make a two-month journey from Emmitsburg, Maryland, to San Francisco to take care of orphaned children after cholera broke out in the city. The seven nuns of the Daughters of Charity traveled from Emmitsburg, Maryland, to New York and sailed to Panama. Two of these Daughters of Charity died of cholera on the journey when stricken with the disease crossing through Panama's jungles on mule-back. The five surviving nuns were given a place to live at Market and Montgomery streets in an area then called "Happy Valley." Sister Francis McEnnis soon established both an orphanage and a school with land donated by three successful resident Irishmen, John Sullivan, Tim Murphy, and Jasper O'Farrell. When Bridget Crow died, the orphanage/school had only been operating for two years, but Mary Ann found a home. For four years she attended school, which included nursing classes and domestic training. The nuns also did their best to attract girls they felt had a future in their order, and these were then sent back east to Emmitsburg for commitments to the Church. The nuns also openly operated as matchmakers for the girls as they grew older, especially with Irish Catholic young men, who filled San Francisco each month.[8]

With the Gold Rush over a decade old, San Francisco was becoming a great place to be in 1860, especially for bright, ambitious Irishmen. The past decade's gold rush had brought thousands to California, and the California Irish were way ahead of their brethren on the East Coast politically, culturally, and often economically. In short, California was becoming civilized.

By 1857, Irishman David Broderick was a U.S. senator; Terrence Bellew McManus was a resident from his escape in Tasmania in 1852 until he died in 1861; John Sullivan was the city's top banker; Eugene Casserly from

Mullingar was a prominent lawyer soon-to-be senator; Tom Hayes was the sheriff of San Francisco; and Peter Donahue was an influential railroad man. In 1867 Frank McCoppin became the first Irish-born mayor in the United States, and the Irish population in California when John O'Neill arrived on horseback in October 1858 was closing in on 9,000, the highest Irish population west of New Orleans. O'Neill must have easily been able to hide out in plain sight.[9]

Thus while many Irish immigrants struggled in poverty in the east, San Francisco was emerging from a building boom, and would show steady growth during the two years John was a resident. O'Neill kept a low profile, living for a year with a railroad watchman, Jonathan Hunt, and in early 1860 working as a laborer and living at the corner of Front and Jackson streets. O'Neill's time in the City by the Bay was often eventful. Just one month after his arrival there was a strong earthquake, and in September 1859 the city was inflamed when a notorious duel was fought between Senator David Broderick, a son of Irish immigrants, and his ex-friend, California Chief Justice David Terry. Both men had hair trigger pistols, and Broderick's went off prematurely into the ground. Terry then calmly shot his old friend, killing him. Broderick became a martyr for the anti-slavery movement, and Terry was acquitted of the shooting, but in truth, both powerful political operatives were as corrupt as any men in the country. Thirty years later, Terry threatened a California Supreme Court Justice and was shot and killed by a United States marshal.

But John O'Neill's mind in 1859 was not on politics or duels. Years later Mary Ann told her son John Hugh, "I met your father in a confectionary store, where I went with some other girls from the convent school to buy some candy. I was then about fifteen."[10] Mary Ann had been living and working at the convent school for a few years, but by sixteen had left the orphanage and gone to work as a teacher for one of the richest men in California, George William Pitt Bissell, likely on recommendations from the nuns at the orphanage.

G.W.P. Bissell was a native of Vermont, but left home early, drawn to the West. He eventually became heavily involved in China trade with the Pacific Mail Steamship Company and became American Consul to San Blas, Mexico. Just after the Gold Rush, he bought Mare Island, north of San Francisco, for $17,500 and sold it a year later to the U.S. Navy for more than $83,000 ($2.5 million today), which became the largest Naval base in the country. He married late at forty-five, to a twenty-five-year-old Virginian beauty, Mary Longbrough.

In 1860, the Bissell family settled into a large property on Folsom between Second and Third streets. They employed seven servants, including a family lawyer. The servants were all over thirty with one exception, sixteen-year-old Mary Ann Crow. There is one other historical reference to the

O'Neill and Crow romance, and it comes from O'Neill's trusted aide, the scurrilous English spy Henri Le Caron, but it does not coincide with what Mary Ann told her son. In his memoir printed more than thirty years later in 1892, Le Caron claimed Mary Ann "was once a Sister of Mercy, had nursed and grown to love him, and disregarding all her vows, had in the end married him."[11] It is ridiculous that Mary Ann was ever a nun, and the Sisters of Mercy records show no nun with the baptized name of Crow. It would be the first, but not the last, of Le Caron's lies and exaggerations regarding the O'Neills. At sixteen she was too young to make her vows, and would have to have been sent back east in any case to formalize her religious education. There is every reason to believe that at her young age, she was placed with the Bissells simply because she was well qualified after five years at the orphanage school, met the stubborn and handsome County Monaghan deserter, and fell in love. Like so much of Le Caron's recounting of John O'Neill's life, there is little proof and many angry accusations.

The romance was turned on its head soon after it began. In the spring, O'Neill serendipitously ran into an old acquaintance, Captain John Adams from Baltimore. It changed O'Neill's life. A teenage Australian woman, left abandoned for years, 7,000 miles from home, raised and educated by Irish nuns who often acted as matchmakers cares for and advises a twenty-year-old headstrong Irish semi-orphan, 10,000 miles from home, wanted by his new nation as a deserter. Nonetheless, O'Neill must have agonized over the decision. Whether it was Mary Ann's common sense, or the self-realization that he was a soldier at heart, O'Neill decided to rejoin the Dragoons and face the music for a two-year absence without leave.[12]

While the majority of the U.S. Army Utah Expedition had returned east after the Mormon War, the 1st Dragoons had continued west to Fort Crook in the foothills of northern California, directly west of Reno, Nevada. Fort

U.S. Army record of John O'Neill's desertion and return on July 8, 1860, when he gave himself up to Capt. John Adams (author's collection).

Crook was two hundred arduous miles north of San Francisco, and consisted of a few log buildings with no bunks for the men. The Dragoons themselves numbered less than a hundred, and they were ostensibly there only to protect immigrants and settlers in the far northwest. In July of 1860, when O'Neill showed up and surrendered to Captain Adams, it was as bleak and remote as any Army post in the United States.

Adams was a West Pointer and second-in-command in 1860 when he came upon O'Neill in San Francisco either on leave or assignment. After the Civil War O'Neill said both Adams and Mary Ann convinced him to return to Fort Crook on July 8, 1860, with a special amnesty. Adams met O'Neill halfway to the fort at Red Bluff, California. After just one week in the stockade, O'Neill was accepted back with the Dragoons with no further punishment, a remarkable accommodation for a two-year deserter in peacetime.[13] Adams must have recognized the ability of the headstrong O'Neill, for such a deal would never have been offered to a common deserter. Private O'Neill would not disappoint Adams again.

Mary Ann Crow had a more disappointing July. After a year with the Bissells, G.W.P. died suddenly at home on the 14th at age fifty-seven, leaving a young wife and two infants. Mary Bissell remarried quickly, this time to another older man, Erasmus Darwin Keyes, a West Point legend, veteran of three wars, and the founder of what is now known as the Napa Valley wine industry. When the Keyes moved to Napa Valley, Mary Ann Crow stayed near the orphanage and worked as a domestic at the home of James L. Watkins in the city. In the short space of two years, Mary had worked for three of the most interesting families in American history. The Loughboroughs were Virginian royalty, the Bissells national entrepreneurs, and the Keyes a family of

John Adams, the West Pointer with Irish roots who recruited young John O'Neill in Baltimore, traveled with him to Utah, and convinced him to return to the Army in California before dying as a Confederate general at the Battle of Franklin, 1864 (Library of Congress).

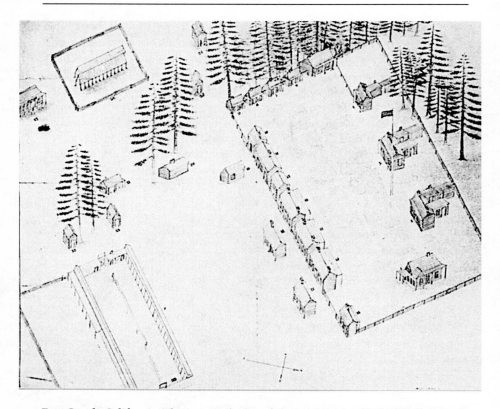

Fort Crook, California. This extremely out-of-the-way post enabled O'Neill to resuscitate his military career. It was formed in 1857 to protect settlers against Indians in northern California and Oregon (courtesy Fort Crook Historical Society).

military distinction, but life with John O'Neill would lead the young Aussie woman in a drastically different direction.

On April 12, 1861, less than a year after beginning his second stint as a soldier and already a sergeant, the North came under attack at Fort Sumter and the Civil War began. California was slow to join the war, as many expected the North to quickly end it. After his one week in the stockade, Private O'Neill was released on July 15 and spent just four months in active duty at Fort Crook. His first action on the West Coast began on August 3, when one officer, O'Neill, a bugler, and eighteen other privates of Company F were sent "to punish Indian tribes northeast of the fort, who had murdered two white men and stolen 800 cattle from immigrants." Over the next eleven days the troopers killed one Indian, wounded three others, and recaptured 350 of the 800 cattle. They did see two hundred other Indians but nothing occurred outside of one soldier accidentally shooting himself in the leg while dismounting his horse. Sergeant O'Neill returned to Fort Crook with his fellow small company after a three-hundred-mile march mostly in Oregon on August 13. The next day Company F returned to the field with two officers and twenty-five privates and, after traveling two hundred and eighty miles over a week through much of the beautiful northwest and without much stressful Indian fighting, returned with five more cattle.

From October 1 to October 5, 1861, O'Neill was involved in one more foray in Oregon, chasing Indians and cattle but returning to Fort Crook empty-handed. They would be the only incidents John O'Neill would be involved in before Fort Crook was closed and the men sent back east to fight confederates. Nonetheless, the Monaghan Irishman had restored his personal reputation and seen much of the country Americans could only dream of seeing for generations. Much of what we know is written in what O'Neill called his "travel reports," which are remarkably clear, concise, pleasurable to read, and rare for a twenty-three-year-old with little formal education. These reports would foreshadow the intelligence and exceptionally profuse pen John O'Neill would wield the rest of his life.[14]

The 1st Dragoons at Fort Crook, with John O'Neill, were reassigned and commanded to the East, and left Fort Crook on November 6, now needed desperately for the new war begun in South Carolina. The Dragoons took a barge from Red Bluff (where O'Neill had surrendered himself just four months prior) to Sacramento and then a steamer to San Francisco. There can be little doubt that in the two weeks the Dragoons waited for the steamship *St. Louis* to leave San Francisco, O'Neill and Mary Ann Crow made plans for their future. The *St. Louis* arrived in Panama two weeks later, and the American soldiers transferred to the steamship *North Star* for the remainder of the 5,700-mile journey to New York City, arriving on Christmas Eve just short of a two months' journey, staying the night on-board ship. O'Neill's daily notes, which survive, give longitude, latitude, depth, sights, weather, sea levels, and daily personal observations. The California Dragoons left New York on Christmas Day by rail, passing within a block of his mother's home in Elizabeth, and arrived in Washington, D.C., two days later, ready to fight. It wouldn't take long.

O'Neill would soon garner a stellar wartime reputation. In a sign of things to come in this vicious American Civil War, Captain John Adams, the Irish American native of Tennessee who signed John O'Neill into the Army and trained and mentored him before allowing him to restart his career in good standing, went absent from the U.S. Army at Fort Crook in June 1861, just after Fort Sumter. Adams also traveled to San Francisco, made the same long journey to New York, then headed home to Tennessee, and declared for the Confederacy. Adams and O'Neill would never meet again, though both would serve on opposite sides in the Western Theater. Adams had a splendid war career, and was a Confederate brigadier general when he was killed in the Confederate attack at Franklin in 1864, in his home state of Tennessee. Adam's dying statement after being shot nine times was, "It is the fate of a soldier to die for his country."[15] Words that his protégé, John Charles O'Neill, certainly understood.

3

Days of Glory

Of this I am convinced—what is called 'Irishness' can be understood only in relation to the homeland. In the long run, I believe geography counts more than genes.—E. Estyn Evans

The California Dragoons arrived in New York after a long journey via the Isthmus on Christmas Day, 1862, were immediately reorganized and renamed cavalry, and sent to Washington, D.C.[1] Newly-promoted sergeant John O'Neill was parceled out to General George Stoneman, once Stonewall Jackson's roommate at West Point and now part of General George McClellan's grand scheme to invade Richmond in the spring of 1862. Stoneman was a serious early advocate of cavalry, as the Dragoons were now named, and McClellan was not.

McClellan, a superb organizer but a plodding commander, landed at Fort Monroe after four months' preparation with 125,000 men, intending to take Richmond, eighty miles north, and end the war quickly. Union troops began the attack first towards Yorktown on April 4 and worked their way slowly towards the Confederate capital for months, but at the conclusion nothing was achieved except a stalemate. McClellan's last troops left the Peninsula from Harrison's Landing three months later on August 16, headed back to Washington, and the closest they came to Richmond was seeing church spires. Despite the Union failure to capture the Confederate capital, the campaign was the largest of the entire war, with a quarter of a million men involved in fierce and savage ferocity. McClellan declared the campaign a victory, but Lincoln, Robert E. Lee, and the men who fought knew differently. It was a horrible sample of war, but it was in this months' long carnage that John O'Neill began his dream of becoming the celebrated soldier he had always envisioned. O'Neill's biographers point to his record in Indiana and the Western Theater, but the Irishman's early fighting began in the East. O'Neill, with his obvious bent for the military, had been in the Army for almost three years, experiencing discipline, training, hardship, and travel, but had never experienced battle. That would change quickly. After an easy taking of Yorktown, Union forces marched slowly north, reaching the next little village of Williamsburg on May 5, 1862.

The Union forces expected little or no resistance, but they were wrong. At the end of the day, one of the most vicious firefights in the war saw 3,742 casualties involving 21,000 men locked in deadly combat on both sides in a matter of hours. O'Neill's job as a bodyguard of the tall and gaunt General Stoneman, who was in charge of all advanced cavalry, saw him intimately involved in the fight at every turn. In recent history, it has become common to denigrate the Union cavalry early in the war, but Stoneman's guard was sensational, clearing the two roads to Williamsburg and catching the enemy by surprise.

The ensuing battle was fought in a pitiless rain, and bodies on the Confederate side were left on the battlefield, some sinking deep into the mud and often run over by artillery and horses. On one occasion, a white Confederate flag was mistaken as a flag of surrender and the Union soldiers stood up to accept the surrender. They were cut down with a savage volley. Stoneman's cavalry, with O'Neill involved, is credited with saving the day for the Union by having a messenger bring up General Hooker's Brigade.

The 7th New Jersey Infantry was in the midst, and lost one third of their men in hours, and the 70th New York Infantry suffered 380 casualties, the most on either side. Mass graves were dug on the Union side, with eighty men of the 8th New Jersey Infantry buried in a grave eight feet wide and eighteen inches deep. Bodies from both forces were looted of any valuables, including shoes.[2] Several of those New Jersey men were Irishmen from Elizabeth, but O'Neill is not likely to have known them, having left his family years prior. O'Neill's personal note said simply, "May 4th, 1862. Left camp in pursuit of the enemy and became engaged with him in the afternoon."[3]

The Union forced a Confederate retreat, but experienced 2,239 casualties of their 12,000 combatants while the Confederate forces under General Joe Johnston lost 1,500 of their 9,000-man force. It was for many, including John O'Neill, their first encounter with the reality of war. Today, Williamsburg is a tourist hangout, portrayed as a Revolutionary War feel-good village. The 1862 vicious firefight that began the Peninsula Campaign is sadly a forgotten memory, with Confederate redoubts in hotel parking lots the only reminder that brave Americans of both the North and South are buried there in mass graves.

Less than a month later in the same long campaign, the Union forces were involved in a bloodbath at Gaines Mills, the third battle of the Seven Days Battles, where the combined armies suffered 14,830 casualties. O'Neill was one of the lucky ones, with only his horse shot from underneath him. General Stoneman praised him "as a brave and worthy officer, in whose judgment I had the greatest confidence."[4] At the conclusion of the ill-fated attempt to conquer the Confederate capital, O'Neill must have had mixed feelings. His first adult job had been as an owner of a bookstore in downtown Richmond, just four years and ten miles from the killing swamps of the Seven Days Battles.

Following the months-long fight around Richmond, many of the 1st Cavalry were temporarily broken up and dispersed as recruiters throughout the North, and John was sent to Indiana to help raise and train their first Calvary regiments. It did not take long for O'Neill to make a mark. By the end of October, every officer of the newly-raised Indiana Home Legion at Burnside Barracks signed and sent a letter to Governor Oliver Morton asking that O'Neill be the drillmaster of the whole unit. "We the undersigned officers of the Home

George Stoneman, West Point roommate of Stonewall Jackson, was O'Neill's first commander in the Civil War. He later championed O'Neill's promotions, and had a distinguished Civil War and postwar career (Library of Congress).

Legion of the State of Indiana [Cavalry service] having been under the instruction of Sergt. John O'Neill of the first U.S. Cavalry part of the time since coming to this camp, and being highly pleased with him as an instructor, and convinced that he is well qualified to instruct a company or regiment in cavalry drill, do hereby recommend him to his Excellency, Governor Oliver Morton." They added, "We are confident that a week or ten days under O'Neill's instruction would accomplish much good for ourselves and company officers, as well as the men of our respective commands."[5]

Helped by the petition and with General Stoneman's express approval, O'Neill was soon promoted to 2nd Lieutenant in December 1862 and assigned to the 5th Indiana Cavalry based in Indianapolis, with cavalry quickly becoming regarded by the Union as pivotal in the fight. O'Neill, now just twenty-four, did not disappoint Stoneman, perhaps with the memory of John Adams as his mentor.

O'Neill was placed in charge of Company I and by war's end, there would be over 110 officers in the 5th Indiana. One hundred were from the Hoosier state, nine from Illinois, and one lone outsider from faraway Elizabeth, New Jersey, which would portend a problem for the soldier born in tiny Drumgallan, County Monaghan.

The 5th Indiana Cavalry was part of the fight by late winter 1862, and within months the legend of the Irishman began to spread throughout the Western Theater. In April, after only five months, O'Neill was promoted again. Enlisted men, other officers, and even an Ohio Archbishop used words such as "brilliant, daring, courageous, noble and gallant"[6] to describe John. By the end of 1863, he had seen, according to a later harsh critic, "enough fighting to satisfy the most exalted Irishman." The innumerable volumes of the *Official Records of the War of the Rebellion* yield up evidence of how the future Fenian fully earned the reputation of being "an unusually dashing officer."[7]

On June 9, 1863, near Glasgow, Kentucky, O'Neill was in command of an advanced guard. They engaged a detached Confederate battalion commanded by Major Oliver Hamilton's Tennessee Cavalry. O'Neill, with his two small companies, fiercely charged the rebels, broke them, and moved to cut off their retreat. Hamilton's command was totally routed, with a loss of forty men, thirty-six prisoners, two guns, and large quantities of supplies and public funds. The Colonel Graham reported this affair, "I take occasion to make special mention of Lieutenant John O'Neill, Lieutenant William Angel of the 5th Indiana Cavalry, and the men under their command. No officer or soldier could have done better than they. O'Neill killed two men with his sabre while Angel shot three men with his revolver."[8]

A month later, on July 19, 1st Lieutenant O'Neill again showed unexampled bravery. Confederate General John Morgan carried out his celebrated "Ohio Raid," designed to threaten the Louisville area, trying to cover General Braxton Bragg's Confederate retreat in Tennessee. With 2,500 men, Morgan boldly crossed into the North, actually marching his men through the streets of Cincinnati. Covering almost a thousand miles in forty-five days, Morgan struck fear into civilians at the same time the Battle of Gettysburg was being waged not many miles to the east. As the Confederates attempted to cross back into Tennessee at Buffington's Bluff they were surprised by Northern forces under Brigadier General Henry Judah, under whom O'Neill was then serving.

Judah later reported, "In less than half an hour the enemy lines were broken and in retreat. The advance of my artillery, and a charge of cavalry made by Lt. John O'Neill of the 5th Indiana Cavalry with only fifty men, converted Morgan's retreat into a rout."[9] As a result, the Morgan Raid ended and he surrendered a week later, the threat to the north via Tennessee never again attempted.

After this incident, O'Neill seems to have been "almost a legendary figure"[10] with men of his regiment, though it is doubtful they were aware he was now just twenty-five. One soldier wrote, "We know of seven rebels he has killed with his own hands. We know he charged and put to rout two hundred rebels with only thirty-three men. We know he charged two regiments of Morgan's command with fifty men, and took three of their guns. Let every officer in the service do that well, and the privates will soon finish the balance."[11]

But the determined Irishman, adored by his own men, was paying a physical price for being in the field constantly for six months. Illness, including the asthma which would plague him the rest of his life, forced the dashing O'Neill to spend almost two months in the hospital with dysentery, first at Cincinnati, and then at Rising Sun, Indiana. O'Neill's reputation had grown so quickly that the illness was a matter of concern to Archbishop John Purcell of Cincinnati.

Henry Judah, an underwhelming Union commander with alcohol problems, was lucky to have Lt. John O'Neill on his staff during Morgan's Raid into Ohio (Library of Congress).

An Irishman from Mallow in County Cork, Purcell had already been the Roman Catholic ruler of Ohio for thirty years, and was one of the most celebrated and powerful religious leaders in America. When informed of John's illness, Purcell said, "There is a remarkably brave officer suffering from diarrhea, contacted in a three-month chase after Morgan, now in St. John's Hospital, in this city in Lieutenant John O'Neill of the 5th Indiana Cavalry. His mother resides in Elizabeth, New Jersey."[12]

O'Neill was released from the hospital in late July and remained at Rising Sun, home of Company I, to recuperate. He applied for a twenty-day leave to visit his "mother and relatives in Elizabethtown, New Jersey. She is sick and a very old lady [Catherine was 58]." For whatever reason, O'Neill was turned down and the news was not well received by the stubborn young hero. The next day he wrote, "I am still sick in bed," and a Dr. Williams of Rising Sun wrote him a note that his patient would be out of action for twenty days.[13]

Mary Ann Crow and O'Neill had continued their romance by letter, not just to each other. Mary Ann, raised in a convent orphanage school, was a devout Catholic, as was Lieutenant O'Neill. Anxious to prove her baptism prior to any Catholic wedding, she advertised for her missing father in Australia, and in late 1861, at age seventeen, she actually found him. Mary Ann informed him of her mother's death, and Patrick Crow, who abandoned his daughter at age seven, responded:

> 15 January 1862
> 245 Clarence Street
> Sydney
>
> My Dear Mary Anne,
> I have received your welcome letter and am happy to learn you enjoy good health. I was not aware you advertised or made any enquires [sic] about me. I have been told since leaving San Francisco your mother was dead, but did not credit it. If I thought such was the case I would not have been so remiss. As to the certificate you have been searching for, you were baptized by the Rev. Dean Coffey of Parramatta near Sydney. Mr. and Mrs. Kennedy of Concord were your sponsors. If any person has insulted you or said you were not christened in the Roman Catholic Church shew [sic] them this letter and if you still require the certificate I will forward it on your reply to this letter. Please let me know what you require it for are you going to be married or what is it for. Please let me know what Mrs. Davis and father are doing and if alive give them my best respects. If you wish to come to Sydney and want means let me know and I will pay your passage. I was about proceeding to New Zealand when I received your letter but will await your reply to this. Mr. and Mrs. Sexton send their kindest regards and please direct your reply to 245 Clarence Street care of E. Sexton. I enjoy good health thank god ever since I left Calafornia [sic]. I remain your affectionate father.[14]
> Patrick Crow

One can only imagine Mary Ann's tumultuous feelings. She was in love with a soldier fighting in the Civil War on the other side of the continent and found a father who had totally abandoned her and her mother in a foreign land and not seen since her since age seven. Her fiancé might be killed any day, and the parent who had abandoned her and her dead mother was now pleased to hear from her. In addition, her employer, the wealthy Bissell, had just died, leaving her working for a widow and two young children.

How Mary Ann was supposed to know the Sextons in Sydney is a mystery, and how she handled the statement "I have been told your mother was dead but did not credit it" from a man that abandoned his wife and child in a tent is unknown. But Mary Ann was trained well by the Daughters of Charity, and their resources may easily have helped locate the Irish ex-convict father. If Patrick had been the one to track down his only child, it would show some love and deep-seated affection, but such was not the case. He never even asked how Bridget had died or where she was buried.

Discovering her soldier boy in dire straits in the Cincinnati hospital,

Mary Ann embarked on a planned journey via the Panama Canal. The trip took almost two months, and the nineteen-year-old met her future O'Neill family for the first time in Elizabeth where they would all begin planning a future Irish wedding. She told her son John Hugh later, "It was the first time I ever saw snow, when I landed in New York."[15] Mary Ann had perhaps another reason to be happy. She had, after all, established a long-distance relationship with Patrick Crow, the father who had abandoned her as a child, and the correspondence would continue for over a decade, with complications one can only imagine.

Mary Ann Crow in an ambrotype only produced between 1855 and 1864—perhaps taken around the date just prior to or at her marriage, it shows Mary Ann about age 20 (O'Neill family collection).

But there was still a war to fight and win. The young lieutenant whose men would follow him anywhere returned to active duty in September, letting Mary Ann, Catherine, and spinster Mary O'Neill plan a wedding in Elizabeth. With Confederate General James Longstreet and Union General Ambrose Burnside about Knoxville, each trying to gain control of the area, O'Neill's star continued its ascent. His name once again enters the *Official Record* with Brigadier General F. W. Graham commenting on his outstanding conduct at Walker's Ford at the Clinch River in North Central Tennessee on December 2, 1863. "Of the officers and men of my command I cannot speak too highly; fighting as they did, five times their number and did so for eight hours before want of ammunition. I must however speak of Lieutenant John O'Neill of Company I, 5th Indiana Cavalry, my acting adjutant general. I take pleasure in recommending him for speedy promotion. He rendered me great assistance in conducting the engagement, was constantly under fire, and was finally wounded and taken off the field." At the end of his report, Graham cryptically adds, "Lieutenant Colonel Butler, 5th Indiana Cavalry, was cool and determined, and at all times kept control of his men."[16]

Shot in the upper thigh, O'Neill's version of the fight did not jive in any way with that of the more politically correct Graham, who may have been trying to preserve morale in the 5th. After the war, O'Neill told a biographer, "I was at breakfast when the alarm was given that the enemy had surprised the advanced guard, and were attacking in force." He continued, "I rallied the company of picked men I commanded and for a long time held the advancing forces of the enemy in check, to give time for the others to form line of battle. But the enemy was rapidly getting in rear of our Union troops and we fell back on the main body of the regiment, just in time to hear Colonel Butler cry out, 'Oh God, all is lost! Save yourselves men, the best way you can. Nothing is left us but retreat!'"

O'Neill's response was predictable. "Not by a long sight," he recalled later. Sword in hand, "I dashed in front of the mob of soldiers, upon whom panic and the example of their commander were rapidly doing the work of the disorganization. Men, all of you who can mean to fight, fall in with me." The effect was immediate. "About one hundred and fifty of the fugitives rallied, and we drove back the advancing columns of the enemy."[17]

There is corroborative evidence of O'Neill's version from a news correspondent from the *Indianapolis Journal*. The reporter wrote,

The rebels, finding we were retreating, determined to drive us into the river. About three hundred mounted men came over the hills, charging through Company A 65th Indiana, and three companies of the 5th, commanded by Col. Butler and Captain Hodge. Our boys began to waver. The Colonel tried to rally them to no effect, when O'Neill rode up and took command. Taking a Henry rifle from one of the 65th boys, he commenced firing, at the same time yelling at the men to charge them, which they did. For about five minutes it was the most frightful scene I have ever witnessed. Out of the three hundred Confederates only about twenty went back mounted, the balance being killed, wounded and dismounted. A rebel officer, afterwards taken, admitted the loss of twenty killed and forty wounded in the charge. This so effectually checked them, and convinced them that a charge would not pay, that we very easily held our ground until the wagons and guns had crossed the river. But our brave Lieutenant, O'Neill, received a wound in the thigh while we were making our last stand. He rode out all day, never seeking shelter, cheering his men. When other officers had given up all as lost, he replied, "Not by a long sight." He met with a hearty response from the men. We afterwards learned that we were fighting three brigades, among them the famed "Texas Rangers."[18]

There is no refutation of O'Neill's version of the battle, then or now, nor is there any record that O'Neill ever misrepresented himself, exaggerated, or lied about his army service during the Civil War. Indeed, just the opposite. Nonetheless, this episode, though covering him in true glory, would bring a price beyond his physical wound, and remind us of his rashness, anger, and unbending nature, which was common to his unusual upbringing. His grievances in this instance were real, and O'Neill should have continued his extraordinary rise as an officer in the Union Army. Such, however, would not be the case.

Lieutenant John O'Neill spent the next seven weeks in the hospital with a severe wound to the thigh but his recovery was made easier to bear when he discovered Brigadier General Graham recommended him for promotion to captaincy, surely a deserved honor. In fact, O'Neill's recommendation by Graham was seconded by Brigadier General Henry Judah, Inspector General of the Army of Ohio. "I deem Lt. John O'Neill of the 5th Indiana Cavalry one of the most gallant and efficient officers it has been my duty to command. His daring services have been conspicuous and I trust he may receive what he so ably merits—a speedy promotion."[19]

There is no question O'Neill was a rare officer, even younger than the Army knew. He was adored by his men and honored by his supervisors, a rare combination. For certain, the travails of the young boy from Monaghan seemed to have been overcome by maturity beyond his youth. With a promotion in his proverbial hip pocket, O'Neill used his absence with leave time to go home to New Jersey and reunite with family he had not seen in nine years, and a beautiful Australian girl he wished to make his wife.

There was no need in Elizabeth to discuss a failed bookshop, a rash desertion, or the long delay connecting with family. Lieutenant John Charles O'Neill was back in Union County, New Jersey, a certified hero, expecting he would soon be a captain—perhaps even a major—of cavalry with a wonderful future. Wedding plans, marriage registration, and Catholic banns would take place in the very near future, war willing. It was, in fact, the first time he had seen any family member for nine years.

O'Neill returned to Indiana in May, and the now twenty-six-year-old was hit by the hammer of disappointment. There was no promotion of any kind. While away, the Indiana politicians had gone to work and promoted several men in the 5th Indiana Cavalry, all Hoosiers. Compounding the insult, Thomas Butler was incredulously promoted to full colonel. John O'Neill, the only officer in the 5th Indiana Cavalry east of Indiana, was ignored, and politics won out. He never saw it coming, and responded as he had his entire life, quickly and rashly. John C. O'Neill resigned on the spot.

Camp near Paris, Kentucky, April 7, 1864

Sir, I have the honor herewith to tender my resignation as First Lieutenant of Company I, 5th Cavalry, 90th Regiment Indiana Volunteers, on account of promotions in the regiment, which have placed men over me whom I cannot consistently serve under. Some of them Captains, have been Sergeants in the same regiment since I have been First Lieutenant; and while I have a high regard for these officers personally, I can never allow myself to be commanded by them in the field. I served in the regular army nearly four years, in Utah, California, and on the Peninsula: as a private, Corporal, Sergeant, and acting Sergeant-Major, and have been in the regiment, as Lieutenant, sixteen months.[20]

But the angry Irishman was not finished, and even one of his most severe Canadian critics later defended him, saying, "O'Neill had a real grievance."[21] O'Neill attacked the decision with the following: "The enclosed copies of letters from Generals Hodson, Judah and Stoneman, with others from the present Colonel of my regiment, and the former, Colonel Graham, recommending me to Governor Morton, for the position of field officer in one of the regiments being organized in Indiana, will show that I am not undeserving of promotion in my own regiment, and that I have some cause to be dissatisfied with not receiving it, and with having officers placed over me whom, in point of military knowledge and experience, I cannot regard as my superiors."[22] The boy warrior ends with a flourish. "I certify, on honor, that I am not indebted to the United States on any account whatever, and that I am not responsible for any government property, except what I am prepared to turn over to the proper officer on the acceptance of my resignation, and that I was last paid by Major Haggerty to include the twenty-ninth of February, 1864."[23]

Though the tone and tenor of the resignation left little to change the decision, General Stoneman replied immediately, and had obviously been working on a compromise to salvage the services of O'Neill.

Headquarters, 23 D Army Corps, March 8, 1864.

I knew Lieut. O'Neill well on the Peninsula, and as a brave and worthy officer, in whose judgment and capacity I had the greatest confidence. I hope he will receive the promotion to which his merits entitle him, that of a field officer in a coloured regiment.[24]

Finally, there was one more direct intervention, and it came from a man who surely not only understood the predicament, but disagreed with it as well.

Headquarters, Cavalry Corps
Paris, Kentucky, April 7, 1864
Disapproved and respectfully forwarded.

This is an excellent officer—too valuable—indeed, to be lost to the service. He was severely wounded near Tazewell, under Colonel Graham, last December, and is estimated as one of the best officers of my command. This is not the only resignation which has been offered on account of the promotions of inferiors having been made in the 5th Indiana Cavalry over the heads of superiors, based upon political or other considerations, and altogether regardless of merit. By this system junior and meritorious officers find themselves cut off from all hope of advancement, and compelled to serve subordinate to others for whose qualifications they can entertain no respect.

Respectfully,
Sam D. Sturges, Brig-Gen Com'g[25]

Sturges, as they say in modern terms, got it. Even though he was from West Point, and graduated with the likes of McClellan, Stoneman, Stonewall Jackson, A.P. Hill, and George Pickett, he came to realize the importance of enlisted men like O'Neill. Unfortunately the Chief of Cavalry in the Army of Ohio was ignored when it counted most.

Headquarters, Department of the Ohio
Knoxville, Tenn., April 16, 1864

Respectfully returned from the Headquarters, Cavalry Corps, to Lieut. John O'Neill,
5th Indiana Cavalry.
There appears to be no remedy for the evil referred to by General Sturges.
By command of Major General John Schofield[26]

O'Neill's friends, and there were many, did not forget him, including the Military Governor of Tennessee, Andrew Johnson, residing in Nashville. Johnson, a five-time congressman from Tennessee who many said had been taught to read by his wife, had admired the hard driving and effective cavalry officer during the 5th Indiana work against Morgan, the Confederate raider. Though finished in Indiana, influential officers and local people in Tennessee where O'Neill had been so active calmed him down and convinced him to take the position of captain of the 17th U.S. Colored Troops on June 1. For a month or two he worked hard in Nashville organizing the regiment, but when O'Neill realized his colored troops would be doing little but guarding depots and digging ditches—not fighting—he resigned again in October, this time for good. Later historians would have O'Neill leading these soldiers into battle, but this is not true. Johnson, a slave owner but staunch Unionist, soon to become Lincoln's vice president, was disappointed, but the friendship was firm, and would play out in the months and years ahead.

The elements surrounding O'Neill's sudden resignation eerily resemble the outcome of another Union soldier faced with disappointment when searching for advancement in the U.S. Army. Ulysses S. Grant, whose life would intertwine with that of John O'Neill in ten years, sat in the office of Illinois Governor Richard Yates for days in 1861 and was more than ignored by all. Yates was Abraham Lincoln's old campaign manager, and no fan of Grant.

Finally seeing the governor, Grant was told, "I am sorry to say captain, there is nothing for you now to do. Call again." Despairing, the future two-time president almost quit. Assigned to a desk command much like O'Neill's "promotion" with Negro troops, Grant said to a friend, "I'm going to quit. I'm going home."[27] Before actually taking a train home to his shopkeeper's job in Galena, Illinois, by a stroke of luck, Yates hesitatingly recognized his value and gave the future president a command.

Both Grant and O'Neill would go through life as poor businessmen, and each was hurt by exaggerated stories of alcohol abuse by enemies jealous of their strong personalities. John O'Neill, unfortunately, did not possess the grit or luck of an older Grant, and gave in to his long time dissociative behavior and headed home to Elizabeth, the town he had abandoned a decade prior, and his Australian fiancée, Mary Ann Crow.

On his travel back home to New Jersey, the Irishman from Monaghan knew his career was over after seven years, with five of active service and two of desertion. At his resignation, he was twenty-six years old—not the thirty he led people to believe—and had served each of those five years with distinction and not one bad review. His files in the National Archives show not a single admonishment from anyone, ever. O'Neill rose from the ranks and earned five promotions, four of which were granted. The ex-lieutenant was actively involved in six states, and had made two cross continental trips, one by land and another by sea.

There were 180,000 Irish who served in the Civil War, and John O'Neill's record ranks among the best. He was not a Tom Sweeny or James Shields, whose courage and leadership are enshrined in American history. O'Neill was also not a leader as renowned as Confederate General Patrick Cleburne or Union commanders Michael Corcoran or Myles Keogh, who not only served but sacrificed their lives serving their country. But Lieutenant John Charles O'Neill and men like him can lay claim to gallantry often overlooked in the history of the Civil War. The Civil War stage of O'Neill's life ended with him being a minor but daring legend of the Midwest. But it was only Act 1; Act 2 would soon see the name John O'Neill on a national stage.

4

Nashville and the Fenians

We all declare for liberty, but in using the same word, we do not all mean the same thing.—Abraham Lincoln

On a cool brisk Sunday in late November 1864, the Rev. Isaac Howell, the pastor whose strategy defused the Know Nothings in Elizabeth a decade prior, officiated at the wedding of twenty-four-year-old John O'Neill and twenty-year-old Mary Ann Crow in St. Mary's Catholic Church. The witnesses were somewhat unusual for an Irish wedding. John's only sister Mary, now thirty-two, was Mary Ann's maid of honor, the young bride having no remaining family with the exception of an itinerant gold miner in Australia who abandoned her as a child. John's best man was his first cousin, George Macklin, now twenty, and not his only brother, Bernard, thirty-four. John and George had only seen each other once in nine years since George was twelve, and though there is no record of discord between Bernard and John, hints like the one above will grow in future years for the two Drumgallan brothers. It certainly would not be the first time two Irish brothers would lead different lives, and the career paths between the grocer and the soldier would widen more with age.[1]

The newlyweds did not settle in Elizabeth, or even New Jersey. John and Mary Ann arrived in Nashville after Christmas, just weeks after the battle at the city of Franklin, Tennessee, that would effectively end the war in the West and marked the death of Confederate General John Adams, mentor to a younger O'Neill.

While O'Neill was getting married, General John Bell Hood led a desperate Confederate attempt to regain the Western Theater, hoping to draw Sherman and his army away from Atlanta. Sherman saw it as a ruse, and continued his attack in Georgia and then famously up the East Coast. Hood foolishly led 20,000 men into a full-frontal assault without substantial artillery support against Union forces entrenched and waiting. Six Confederate generals were killed; seven more wounded; and Hood's forces suffered more than

7,000 casualties in five hours. The first general killed in the initial assault was John Adams, who had first recruited John O'Neill in Baltimore in 1857, and then saved his Army career with intervention in San Francisco in 1860.

After Adams left Fort Crook and followed his Tennessee heart with service in the Confederacy, he was made a captain of cavalry in charge of Memphis. Within a year he advanced faster and higher than his protégé O'Neill, and by December of 1862 was made a brigadier general. At Franklin he urged his men forward on his bay horse "Old Charley" and rode headlong toward the Union parapet in a spectacular assault. Colonel W. Scott Stewart of the 65th Illinois shouted to his men to hold their fire, recognizing a courageous act.

Although a conspicuous target, Adams at first appeared to be immune to bullets flying all around him as he rode straight for the colors of the 65th Illinois. A Union soldier who watched Adams said, "We hoped he would not be killed. He was too brave to be killed," but it was too late as nine bullets drove Adams backward; he would die fifty yards from another Irishman, General Patrick Cleburne. Both their bodies would soon lie side by side in an ambulance, great losses to America and Ireland.[2]

Both Adams and O'Neill had come a long way in seven years. Adams, a first-generation Irish American with roots in County Tyrone and a West Point graduate, and O'Neill from nearby Monaghan, an underage Dragoon with a suspect past. They became friends and great soldiers. The newly-wed O'Neill surely learned of his demise, as Franklin is only twenty miles from Nashville, and the Franklin Massacre was widely reported.

The move to Tennessee made perfect sense for the newlyweds. Except for family he did not identify with, New Jersey offered few prospects for the new bride and groom, while in Nashville the name John O'Neill was honored, his prospects great. With the Confederate threat eliminated, and peace on the horizon, civilian John O'Neill opened a real estate and claims agency, O'Neill and Mitchell, at Cedar Street in May 1865. John and Mary Ann lived just blocks away, on Russell Street, in the fashionable Edgefield neighborhood. The 1866 Nashville Directory had a full-page ad for the O'Neill claims agency, and identified him as a "military attorney," proof of the non-schooled Irishman's intelligence. The references for the now twenty-six-year-old O'Neill included six ex–Union generals and one governor, all residents of Tennessee.

The *Nashville Morning Times* stated, "Without a doubt, the most extensive claims of its kind on this side of the Alleghenies is in 35 Cedar Street under Captain John O'Neill. More than a million dollars lie upon his shelves in the shape of claims of every description. The present prospect is that this winter will bring in a million dollars' worth of claims per month. Captain O'Neill has established branch offices throughout Tennessee, Alabama, and Georgia—all under charge of prominent citizens."[3]

The future for the O'Neills could not have looked brighter. The history of the Irish in America is often portrayed as an Eastern ghetto, and though the majority did indeed live as "first-boat Irish," clinging to the Eastern Seaboard, there was Irish vibrancy nationwide. New Orleans, San Francisco, St. Louis, and Chicago were teeming with Irish, even during the Civil War, but it's a surprise to many that Nashville, Tennessee, was heavily Catholic Irish and, because of the war, a booming city.[4]

Andrew Johnson, soon to be the 17th United States President, had been a resident of the town since his appointment as military governor in 1862. Nashville was a prime shipping port on the busy Cumberland River and the number one depot for the Western Theater of the Civil War. Unlike many southern towns and cities, Nashville emerged with fewer physical and political scars since it was never really attacked during wartime. It was

The State Insurance Company of Nashville. See page 24.

A. A. SPENCER & CO., Commission Merchant   Church Street.

208   KING'S NASHVILLE CITY DIRECTORY.

JOHN O'NEILL
LATE CAPTAIN IN THE 17th U. S. C. I.

SOLICITOR OF CLAIMS,
AND

Military Attorney,
NO. 35 CEDAR STREET, UP STAIRS,

NASHVILLE, - - TENNESSEE.

Prosecutes Claims against the Government for property taken by, and for the use of the Army, Bounties, Pensions, Arrears of Pay, Commutation of Rations for Prisoners of War, Prize Money, AND HORSES LOST IN THE SERVICE.

Special attention paid to making up ORDNANCE, QUARTER-MASTERS' and MEDICAL RETURNS. Certificates of NON-INDEBTEDNESS procured in a short time. Quartermasters' Vouchers collected, and Patents procured. Being connected with a well established office at Washington, D. C., I offer peculiar facilities for the prompt Collection of Claims, not surpassed anywhere within the United States.

REFERENCES:

Initial career move of John O'Neill following Civil War and marriage: opening claims office in Nashville. Choosing the Fenians over career and Ireland over America were perhaps O'Neill's worst family decisions (Nashville Public Library).

a city of renovation, not reconstruction, and Tennessee became the first secessionist state to be readmitted to the Union in 1866. Nashville escaped most of the ravages of the war, and avoided the heavy physical and emotional prices that Vicksburg, Chattanooga, and Memphis paid.

In 1850, the population of Nashville was 11,000, and by 1870 there were 26,000, with 11,000 African Americans, many of whom had begun a soon-to-be century-long trek north after the Emancipation Proclamation. Unlike other southern cities, many of the newcomers were from the north, ex-soldiers like O'Neill who sensed new opportunities in a changing world. Soon, like the African American migration, there would be 9,000 Irish or Irish

Americans. It was a reluctant partnership between southerners and northerners, blacks, and Irish, which at times struggled to cooperate with each other, but Nashville was way ahead of most of the country.[5]

The economy boomed after the war as well, and it brought to Nashville advanced education and culture. There were soon five colleges around town: Fisk, Central Tennessee, Roger Williams, Peabody, and Vanderbilt. O'Neill's business thrived, handling the pension and claims requests of ex-soldiers settling in the area. Cedar Street was in a high-class neighborhood and years later O'Neill would claim he lost a fortune when choosing Ireland and the Fenians over family and business life in Nashville.[6] But choose Ireland he did, without blinking. Perhaps, as he lay dying in Omaha, O'Neill wished he had stayed in Nashville, an esteemed, perhaps portly and revered Irish American.

The Fenian Brotherhood was formed in 1858, and like most Irish organizations past and present, the aim was to unite and free Ireland, though it always entailed divisions between Irish and Irish American approaches to the same problem. Who would lead, who would collect the funds, where the funds would best be spent, whether to attack with violence or with the ballot, and who would be in charge were always questions. Two veterans of the failed 1848 Young Irelander Rebellion founded the Fenian Brotherhood, the American branch of the Irish Revolutionary Brotherhood (IRB), in 1858. Writer Michael Doheny eluded arrest in Ireland and escaped to New York where he worked as a lawyer, but died unexpectedly in 1862 before the Brotherhood became a national movement. His best friend, John O'Mahony, became the driving force and lightning rod of the organization until his death in New York City in 1877. The FB, or the Brotherhood, as it became most easily known, became a significant Irish nationalist force in the United States, though most modern Americans, especially Irish Americans, are unaware of its history. In truth the Fenian organization soon became the most popular and most powerful ethnic organization in United States history.

The concept itself was simple but brilliant. Ireland was and had been unfree for centuries. Its people were subjected to famine, poverty, lack of representation, and subjugation from Britain for generations upon generations. The seeds of Irish nationalism in America were thus easily found "in the realities of loneliness and alienation, poverty and prejudice," especially after the Famine.[7]

The odds of rebellion were still small but in America the seeds took hold after 1.3 million emigrants began new poor lives as a result of the Famine, free from the English yoke. The influx of Irish immigrants was overwhelming. In 1851 alone, 221,000 Irish arrived, and a decade later many of these were of military age. Once the Civil War began, perhaps two hundred thousand Irish and Irish American boys and men, North and South, became trained soldiers.

They fought in hand-to-hand combat, died by the thousands via cannon and disease, and learned the hard way about the monstrous art of war. The Fenian Brotherhood, a secret Irish society that never was anything but public, recruited nationwide from 1858, but during the Civil War reached its zenith. Both Confederate and Union commanders for years during the Civil War allowed Irish recruiters to cross battle lines with official permission or free passage with escorts to convene and recruit their men to a Fenian oath, and there were few regiments in either army without a Fenian "circle." Some commanders commonly gave twenty-day passes to officers and men to attend Fenian conventions or to recruit.[8]

In the most high-profile case, Union General Tom Sweeny reportedly conferred with Confederate Major General Patrick Cleburne, just prior to Cleburne's death at Franklin, in a clandestine nighttime discussion about joining the Fenians. Sweeny, under a flag of truce, sent a message to Cleburne that "after the war was over" they both would raise a Fenian army and "liberate Ireland." Cleburne reportedly answered that after the war both would have had enough fighting for a lifetime, and declined.[9]

The organization suffered a major blow with the sudden death in 1863 of Union General Mike Corcoran, a former cop from Sligo and the soul of the Irish Revolutionary fight in America, and Cleburne the following year, but nonetheless Irish Americans of all kinds embraced the Brotherhood with alacrity as the war wound down.

Few written records were kept, but estimates of men who signed the Fenian pledge ranged from 125,000 to 200,000. In 1863 the Brotherhood held their first national convention in Chicago, with eighty-two delegates from

The Fenian poster of the Brotherhood. Begun in 1858, it combined to show solidarity between the U.S. and Ireland. The American flag in foreground, green flag in background with harp and shamrocks, and all in red, white, and blue.

twelve states, but less than two years later, at the second convention in Cincinnati, there were 348 delegates with 273 circles.

Each member paid a one-dollar initiation fee and weekly dues of ten cents. The Fenian Brotherhood could be found everywhere, with one report stating there were more than five hundred circles across the country and another eighty in Canada. It was an ambitious organization with initial hard-cash support, and definitely a by-product of the Civil War. Money was not a problem in these early days, though it would dry up significantly through lack of interest and mismanagement. Nonetheless, in the first few years of enthusiasm for the cause, there were times when between $5,000 and $15,000 a day rolled into its New York City coffers. The FB eventually became the only organization in United States history that armed and drilled publicly anywhere it wished on American soil, and flew its own flag. The original headquarters were on Duane Street in lower Manhattan, but by 1865 the Fenian executives, led by a president and senate, purchased one of the finest buildings in America on Union Square. Known as the Moffat House, it was a five-story mansion of pure opulence, reportedly rented for eighteen months for $25,000, proof of the Brotherhood's membership and finances. It still stands today as a Barnes and Noble bookstore, but then operated in effect as a sovereign embassy. Immediately after the war, the Fenians began purchasing arms, ammunition, and even ships, many directly from the U.S. government.[10]

At the end of the Civil War, the American portion of the Brotherhood had one simple aim: Declare war on England to free Ireland. O'Mahony wanted the Brotherhood to foment a rebellion in Ireland, but the majority of the organization realized this was impossible. England controlled the sea and invading Ireland with thousands of men with arms and artillery was impractical. Controlling Canada was a shorter, more reasonable route, and would force England to commit serious numbers to defend its northernmost Dominion, thus enabling an armed revolt back home in Ireland against minimal defenses.

What made the Fenian plan incredibly viable was that by 1865 it was approved and backed silently by the United States government. As bizarre as this sounds today, it was more than reasonable in 1865. The Fenians were serious business, though many English historians have tried to write them out of history books. In addition to the thousands of Fenian Irish ready to fight, it also made sense to the new chief executive of the land, President Andrew Johnson, and many other politicians. For starters, the Canadian provinces were vulnerable. Some among the Brotherhood said if Texas could have been annexed in 1836 in similar fashion, surely a stronger Irish organization could capture Canada. There is no doubt the American seizure of land distressed many of its neighbors. Besides Texas, by 1865 the United States had acquired by less than honorable means Florida from the Spanish and

California, New Mexico, and Arizona in a questionable war with Mexico. Some restless entrepreneurs in Louisiana and Texas were even plotting to procure Cuba. At the highest level of government, Secretary of State William Seward made no secret of his aim to buy or annex Canada for years.

In addition, the Americans still seethed over British support of the Confederacy, especially presidents Johnson and Grant, both of whom demanded reparations while in office. Nobody had forgotten that Britain had helped arm the South and sold them warships, and the government sued Britain for $15 million in reparations. Other non–Irish Americans believed that America should include all of North America, a north-south version of Manifest Destiny. Finally, there was still incredible anger over Canada permitting Confederate spy rings to operate openly during the Civil War, partially blaming Canada for the very recent assassination of Abraham Lincoln. Both Johnson and Seward openly linked the Lincoln assassination with Canadian input. Left unsaid but clearly understood by everyone was the need of all politicians for the huge Irish vote.[11]

Seven years after its initial forming, the organizational infighting often found among the Irish came to an end after the third annual convention of the Brotherhood in Philadelphia in October 1865. Six hundred delegates from thirty states elected John O'Mahony, one of the founders in 1858, president; fifteen senators were chosen nationwide; and former Union General "Fighting" Tom Sweeny was selected as secretary of war. O'Mahony began the organization yearning for an Irish revolt in Ireland, but the Brotherhood in America believed, all too correctly, this was a risk not worth taking, and O'Mahony was quickly pushed aside by the Americans, who were determined to take the fight to Canada. The new chief executive was Corkman William Randall Roberts, a wealthy New York merchant and consummate politician.

But if the Fenian Brotherhood ran its embassy from the Philadelphia/New York axis, the blood and guts were found in the Midwest, especially in Indiana, Tennessee, Ohio, and Illinois. The Fenians were popular throughout the South, and circles could be found in Savannah, Charleston, Mobile, and throughout Texas. New Orleans had seven circles. Nashville in particular was a hornets' nest of Irish nationalism. D.L. Mundy was a local Fenian leader from the beginning of the Civil War; Dennis Murphy was a Nashville Fenian selling Fenian bonds; and in 1866 the *Nashville Daily Union* reported on the vibrant Fenian activity in the town in almost every issue.

By 1863 the Nashville Fenians had already built a Catholic orphanage and supported a large Saint Patrick's Day celebration. Firebrand John Mitchell lived in nearby Knoxville, and James Stephens, a founding member of the FB with O'Mahony, had visited the southern city. Stephens, a thirty-nine-year-old veteran of the 1848 uprising, had studied in Paris and allegedly spoke sixteen languages, few of which impressed the local residents. Stephens spent some time in Nashville, and reported "some of these men are excellent and the majority average."[12] General Tom Sweeny, the future commander of the initial Fenian army, was stationed in Nashville directly after the Civil War, and was already regarded as a hero in much of America, and all of Irish America. The Nashville circle would eventually number over three hundred recruits, none more vocal than the legendary Thomas J. Kelly. The Galway-born Kelly, who had been raising Irish consciousness since he moved to the Tennessee town in 1857, would eventually become an international Irish rebel, working for Irish freedom until he died in 1908 at seventy-five. In the years following the Civil War, Nashville was a beacon in the nation with an all-star cast of fighting Irish, and John O'Neill soon became one of the leading players.

Throughout the land, thousands of survivors of the long Civil War began the process of repairing, reinventing, or beginning new lives, and John O'Neill had a head start on most. With a sterling reputation, honored and respected as a veteran who had done much fighting, O'Neill's future appeared bright, and his business, according to his later testimony, was very successful that first year. But the one disconnect in John O'Neill was his fervent hatred of England and his desire for Ireland to be free of its yoke. No business, family, or friendship could overcome his desire for Irish freedom. It would propel him at one point to national prominence, becoming a general and friend of a president. It would also make him bitter enemies and cause grief and hurt within his own family.

In the summer of 1865, businessman John O'Neill officially became a Fenian, along with fellow Nashville Irishmen James Brennan, Michael McCormick, and Dan Daugherty, joining at least 100,000 others in America, Canada, and Ireland. Sometime soon after, so did another retired Union soldier, Henri Le Caron, who had also moved after the war to Nashville.

> I, John O'Neill, solemnly pledge my sacred word of honor, as a truthful and honest man, that I will labor with my earnest zeal for the liberation of Ireland from the yoke of England, and for the establishment of a free and independent government on the Irish soil; that I will implicitly obey the commands of my superior officers in the Fenian Brotherhood, that I will faithfully discharge the duties of my membership as laid down in the constitution and by-laws thereof; that I will do my utmost to promote feelings of love, harmony, and kindly forbearance among all Irishmen; and that I will foster, defend, and propagate the afore-said Fenian Brotherhood to the utmost of my power.[13]

Though a relative latecomer to the Brotherhood, O'Neill was well aware of its aims and ambitions, and soon was one of the leaders of the Nashville circle. He became a delegate to the Fenian Convention at Pittsburgh in February 1866. Within a month, these Nashville Fenian soldiers and their officers would prove James Stephens very wrong about their mettle.

Everyone has his own path, and the hatred of England bred in the bone of young John O'Neill from Monaghan was about to take possession of his soul. Within months, he was named a colonel of the 13th Nashville Fenian Regiment, and soon Colonel John O'Neill had his 120-man regiment fit, willing, and ready to fight for Ireland.

Before Christmas 1865, Fenian Secretary of War Tom Sweeny had put on paper a detailed approach to a three-pronged Fenian invasion of Canada, and Tom Sweeny was no lightweight. Born in Cork, he fought valiantly in Mexico, wounded in the groin and losing an arm at the Battle of Churubusco. Despite this, Sweeny remained in the Army before being named a brigadier general in the Civil War. At Shiloh, he was shot in the leg and his remaining arm, but stayed in the fight. Later in the war he beat up his corps commander, General Grenville Dodge, a political appointee, in a fistfight with one arm. Awaiting court martial, he went to Nashville, where he became known to O'Neill and other Nashville Fenians. In the summer of 1865, "Fighting Tom" was acquitted and considered a hero by the average soldier, especially by an ex-cavalry officer in the 5th Indiana who had a similar history of being mistreated by political appointments.[14]

Tom Sweeny and John O'Neill were more alike than perhaps they or anyone else realized, and both have been relegated in history unfairly in a fragmentary fashion. Sweeny was fifteen years older than O'Neill, but like the younger Monaghan man had wished for nothing else than a military life. Both were 5'9" and had black hair and dark eyes, and neither was quiet when their ire was raised after a drink. Sweeny, a stalwart in the Civil War, had fought bravely in Mexico and against the Indians, rising through the ranks after enlistment much like O'Neill would do a decade later.

Neither man knew their fathers, who died in Ireland, and each arrived as the youngest children in their respective families. Both joined the Army for an active,

General Tom Sweeny, one of the more underrated soldiers in American history. Though his Fenian career was clouded, his place in American history is still admired.

not philosophical, life, seeking adventure away from the quiet home life their mothers had fashioned for them in the East. A description of Sweeny could easily pass for O'Neill. "Sweeny was brave, often to the point of rashness, efficient, resourceful, self-confident, careful of the safety and comfort of his men, and capable of enduring the most trying hardships. He was quick to damn incompetence, and quicker still to resent any slight, real or imaginary."[15]

Fenian fervor swept the country. It was just a matter of time, and John O'Neill, for one, couldn't wait.

Almost a year to the day that ended the Civil War, the Fenian leadership determined it was time to act. President Roberts had spent an untold amount of Fenian money on arms and ammunition, and the false alerts spread by fidgety members and offensive press were beginning to wear thin. Sweeny was convinced he had upwards of 50,000 trained men spread throughout the country, most of them veterans, and thousands of sympathizers. Roberts had even met with President Johnson regarding the attack, and Johnson agreed "to recognize the accomplished facts" and acknowledge an Irish Republic in exile if the Fenians established a foothold in the North Country.[16] With less than 400 U.S. military on the entire Canadian-American border, General Sweeny believed his forces could easily measure in excess of 20,000 men at various attack points across the 4,000-mile border, and even purchased three warships from the U.S. Navy.[17] The leading Canadian Fenian, Toronto's Mike Murphy, convinced Roberts, but not Sweeny, that after defeating the initial Canadian (British) defenders, thousands of disaffected Canadians, one third of whom may have been of Irish descent, would rise with his troops.[18] The frenzy for Irish freedom continued when a crowd close to 100,000 rallied in support of the Fenian Brotherhood in Jones Wood in Manhattan and raised $50,000. There was, it appeared, no stopping the Brotherhood in 1865.

The audacious invasion plan was approved on February 19, 1866, with a date of May 31, giving the inevitable loose lips plenty of time to give it away, and they did. The Canadian government, led by the brilliant, hard-drinking John A. MacDonald, was always fearful of American intentions and planted Fenian spies throughout the Northeast.[19] In Nashville, one would become the bane of the entire organization, especially the life and career of John Charles O'Neill.

In March, John and Mary Ann O'Neill were living the American dream—they had a nice home in a fashionable neighborhood, a thriving business, a leadership position in the Fenian Brotherhood, and their first child. A question of priorities surely crept into the lives of Mary Ann and John O'Neill. On March 2, 1866, John Hugh O'Neill was born in Nashville and baptized on March 14 at the Catholic Cathedral. His godfather was the same George J. Macklin of Elizabeth, New Jersey, who had been the best man at the colonel's wedding. George was now twenty-one, and had moved to

Nashville working as a clerk in O'Neill's agency. There is no record of another Macklin or O'Neill present at the baptism, but traveling would have made it difficult.[20]

It was a glorious day for Mary Ann, the beginning of her life as a mother after arriving in America as a young child herself. She was educated by the Sisters of Charity in San Francisco, worked as so many thousands of Irish immigrant girls did as domestics in the homes of wealthy American families, and fell in love with a handsome Irish young man with a sense of morality, courage, and conviction. Mary Ann's much honored and beloved husband surely could feel similar but distant thoughts—a son born, whose middle name was in honor to the greatest Irish revolutionary leader of all time, Hugh O'Neill of Tyrone, with the greatest Gaelic title possible, "The O'Neill." John O'Neill of the Fenian Brotherhood must have felt some pangs of emotion knowing he was present and alive at the birth of his own son, with the memory of his fatherless birth and upbringing etched upon his mind. There would be no doubt, of course, where the expansive John O'Neill stood on the invasion issue.

Nonetheless, March must have been an excruciating month. A week after his son's birth, 100,000 Irish demonstrated in Jones Wood, New York, and raised $50,000 for the Brotherhood.[21] His son was just baptized, and war with the Fenians seemed just a few short months away. What O'Neill couldn't—and would never—know is that just days after his son's welcome to the Catholic Church, a Nashville Fenian friend would begin a lifetime betrayal of the cause and John Charles O'Neill himself.

Henri Le Caron, a.k.a. Thomas Beach, wrote to his father John Beach in England, who reported the following to British authorities. "I have a son in Nashville, Tennessee, who continually sends communications connected with Fenianism ... my son is surrounded by Fenians in Nashville, and is also intimate with Capt. O'Neill.... If I can be of any service I shall be happy to do so."[22]

But a fight was brewing, and John O'Neill was ready and willing, son or spy notwithstanding.

5

Ridgeway

O'Neill's history incontrovertibly illustrates as noble, determined and daring a character as ever led a brave but enslaved people to victory.—The Irish-American, 1868

General Tom Sweeny wisely appointed retired, experienced Civil War officers in his invasion plan. Brigadier General William Lynch would lead 5,000 men across Lake Erie and the Niagara River from Cleveland and Buffalo; Brigadier C. Carroll Tevis would attack from Chicago and Detroit with 5,000 hoping to lure British forces westward; and Brigadier General Sam Spear would lead 16,000 from Vermont and New York. The plan was sound, and Sweeny had purchased 10,000 arms and 2,500,000 cartridges from U.S. arsenals, with government approval. Tevis, a West Point graduate from Philadelphia, legally purchased 4,220 of the guns from the Bridesburg arsenal in the northeast section of the city. Armed men from towns and cities left families convinced in their hearts they would free Ireland, but, as boxer Mike Tyson once said, "Everybody has a plan until they get hit in the mouth."[1] Logistics became the Irish's punch in the mouth.

If John O'Neill had any second thoughts about leaving his newborn son and wife, it is unknown. The record also fails to mention O'Neill's reaction about the Memphis riots of May 1–3 that occurred just two weeks before his regiment of Fenians embarked for Canada. For five months, from July to October 1864, John O'Neill was the commanding officer of the 17th Colored troops recruited throughout Tennessee. Frustrated when his new regiment was relegated to guard duty, repairing bridges and roads, O'Neill, the ultimate warrior, resigned, frustrated that he and his men would see no active fighting. Less than a year later, in a combustible scene in Memphis two hundred miles southwest, that city's two lowest ethnic groups battled for three days, leaving all but two African Americans dead, with fifty total casualties. The Irish in Memphis, twenty percent of the population and ninety percent of the police department, were still regarded by most as "lower class whites." Much of the old Memphis population was upset that black soldiers were being used to patrol the town under General George Stoneman, an old O'Neill mentor. On May 1, a fight between three black soldiers and four Irish cops began three days of mayhem. Five rapes, the burning of four churches, ninety-one homes, and eight schools, and forty-eight dead was the reported total of African American community damages. Two white people were dead, one of these self-inflicted. The white mobs were all Irish. Though it remains one of the major blights on Irish American history, you have to wonder what the young Fenian Colonel John O'Neill thought as he prepared his Fenian regiment to head north. Records show that of the black soldiers in Memphis, none were in O'Neill's 17th Regiment, a unit he was proud to lead just a year prior.[2]

But Memphis was, and still is, a distinct southern city, and Nashville was not. Not one racial incident was reported in Nashville, and soon, along with his adjutants, captains Lawrence Shields and Rudolphus Fitzpatrick, and the other 114 men of the 13th Tennessee Cavalry, O'Neill was ready to leave home, hearth, and even new-born for Irish freedom. On May 10, Brigadier General C. Carroll Tevis sent orders for O'Neill to prepare his men to head to Sandusky, Ohio, where the regiment would receive final orders.

On the same day, the fifteen Brotherhood senators issued a national proclamation to all FB circles from Fenian headquarters in New York, with no masking of intentions. "Brothers: Your Senate has, for the last time, assembled together: and we desire to make our demands on your patriotism, both for the purpose of furnishing our soldiers with all the little necessities and comforts you can.... In making this appeal to you, we desire to say that the day which is to decide our fate approaches, we feel deeply the responsibility which you have imposed on us."

The invasion of Canada would soon be a reality, and the Fenian Brotherhood cared not a whit who knew it. Leaving no doubt of the Brotherhood's intentions, the Brotherhood Senate continued with direct orders to all circles nationwide.

> Your patience, my brothers, is about to be rewarded by the performance of deeds which will strike terror to the heart of the tyrant and carry hope and joy to every Irish hearthstone throughout the world. We know the promulgation of marching orders, which will follow this circular, will be more welcome and rouse more enthusiasm than any language we could use, and therefore we proceed to lay before you the instructions we deem necessary.
>
> Each man should be supplied with the following articles ... towels, soap, combs, coarse needles and thread, socks and if possible, a change of under-clothing. Immediately upon the announcement of a landing of our troops on the soil of the enemy, and the unfurling of the green flag of the Irish Republic over an Irish Camp, you will call public meetings, parade the streets with flags and music.... There will be no more excuses, then, no more talk of waiting for the striking of the blow.[3]

With the thought of more than 20,000 troops invading Canada in three or more locations, the Brotherhood senate couldn't restrain its optimism. They had guns, ammunition, and perceived government approval. Sweeny wrote a last message to his troops. "After the first victory, the enemy will be pursued with the sword at his loins, until triumph, final and certain, crowns our efforts. There will be no rest, no relaxation. Brothers, the next Circular from us will be after our army is in motion…. May the God of battles and of justice, crown our arms with victory." An American invasion of Canada was about to begin.[4]

A week later, on May 17, Tevis instructed O'Neill by telegram to meet in Cincinnati with other Fenian regiments from Tennessee and Kentucky, and six days later Sweeny directed them to advance to Buffalo. After a boisterous May 25 rally at the Masonic Hall, the Nashville contingent left in the morning, headed north. O'Neill left his trusted cousin George Macklin in Nashville to help Mary Ann and his godson John Hugh, and placed him in charge of the Nashville claims agency. Along the way they picked up the 17th Regiment under Colonel George Owen Starr at Louisville, the 18th Regiment from Cincinnati, and a small company from New Orleans under Captain J.W. Dempsey before rolling into the Cleveland train depot with under five hundred men.[5]

Along all routes north, men boldly chanted the song they had used during the drilling of the winter and spring:

> We are the Fenian Brotherhood,
> Skilled in the arts of war.
> And we're going to fight for Ireland,
> The land that we adore.
> Many battles we have won, along with the boys in blue.
> And we'll go and capture Canada, for we've nothing else to do.
> Fenian Soldier's Song

Wearing working clothes as a disguise, but fooling absolutely nobody, the Fenians, whose plans were always public secrets, discovered no boats, no superiors, and no orders in Cleveland. Not even Brigadier Lynch was to be found. After waiting anxiously for twenty-four hours, a cable from Sweeny told the four hundred to move to Buffalo. Upon arrival Fenian men of the Buffalo circle billeted them throughout the area.

The Western attack plans were even more poorly executed. Though only 1,500 of the 3,000 expected men showed up, they had no horses as the local railways and boat companies would not transport them, thanks to American and Canadian press efforts. In the East, 16,000 were to arrive in Vermont and New York, but again, prior knowledge of the secret invasion enabled most of the men from the Northeast to be delayed or halted by American authorities far from the border.

The historically audacious plan was already becoming a fiasco. Roberts was seemingly lost in his role as President, giving credence to Irish rebel leader John Devoy in his assessment of the Brooklyn merchant, whom he described as "successful, vain, and shallow, but showy."[6] John O'Mahony was even more critical, calling the Brotherhood president a "half-educated shopkeeper, and son of a shoneen baker."[7] It was clear from the beginning that Irish nationalism was not made for the softhearted.

Newspapers throughout the country were reporting mass movements of men, many moving in different directions. Worse, leadership of the attack fell apart. General Sweeny, though he had chosen men with solid credentials to lead, was let down by a combination of poorly organized local circles, bad luck, and perhaps hidden agendas.

Brigadier William Lynch was a solid choice for the attack from Lake Erie. Born in Rochester, he graduated from Notre Dame and served with the 58th Illinois Infantry throughout the Civil War, ending as a brigadier general. Lynch was too sick with a fever to appear, though later critics believed he stayed out of the action in order to stay in the Peacetime Army, which he did until he retired in 1870.

General Charles Carroll Tevis did nothing at all, and was later tried for cowardice before finally being dismissed for desertion in the face of the enemy by Sweeny. Tevis had outstanding credentials but was an eccentric. He was a West Point graduate who converted to Catholicism and served in the Papal Army before returning for the Civil War as an exceptional officer in a Delaware artillery regiment. Following Sweeny's dismissal of him, he went to Europe and fought in Turkey, Bulgaria, and France, where he became a French citizen. It was discovered after his 1900 death in Paris at age 72 that he had volunteered to the British to become an informer and had been on the British payroll since 1867.[8]

Only fifty-year-old Sam Spear of the three major generals in charge fulfilled his orders on the eastern front in Vermont, but he was hampered by newspaper accounts which helped railroads delay arrivals, lack of coordination by New York and Massachusetts circles, and bad luck. His men would arrive for a fight, but it would be too late to be effective. Spear was a career military veteran of three wars: the Seminole, Mexican-American, and Civil. He enlisted as a private and by the end of the Civil War was a colonel of the 11th Pennsylvania Cavalry.

With his chain of command disintegrating completely, Sweeny ordered Lynch's adjutant, Colonel Ed Sherwin, to take command, but he also failed to appear, saying he could not get there in time. Exasperated, Sweeny sent a telegram ordering the most senior officer in Buffalo to take charge as acting brigadier. All historians have been convinced that this choice of an obscure O'Neill was by default, and while this makes a great story, there is little doubt

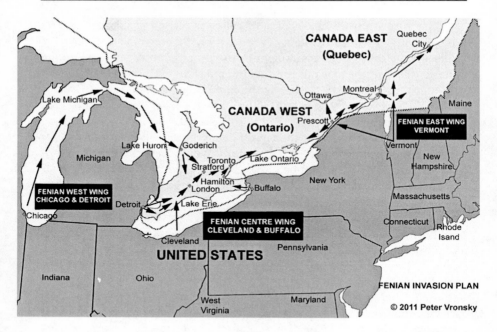

The Fenian Brotherhood plan to invade Canada in 1866. The Sweeny plan involved three attack points, but only the one from Buffalo was initiated, and successful—to a point (© Peter Vronsky).

Sweeny and Tevis had known O'Neill intimately in Nashville, were impressed by both his history and his nature, and thus made a comfortable and knowing decision. In a letter from the previous May even Brigadier Tevis ended with a personal note to O'Neill giving his best wishes to "Mary Ann and son," hardly a remark of an unfamiliar officer. But whether by design or luck, it was a brilliant choice.

After five days on trains and in warehouses, John O'Neill was thrust into history, but he was ready. The engaging, persuasive, and impulsive O'Neill was a natural leader and a most loyal Fenian soldier looking for a long-awaited fight. The Brotherhood oath was ingrained on his heart, especially the phrase, "I will labor with my earnest zeal for the liberation of Ireland from the yoke of England."[9] There were thirty-one Fenian colonels, all Civil War veterans, on Sweeny's invasion plan from across the country, but only one ex-cavalryman excitedly accepted the challenge. O'Neill was proud and honored to play a supporting role, and would get after Canada just as he did Morgan in Tennessee, head-on.

On May 30 O'Neill made his headquarters in the heavily-Irish Buffalo with eight hundred men—the three units from Tennessee and Ohio and the remainder from Buffalo and Indiana. Before he could even think of getting started, neither Canadian nor American vessels were allowed to operate between 4:00 p.m. and 9:00 a.m. on May 31, and Canadian detectives were shadowing every move.

Despite the disorder, O'Neill and his men rose to the challenge. They were without maps but had advance information about Canadian defenses from Canadian Fenians. Their own attack would become more difficult: the Buffalo city authorities were attempting to stop Fenian movements; the Canadian forces were gearing up slowly from Toronto to meet them; and worst of all, the USS *Michigan,* on orders from President Johnson, was patrolling the Buffalo harbor with a U.S. Marine guard to prevent their passage.

O'Neill was thrust into this position and no one would have blamed him had he stood down—everybody else did. But his natural tendency to fight, his impulsive nature to make quick, even rash decisions, and the deep yearning for Irish freedom made his actions of the next forty-eight hours no surprise to anyone who knew the Monaghan-raised John O'Neill.

There were five regiments that made it across the narrowest point of the river, about three miles north of Buffalo proper, most wearing different uniforms. O'Neill's regiment, including forty-four Memphis men, had about 300 men total. The local Buffalo regiment added 150; the Louisville, Kentucky, and Indiana regiments were mostly in full blue uniforms, and led by the man who would stay with O'Neill for years, second-in-command Colonel Owen Starr, who commanded approximately 260 men. There was one other group of similar size, the Cincinnati "Irish Volunteers," who had another 200 men. There was a small group from Cleveland, and of course, no Irish fight could begin without some "Louisiana Tigers" from New Orleans, who wore their Confederate grey. There may have been only twenty or so but they may have been the best fighters and the most difficult to discipline, if their history during the late war is any indication. At first glance, they were a motley crew— none from the East Coast at all—all eager for a fight, and within hours they were being run expertly by the young Nashville man dressed in drab civilian clothes, who looked, as a witness later said, "pale and freckled, more like a dry goods clerk than the leader of a marauding party." O'Neill's brother Bernard, back in his grocery store in Elizabeth, New Jersey, would have chuckled.[10]

At about midnight, this force made a dash for the Buffalo docks. No one knows how many crossed but a good estimate can be settled at eight hundred men. There may have been others, but if so, they probably returned to Buffalo before any fighting began. The barges and canal boats were towed across the Niagara River at a distance of only about eight hundred yards, and slipped past the *Michigan.* Starr's initial group landed on a wharf on Canadian soil, Fort Erie, at 1:00 a.m., the first forces of the Brotherhood that could later walk proudly amongst their fellow Fenians, as Colonel Owen Starr planted an Irish standard. O'Neill would arrive with additional hundreds of men about two hours later. After a brief rest, breakfast, and settling in, O'Neill moved out of Fort Erie on a nice requisitioned horse, which he returned to its owner in three days. Fenian spies, whether from the circle on the *Michigan* or Canadian locals, had given O'Neill one of his few advantages, and he had his men with their back to the river and in great position for a fight. It would be one of the few times that the Fenian spies would prove superior to their Canadian counterparts.

O'Neill gathered the leading local citizens and demanded provisions for 1,000 men; they burned some bridges and cut telegraph wires. But O'Neill was determined not to abuse the locals. He distributed a proclamation from General Sweeny that read in part, "We come among you as the foes of British rule in Ireland.... We have no issue with the people of these provinces.... Our weapons are for the oppressors of Ireland.... We are here as an army of liberation." The food was given but not one local Irish Canadian joined with the Americans, a sign of things to come.[11]

The Canadian forces now realized that indeed this was not a fictional invasion, and within forty-eight hours 20,000 men came forward to serve their country, including students, farmers, and doctors, but none were within fifty miles of O'Neill. They were eager, but for the same two days they would face a professional soldier with no fear, now called General John O'Neill. Unfortunately, the Fenian executives' predictions that a third of Canada would rise up and join the invasion proved ridiculous. O'Neill divided his small forces into two groups, one headed west toward Port Colborne and the Welland Canal under Owen Starr, the other to search for horses and food. By midmorning O'Neill had enough horses for a small detachment of cavalry, his favorite weapon.

Meanwhile there was a serious sense of urgency on the American side. Generals Meade and Grant, still U.S. Army commanders, both hurried north, Grant to Buffalo and Meade to Vermont, to head off any future Fenian ideas. But the victor of Vicksburg and the future 18th president could do nothing to stop O'Neill, already on Canadian soil.

By 7:30 a.m. the next morning fighting began in earnest. The Canadian volunteers skirmished for two hours, but when the Fenians saw for the first time British redcoat uniforms, their eyes lit up, and the local Canadians, who had fought so well, were overwhelmed. As Peter Vronsky described it, "The Fenians, seeing the Canadian lines wavering, began to press their advantage, and fixing bayonets, formed up to counterattack. They advanced downslope firing volleys into the confused mass of men below them. The Canadian lines on the road bucked as the dead and the wounded began to fall around them."[12]

O'Neill's quick decision to order the bayonet charge was the difference.

The Fenian forces drove the Canadians and British through Ridgeway, and the battle was over, a complete victory for the Irish. These Midwestern Fenians had routed a British force of the Queen's own soldiers and O'Neill's men would occupy the town for hours, but with scouts reporting a large reinforcement of British, the Fenian forces headed back toward Fort Erie, awaiting orders from General Sweeny.

But the fight at Fort Erie, though victorious, was not quite so easy. After the short but stubborn resistance of local volunteers struck down several Fenians, only O'Neill's presence may have stopped the Canadian prisoners from being shot. The two days of fighting was soon over, and with no reinforcements, John O'Neill needed to get his men back to Buffalo. O'Neill's men had fought one major and one minor engagement against courageous but inexperienced British and Canadians and were tired and hungry though victorious.

The *New York Herald*, playing to their Irish readers and the still anti–Canadian Civil War animus, said on June 3: "The Fenians have drawn their first blood on the enemy's soil. They have had their first battle, advancing to the work with the steadiness of veterans and driving the enemy before them. They have shown that upon anything like equal terms the Canadians are no match for them and that the Roberts-Sweeny organization are resolved at least to give the Saxons some convincing proof that they mean to strike him where they can most conveniently find him."[13] The Toronto *Irish Canadian* reported: "The Irish Republican Army, under command of Colonel John O'Neil, met the British troops at a place called Ridgeway.... The British outnumbered the Irish Army two to one. The fighting was desperate, and lasted about three hours, during which time the Fenians were twice driven back, but regained their position. Finally, the Irish Army charged the British at the point of the bayonet, and drove them from the ground and remained masters of the field, which their Irish valor had so nobly won."[14]

As thousands of Canadian forces gathered around the small Fenian units, O'Neill realized he had to withdraw and return his men to safety. He sent a telegram to Sweeny saying, "Our men isolated. Enemy marching in force from Toronto. What shall we do?" Sweeny responded that if O'Neill couldn't hold his position to fall back.[15] Additional reports notified him that General Grant had stopped all movement from the American side, and arrested many Fenian leaders. The O'Neill invasion, a minor but very successful military incursion, became newsworthy and a rallying cry for all disaffected Irish worldwide. His men had marched and fought for two days with little food or sustenance, and everyone praised their leader, John O'Neill.

All critics, both Canadian and American, have remarked on the military preciseness of the three-day Fenian invasion. "There was no wanton killing, and the enemies were treated with respect. General John O'Neill and his men performed admirably."[16] There was no looting, disorder, or uncontrolled mayhem, and O'Neill is even said to have threatened to bayonet one soldier who tried to steal a shawl from a tavern. The evidence is overwhelming. His strategy and tactics were sound, and the revered Canadian historian C.P. Stacey praised O'Neill's martial ability, saying he possessed "something of the Napoleonic coup d'oeil, and considerable courage."[17]

At one point during the Battle of Ridgeway, General O'Neill found British Lieutenant Percy Routh lying on the floor of a cabin with a terrible chest wound, abandoned for dead. According to Routh, O'Neill was concerned that Routh's sword was causing him discomfort and tenderly removed it. Routh offered to surrender his sword to O'Neill, who refused to accept it, saying, "No, I will not take it; its possession may be a solace to you. I will leave it by your side." Routh replied, "Thank you but some one less kind may come and take it." O'Neill then carefully hid the sword under Routh's blanket before bidding him farewell.[18]

British Major George Taylor Dennison, of Toronto, said in his later report, "I spent three weeks in Fort Erie and conversed with dozens of the people of the place, and was astonished at the universal testimony borne by them to the unwavering good conduct of the rabble while among them." Denison added, "The Fenians, except so far as they were wrong in invading a peaceful country, in carrying on an unjustifiable war, behaved remarkably well to the inhabitants. They have been called plunderers, robbers, and marauders, yet no matter how unwilling we may be to admit it, the positive fact remains, that they stole but a few valuables, that they destroyed, comparatively speaking, little or nothing and they committed no outrages on the inhabitants but treated every one with unvarying courtesy. On taking prisoners they treated them with the greatest kindness, putting the officers under their parole and returning them their side arms."[19] According to Canadian Peter Vronsky, "Ridgeway may have been the first modern battle fought by Canadians, but it was probably the last one fought with Old World gallantry."[20]

By the early hours of Sunday, June 2, the Fenians abandoned their camp, but not before General John O'Neill addressed the prisoners captured during the three days' fighting. O'Neill told the Canadians they were free to go. He bade them goodbye, said he hoped they would treat their Fenian prisoners as well as they had been treated, and, with a rifle volley salute, the barge was towed toward Buffalo. O'Neill said he would return, and the Canadians were more aware of the promise than the Americans. The raid was a definite reminder to Americans that the Irish had not totally assimilated and they had indeed invaded Canada, won, and lost.

6

Irish Hero,
American Celebrity

I knew O'Neill, and his fine regiment in the Civil War. He was a perfect specimen of the dashing, daredevil Irish soldier, and his men adored him.—J.F. Dunn, 50th Tennessee Infantry

The two barges, carrying seven hundred or so ill-clad, tired, and hungry but proud Irishmen, did not make it halfway across the Niagara River before they were stopped by an armed United States tug, the *Harrison,* and forced to surrender early in the morning on Sunday, June 3. The USS *Michigan* anchored just behind them to foil any escape plans the rest of the day, and O'Neill and his men were arrested, the barges tied to the *Michigan.* William Leonard, a mate on the *Michigan,* had previously recruited a Fenian circle of seventeen sailors in February, and the Brotherhood on board had done much advance spy work of the Welland Canal and Fort Erie area for the invasion, but there was little they could do to help O'Neill now.

The *New York Herald* greeted the invasion with a one-word headline: "WAR."[1] When informed of the arrests, President Johnson replied to confidants, "We have a white elephant on our hands," and did nothing for three days.[2] The young leader of the invasion was not as reticent, writing letters even while under arrest on the *Michigan.* "Please tell our friends that no demonstration towards rescue, or anything of the kind, must be made when we go to the city," O'Neill wrote to Buffalo Fenian leader Frank Gallagher. "We have no fear of the consequences and believe that our good cause would dictate this."[3]

Media accounts depended on whose side of the fence you were on: The anti–Irish *New York Times* on June 3 reported, "Fenians were throwing away their arms and taking to their legs,"[4] and on June 5, the *Times* reported the Brotherhood slogan should be, "He who fights and runs away, may live to run another day."[5] In the same city and the same day, the *New York World* said, "The Canadian invasion was a spirited and gallant fight."[6] Perhaps the *New York Post* captured the viewpoint of many other Americans: "Between the Irish and the English, few Americans have a preference. If these people should fight for ten years we should deplore the blood, but hardly lift a finger to help either."[7]

Finally, on Wednesday, June 6, President Johnson stepped up to the plate and gave a tepid statement, simply an "enterprise" that just came across his desk.

Andrew Johnson, an early friend of O'Neill's during the Civil War and later president, was a political fan of the Fenians, turning a blind eye to their activities much like John Kennedy during the Bay of Pigs invasion (Library of Congress).

By the President of the United States of America—A Proclamation.

Whereas it has become known to me that certain evil-disposed persons have, within the territory and jurisdiction of the United States, begun and set on foot, and have provided and prepared, and are still engaged in providing and preparing, means for such a military expedition and enterprise to be carried on from territory and jurisdiction of the United States against colonies, districts and people of British North America within the dominions of the United Kingdom of Great Britain and Ireland, with which said colonies, districts, and people, and kingdom, the United States are at peace; and whereas the proceedings aforesaid constitute a high misdemeanor, forbidden by the laws of the United States as well as by the laws of nations.

Now, therefore, for the purpose of preventing the carrying on of the unlawful expedition and enterprise aforesaid from the territory and jurisdiction of the United States, and to maintain the public peace, as well as the national honor, and enforce obedience and respect to the laws of the United States;

I, Andrew Johnson, President of the United States, do admonish and warn all good citizens of the United States, against taking part in or in any wise aiding, countenancing or abetting such unlawful proceedings; and I do exhort all judges, magistrates, marshals and officers in the service of the United States to employ all their lawful authority and power to prevent and defeat the aforesaid unlawful proceedings, and to arrest and bring to justice all persons who may be engaged therein, and in pursuance to the Act of Congress.

I do further authorize and empower Major-General G.G. Meade, Commander of the Military Division of the Atlantic, to employ the land and naval forces of the United States and militia thereof, to arrest and prevent the setting on foot and carrying on the expedition and enterprise aforesaid.[8]

Johnson never mentioned the words Irish, Fenian Brotherhood, or even Canada. This political group that armed thousands with weapons bought from the government, recruited for years with tacit approval, drilled in public for months, and had eight hundred men invade a country, killing and wounding people along the way, were described simply as "evil-disposed," and President Johnson only admonished the public that any more such attempts were "unlawful" and subject to arrest.

Of course the horses were already well out of the barn. The government had already given nominal bail to the hundreds arrested in Buffalo, and the War Department amazingly paid rail tickets home for 7,000 Fenians (with their weapons) if they promised never to participate in another attack on Canada. Great Britain, Canada, and much of the United States were in shock.

The Canadians, in particular, and understandably, were furious. Their country had been invaded, their men killed, wounded, and captured. Though overall the casualties were comparatively small, with only twenty killed, seventy-four wounded, and dozens captured, the mood in Canada was violent. A dozen or so Fenian forces suffered similar numbers, though no written records survive; perhaps a dozen were killed on Canadian soil, a few died in Buffalo of wounds, and two more died traveling home. Four local men from Buffalo died including Lt. Colonel Michael Bailey. Six were from Cleveland, two from Cincinnati, but there were no fatalities from O'Neill's Nashville unit. But fifty-eight Fenians were captured and held for trial in Toronto, mostly pickets unable to join the retreating force of O'Neill. All of Canada rose up in indignation, wanting justice. Of all the aims of the Fenian Brotherhood's invasion plan, the idea of the Irish Canadians raising up to support them once they landed on Canadian soil, was surely the biggest mistake. At the 1865 Fenian Convention in Illinois, Canadian Mike Murphy led 44 circles in attendance, and told the senators he represented 125,000 members. Like so much of Fenian lore, exaggeration often ruled.

But in America, there were few thoughts of the prisoners. Overall, the invasion was a massive disaster, which newspapers were quick to point out. Sweeny and Roberts were briefly arrested and quickly paroled, but the Brotherhood immediately grabbed on to its new shining star, the hero of Ridgeway, John O'Neill. The Fenian Brotherhood considered the small work done by O'Neill a "glorious victory."[9] John MacDonald, captain and Canadian minister of militia, said of O'Neill, "The skillful disposition he made of his forces were commensurate with the ability of a high-class tactician," and added, "General O'Neill coolly awaited the arrival of the Canadian troops, who were advancing from Ridgeway totally ignorant to the fact that there was a lion in their path."[10]

O'Neill was soon paroled after being detained on the *Michigan* and when he, Owen Starr, and other leaders of the raid were brought before the magistrate of Erie County, local sympathizers furnished bail and they were discharged to great applause in the courtroom. O'Neill was hailed in the local paper as a "pleasing, modest, unassuming and altogether very agreeable gentleman."[11] Many of the arrested Fenians were represented by a local twenty-nine-year-old Buffalo attorney named Grover Cleveland, soon to be a two-time American president. One individual proposed three cheers for O'Neill, and the Nashville veteran received a standing ovation. When followed to the Mansion House, the biggest hotel in Buffalo, O'Neill was greeted with clamorous applause and said to the crowd assembled, "Gentlemen! You may not be aware that I am not a speechmaker. The only kind of speeches I am accustomed to making are made from the cannon's mouth. Situated as I am at the present, I can only advise you to retire to your homes, peacefully and in an orderly manner. Good-bye!"[12] O'Neill left Buffalo, but didn't follow his own advice and go home, as most historians have depicted. Instead he headed east to Vermont trying to rally Fenians gathered near the border at St. Alban's. Three thousand of them, not the anticipated eight thousand buoyed by the Battle of Ridgeway, were late to the party but eager nonetheless. U.S. forces under General George Meade stopped them before any further incursions could be made, ending completely the 1866 invasion. O'Neill was detained briefly by the authorities in Ogdensburg, New York, before he could reach them, and only then did he return to Nashville, Mary Ann, and John Hugh.

Three facts emerged from this first invasion of Canada. First, the Fenian Brotherhood's grand plans were reduced mightily, though the Irish vote in the United States was not only tolerated but obviously too important to jail anyone just for invading another country. Sweeny and Roberts were arrested, but only as a political response; Sweeny's Fenian career was all but over, and Robert's role diminished. Second, Canada realized the true danger of attack by the Irish and strengthened its defense systems and continued the process that soon resulted in confederation. Third, John O'Neill was recognized as a national star, the man who backed the British down, if only for a moment. Irishmen throughout the land sang the praises of O'Neill. Indeed, his quiet courage and courteous manner had earned it. The failure of the overall plan incurred derision in much of the country, but post-war Irish American nationalists responded not with regret or apology but with utter defiance.

On Friday night, July 12, only a month after Ridgeway, Colonel O'Neill began taking advantage of his newfound celebrity. He told a huge crowd in Nashville, "I feel that eloquence will not do, unless it is for that which flashes from the cannon's mouth—such as we had at Ridgeway and Erie." Speaking for an hour before an enthralled assembly, he continued to defend the Fenian attempt. "We invaded, not as plunderers, not as murderers but as Irish patriots who had given up all that was dear to strike a blow for their country." With applause ringing, he continued, combining Irish freedom and American independence. "Who are we? What are our antecedents? Let me tell you nearly every man with me in Canada fought for the stars and stripes, some of them right at Andy Johnson's home." O'Neill ended the night with a political note. "I will tell you what I intend to do myself. I never voted in my life. I thought it was enough to enjoy living in America, and to fight for the land of my adoption, but henceforth my feeling shall be to order the party that is the friendship of Irish independence. The friend of the Fenian shall be my friend, and he shall have my vote."[13]

The following evening, July 13, the Fenians of Nashville serenaded General John O'Neill at his residence in Edgefield. "The General was taken by surprise by the music that roused him from his slumbers. With true Irish hospitality he invited the whole party indoors and music, patriotic songs and speeches enlivened the company." If there was any doubt about the new exaggerated reputation of John O'Neill, the last song played was "a magnificent version of 'Hail to the Chief.'"

Nashville Fenian Captain Mulroy read the address to O'Neill, in part, "To us, the Irish Republicans of Nashville, you have been as an elder brother; and no matter where you go, or whatever elevated position to which your talents raise you, with pride we shall claim you as ours. Your public reputation, commands our respect; but your personal character and private worth, has won our love." The local admiration was never in doubt, but Mulroy then touched on the future fame of O'Neill nationally. "Our countrymen, all over the world, honor you as General O'Neill, who fearlessly led to victory the vanguard of Ireland's liberating army against the embattled hosts of the hoary oppressor.... You are to us, General O'Neill, the simple, pure, inflexible patriot ... firm in purpose, pure in motive, strong in faith, ardent in love of country, a champion of human liberation, and a soldier in the army of human progress."[14]

As a Fenian colonel, the handsome John O'Neill led the Brotherhood to victory in Canada in June 1866 at age 28, soon becoming an Irish American nationalist celebrity (courtesy Holt County Historical Society).

But though O'Neill was a local and soon to be a national celebrity, his return to Nashville was met with a family scandal, much to his surprise. Cousin George Macklin, the best man at his wedding and the godfather of his only child, had in the space of two weeks "run with as much cash as he could lay his hands on" from the profitable claims agency, and hightailed it to Texas. If the O'Neill/Macklin family dynamics were fragile to begin with, they now became toxic.[15]

What drove George is impossible to know. He had, like his cousin John, fought honorably for four years in the Civil War with the New Jersey 3rd Infantry, and saw action at some of the worst battles of the war. His unit was involved at Malvern Hill, Spotsylvania, Cold Harbor, Antietam, Fredericksburg, and Gettysburg, before being discharged as a corporal in 1864. George remained a roamer the rest of his life, working as a bookkeeper and laborer before settling ignominiously at the Bowery in Manhattan, dying unnoticed sometime after 1900. His name was never again mentioned publicly by any O'Neill, but surely his actions did not help the already delicate family relations.

Throughout the remainder of 1866 O'Neill stayed in Nashville, but at the urging of Fenian executives, spoke at Brotherhood assemblies around the Midwest and Chicago. He repeatedly parodied the FB's party line, saying that it was his old friend Andrew Johnson's fault. At a Memphis rally in August, O'Neill said, "His party has sold the Irishman, and would sell him again. Had it not been for the duplicity of the President's party, this day's sun would rise upon 200,000 soldiers of Canada fighting for Irish freedom."[16]

A month later, O'Neill was in Baltimore at the annual Fenian "pic-nic" at Daltrey Park. Roberts was not present, but the general was the featured speaker in front of three thousand men. He gave a "stirring" speech. O'Neill continued to hammer home that the only failure was owing to the "deception practiced by high officials of the government." O'Neill predicted a very different result next time the Fenians would "strike a blow."[17]

In Buffalo, with his popularity ascending, O'Neill again accused the Fenian president, his old mentor from Nashville. "The interference from the government was needlessly severe." "The President may be against us, but the people are with us."[18] It was becoming clear to the leaders of the Fenian Brotherhood that though John O'Neill professed not to be a public speaker, he was getting much better. His good looks, rich voice, and bilingual use of Irish and English was appealing to many. It was common that Fall to see O'Neill highlighted throughout the country, as he was at the Masonic Temple in Nashville in November, again with more than three thousand men hanging on to every word.

As the autumn of 1866 approached thoughts of further Fenian physical involvement in Canada were diminishing, and the plights of the prisoners in Canada now became front-page news. With fifty-seven men in Toronto jails facing execution, the Fenian Brotherhood had to regroup politically, physically, and financially.

When the dust of the summer's invasion settled, the Fenians gathered at their annual September convention and recriminations abounded, especially against Roberts and Sweeny, each of whom blamed the other. Sweeny took the high road, as he did his entire military and personal life. "Friends, countrymen, and Brothers":

> Accept my warmest thanks for the welcome you have extended to me. I come among you as a friend, a brother, and an Irishman.... Since my early youth the freedom of Ireland from the British yoke has been the dream and passion of my soul.... I gladly threw my sword in the scale, and offer, my life, my fortune, and my sacred honor upon the altar of my native land.

The former brigadier general who fought Mexicans and Confederates with ferocious honesty, continued: "I need not say to you, and certainly not to anyone who knows me, how deeply I deplore the difficulties which have arisen in our Brotherhood, or how cheerfully I would have made any sacrifice compatible with my honor to have healed them—I am satisfied, however, that the time has passed when words or arguments could do so."[19]

The first Brotherhood secretary of war, whose life would end quietly in 1892 at age 72, remained stoically eager for another fight and took a veiled swipe at Roberts and the businessmen who he felt forced his hand in attacking Canada too early. "I will fight for Ireland to the last drop of my blood, and I will lead all who desire to fight with me, but it must be on what I think the path of at least probable success; and not of certain defeat and slaughter—there has been enough Irish blood shed on improbable plans and visionary schemes."[20]

But the delegates at the convention took the obvious road, praising O'Neill and appointing him Inspector General of the Brotherhood. O'Neill, whose appointment by Sweeny just months before created his sudden promotion, watched quietly as Sweeny resigned and eventually returned to his Long Island home to live life as an army pensioner, often sharing letters and pictures of his grandchildren with old comrade General William T. Sherman. In the end these two extreme Irish nationalists, Sweeny and O'Neill, so much alike, would differ as their Fenian shadows fell. Sweeny walked away discouraged and disheartened, while his protégé O'Neill fought the gods.

Only O'Neill, the original unsuspecting hero, emerged with his reputation not only intact, but elevated. He was unanimously thanked in a proclamation that read, "General John O'Neill and the officers and men of his command gallantly upheld the honor of our flag and vindicated the traditional heroism of our race."

Roberts did not help his own cause when his role regarding the captured Fenians came to light. On July 26, President Johnson supported a House of Representative resolution urging Great Britain and Canada to release the prisoners, but the Canadians did not agree and soon twenty-five of the Fenian prisoners were found guilty and sentenced to death. Brotherhood President Roberts threatened to march upon Canada with 21,000 armed men; this despite the fact that Roberts, a non-soldier, had orchestrated such a previous failure in the June invasion, pushing it forward too quickly despite Sweeny's advice to take more time. With Canadian Premier John MacDonald leading the negotiations between both Britain and America, a quiet diplomatic deal was struck as the British Home Office intervened, gently and covertly asking the sentences to be commuted so as not to create Irish martyrs (a lesson the British would forget fifty years later in 1916). One prisoner died awaiting trial, and the others were all released by 1872. Fenian President Roberts, already politically wounded by his role in the invasion, was crushed by the negotiated settlement.

In a December letter to prisoner Colonel Robert Lynch of Kentucky, Fenian Brotherhood President Roberts said, "I regret to tell you that you are not going to be hanged." The prisoners' deaths, continued Roberts, "would make every Irishman in America a Fenian, and raise enough money to expel the British."[21] The first comment must have made Lynch much more comfortable about his situation. Roberts was re-elected, but the job was wearing on him. One historian also claims O'Neill wanted Lynch to be a martyr and in Nashville publicly accused Lynch of cowardice for not wanting to die for the cause. Lynch also claimed O'Neill never answered one of several letters he had sent to the newfound hero of Ridgeway, asking for assistance in his defense. In a November speech O'Neill attempted to divest himself of the Lynch issue, saying he believed Lynch testified at his Canadian trial he was simply a reporter, not a soldier, and therefore not worthy of Fenian defense, knowing full well this was not true. One has to wonder if O'Neill would have felt the same if Lynch was from Nashville, not Kentucky, or in the 5th Indiana Cavalry.

Cork-born William R. Roberts was the political mentor of O'Neill, handing him the keys to the presidency in 1868. Diplomat, Fenian, and businessman, he died in New York at age 67 (Library of Congress).

While Roberts took a political hit for treating Lynch poorly, no such rebuke stuck to the hero of Ridgeway. The twenty-eight-year-old inspector general of the Fenian Brotherhood returned to Nashville, and some Americans, perhaps even family in Elizabeth, New Jersey, may have wondered if this sudden fame would change the measure of the man. O'Neill had fought his hated English enemy on Canadian soil and spent the following six months accepting invitations to speak all over the country. O'Neill was without question the rising star of Irish nationalism in the United States. But there were warnings. "One name alone survived the wreck of reputations following the failure of the expedition—that of John O'Neill. I fear the adulation showered upon that officer turned his head, for very soon, from being a quiet, unostentatious man, he became unpleasantly conscious of himself as a victorious general."[22]

The British government, however, didn't give a damn about John O'Neill's newfound celebrity—they wondered only if he would ever unmask their secret Fenian spy, John O'Neill's newest friend and aide, Henri Le Caron.

7

The General Becomes
a President

Gablanach in ret an Sceluighecht (storytelling is a complicated matter).
—12th Century Irish scribe

As the hero of Ridgeway settled into newfound celebrity life in Nashville, he was reminded many Americans were not in favor of the Irish in general or the Fenian Brotherhood in particular. Though Americans and politicians remained anti–English, that did not translate to pro–Irish. A June 1866 article called the Ridgeway victory "just a deserted dunghill," and added, "The Irish were not heroes, unless they were heroes of the same stamp who bravely led the retreat at Bull Run, and who helped make up the great army of bounty jumpers. These people are the curse of the American society."[1] Despite their popularity, not all Irish supported the FB either, with many of them happy to simply assimilate into mainstream America, including the O'Neills and Macklins of Elizabeth, New Jersey.

But O'Neill was now the herald of Irish republicanism, and the anti–Irish New York Times especially singled him out with falsehoods beyond the pale. "Not only was he a Confederate but a Confederate friend of the infamous Wirtz of Andersonville," one article said, comparing the former heroic Union officer from Indiana with Wirtz, the only man ever executed for war crimes in the Civil War, without knowing or caring that O'Neill was far from a Confederate and had never been to Andersonville or met Wirtz.[2]

It would be the beginning of a fight John O'Neill would attack head-on for years, as was his wont, but never win. The boy with a hedge school education would grow into a prolific writer and earn ovations from a crowd in New York of more than 50,000, but ultimately discovered he was a naïve politician, and while he convinced general audiences, he could never overcome the press or backroom intrigues of more sophisticated Irish.

In the summer of 1867, Fenian President William Roberts went to Europe to attempt a detente among the differing factions of the Fenian Brotherhood on both sides of the ocean. Despite his political acumen that would later result in two terms as a congressman and an ambassadorship to Chile, Roberts was unable to bring his fellow Irishmen together, a task many have failed to achieve, before and since. He returned to New York and prepared for the annual Fenian Convention in Cleveland with a plan to leave the Fenian Brotherhood, a move that would propel the hero of Ridgeway into even greater prominence.

John O'Neill would say later, "Most of 1867 I labored quietly in the ranks, without a thought of official connection with the Brotherhood," but even the dogs in the street knew this was an oversimplification.[3] O'Neill had left Nashville for Washington, D.C., in mid–July, setting up a new pension claims office at 211 Pennsylvania Avenue, opposite the Willard Hotel, two blocks from the Capitol building. It was a long way from Cedar Street in Nashville. There can be little doubt his uptown address in the nation's capital was a direct result of his new stature, and O'Neill was already developing a friendship with Frank Gallagher, the leading Buffalo businessman and Fenian he first met on the way to Ridgeway. The O'Neills lived in the same house as the family of General William Shafter, a Civil War Medal of Honor recipient who would later become famous as "Pecos Bill." Shafter and O'Neill were already friends, as Shafter was colonel of the 17th Colored Troops in Nashville in 1864 and had O'Neill as his captain. That celebrity was not lost on the Brotherhood executives, who were eager for new blood to continue the fight.[4] President Roberts was looking for a diminished role, and Vice President James Gibbons of Philadelphia, the owner of a printing business at 333 Chestnut Street, was already being referred to dismissively as "the old man."

At the September convention in Cleveland, O'Neill was elected as a senator, a precursor to the moves Roberts and Gibbons planned for the new year. In what would foreshadow Fenian developments for years, a motion was made from the floor to admit women as full members. It was soundly defeated because the majority felt women "could not keep secrets."[5] The Brotherhood was beginning to show a small dip in finances; they had taken in $140,000 in the first nine months of the year, but only had a $25,000 balance. It had spent $32,000 on uniforms, another $31,000 on supplies and salaries, and very little on arms and ammunition, intelligence gathering, or military plans. The pendulum was showing preliminary signs of tilting towards a social organization, rather than an army. The slight backslide needed to be reversed and Roberts and Gibbons, who understood their membership well, looked for a military man to help, and once again John O'Neill was in the right place at the right time.

Just as at Ridgeway, O'Neill would not be the premeditated choice. The man destined for the job early on and most dedicated to the cause was General

Michael Corcoran, but he died tragically three days before Christmas 1863 when thrown from a horse while on parole as a Confederate prisoner of war. Corcoran emigrated in 1849 from Sligo, enlisted as a private in the New York militia, then a citizen group, and in 1859 was appointed colonel of the regiment. By 1860 Mike Corcoran was the epitome of the smart, tough, and politically-savvy Irishman in New York, and he hated the British perhaps more than O'Neill. In 1860 Edward, the Prince of Wales, undertook the first visit to America by British royalty since the American Revolution. Edward was met by vast crowds, took tours with President Buchanan, visited Niagara Falls, and dined with Anglo American elite, including Longfellow, Thoreau, and Oliver Wendell Holmes. But Prince Edward did not impress the Irish or Mike Corcoran. New York greeted the prince with a military parade, but Colonel Corcoran refused to parade with his men, and Irish all over the country were elated. Corcoran was arrested by the embarrassed New York elected officials, leading to court martial. But when the Civil War broke out, he not only was released but put in command of what would become the world famous New York Fighting 69th.

Corcoran's death cast a pallor over the country. Songs and poems have been composed about the 69th Regiment through two world wars, and the Corcoran memory is still alive in New York. A monument was unveiled in New York's Calvary Cemetery as late as 2006 by Mayor Michael Bloomberg, and underneath the memorial a piece of steel from the World Trade Center lies poignantly. Corcoran was an early and enthusiastic Fenian, and most of his command followed its colonel in accompanying him into the Fenian Brotherhood's official ranks.

The same was true of another Irish nationalist, Confederate General Patrick Cleburne, who was killed in the Confederate attack at Franklin, Tennessee, toward war's end in 1864. A Corkman like Sweeny, Cleburne was the consummate professional soldier. The son of a doctor, he served in the British Army for three years before arriving in America with two brothers and settling in Arkansas. An extremely popular citizen and businessman, he joined the Confederate Army for one singular reason—affection for the southern populace that treated him as their own. Enlisting as a private, Cleburne was a general within two years. When he sensed the war was lost early in 1864 due to a diminishing supply of white Confederate soldiers, Cleburne called a meeting of the Confederate leadership and proposed allowing slaves to join the army. He was immediately finished politically, and when killed in the attack at Franklin, Tennessee, in late November, more than a few believed he was sent to his death in retaliation. Cleburne rejected a Fenian overture just before his death, but was as loved in the Irish South as was Corcoran in the North. A Fenian circle was named after him in Algiers, Louisiana.

Fenian executives eventually met with General Phil Sheridan, who had no intention of getting involved even remotely. Sheridan's family was originally from County Cavan, but he never considered himself anything but American and never showed any real interest in the homeland. Sheridan stayed a soldier, fought Indians in the west, and made a personal crusade of the protection and evolvement of Yellowstone National Park. He died at fifty-seven in 1888, a great American, never caring a whit about Ireland.[6]

Lastly, the Fenians had for years tried to lure Thomas Francis Meagher into the fold. Meagher was an Irish hero, transplanted to Van Dieman's Land because of oratorical crimes in Ireland in 1849. His fame grew worldwide when he escaped penal servitude and arrived in America. Meagher married into wealth in New York, and, though he openly supported the South prior to the war, led the Irish Brigade when Corcoran was captured. But Meagher was as poor a soldier as he was a brilliant orator, and eventually was replaced and given minor positions in the Western Theater until war's end.

THOMAS FRANCIS MEAGHER,
CAPTAIN COMPANY K, ("IRISH ZOUAVES,") 69TH REGIMENT, N. Y. S. M.

Thomas Meagher was and wasn't a Fenian, but he was the ultimate politician and orator. Considered by many an Irish hero, he died in the Missouri River in still mysterious circumstances, his body never found (Library of Congress).

Even with the Fenians, Meagher "negotiated" his involvement, as a recent favored biographer phrased it.[7] In 1863 this professional ethnic finally took the oath of the Brotherhood after years of prodding, but only to keep his name in the game. His heart was never with the Brotherhood, just his golden voice. In October he was asked for help in raising $500 for startup money for the *Irish People*, but he did little or nothing, and the paper, which became the voice of the Fenians, began in November in dire financial straits. Meagher, who always liked the attention, never attended a single convention. In early 1866 an Irish newspaper reported he might become involved in a leadership role of the 1866 Invasion of Canada. Handsome, eloquent, and with a good heart, the Waterford orator, now just an American politician, went into panic mode and denied it vociferously to everyone. The Fenians mourned like the rest of Irish America when Meagher, then Acting Governor of Montana, drowned in the Missouri River on July 1 when he fell or was thrown off the boat just one month before the 1867 convention, but they were probably saved future embarrassment. The end of 1867 left Roberts and his executive entourage with the younger, handsomer O'Neill, the shining light of Ridgeway.[8]

On the last day of December 1866, Roberts, Gibbons, and P.J. Meehan, publisher of the *Irish-American,* put their plan to revive the Brotherhood into action. Gibbons resigned as vice president, and O'Neill was chosen to succeed him. Two days later Roberts resigned as president, and by constitutional rule the job went automatically to Vice President General John O'Neill. This majority Senate Wing of the Brotherhood had placed the future promise of Irish American nationalism in his hands, hoping the O'Neill magic could strike twice. The young and impressionable O'Neill cast his future with Roberts and Gibbons, though his true nature would have found more favor with the minority O'Mahony wing, later run by John Savage.

Later, in 1870, O'Neill would proclaim "this was done at the earnest solicitation of P.J. Meehan and other leading men of the Fenian Brotherhood." The general said he stepped into Roberts's shoes "only if they gave me their solemn promise they would unite with me in preparing for a fight that year."[9] The upper hierarchy surely did this of their own volition; O'Neill was popular but not powerful enough to pull this move off by himself. This was not, however, a surprise to O'Neill, as he was certainly part of the plan. To say otherwise would be disingenuousness. The general likely was telling the truth, and it is just as possible the Brotherhood was still itching for a fight, but little did they realize they were dealing with a twenty-nine-year-old fanatic heart, not a wizened and mature veteran of both the battlefield and the backroom. Both O'Neill and the Fenian Brotherhood would later come to feel betrayed by each other.

It took less than a week for the brash new president to put his stamp on the Brotherhood and create great controversy, both of which would become O'Neill's trademarks. Three weeks prior to his ascension, Fenians in Ireland planted a bomb outside Clerkenwell Prison in London, attempting to free a sole prisoner and Fenian arms supplier, Richard Burke. The breakout failed to free Burke or anybody else, but the bomb succeeded in killing twelve civilians and injuring 120 people. The atrocity enraged both Great Britain and America. The Fenian Brotherhood in Ireland was unapologetic, as were some American Fenians.[10] But the newly appointed Brotherhood President John O'Neill was infuriated, and he acted swiftly, using the Fenian news organ, the *Irish-American.*

The New York paper printed a proclamation quoting O'Neill, who said "such acts were not authorized by the members of the Fenian Brotherhood [in America]" and disowned assassination in any form.[11] Members of the Brotherhood from Chicago, who always felt that there was too much control in the East, blistered O'Neill for his soft stance in their rival Irish paper, the *Irish Republic*. Only a week in office, O'Neill responded, as always, with alacrity and impetuous sincerity. He called the *Irish Republic* a "concealed adversary, sapping Irish strength from within." He went further, accusing the editors of opposing the leaders of Fenianism because most of them "were Catholics, devoted to their religion." Lines were thus quickly drawn, but in O'Neill's view, "We can neither sell our country, nor deny our God." O'Neill, the extreme nationalist and conservative Catholic, was far from soft. He explained, with deep conviction, "Rivers of blood will have to flow before Ireland can take her place in the nations of the earth; but not one drop should ever flow by the dagger of the assassin." He concluded, "It shall be done in fair and honorable fight, and no other way."[12] If anyone ever doubted the vision of President John O'Neill, by February 1868 it was abundantly clear, especially when he openly called the editors of the *Irish Republic* "rats and driveling idiots."[13]

In Brooklyn on April 29, thousands showed up at Commonwealth Hall, where O'Neill was treated like a rock star. Continually interrupted by applause during a fiery speech, he reiterated the Irish dilemma in America. "I would rather forget the past history of Ireland. Today it matters not to us or to the Irish people who are now in bondage in their native land, while we, my friends, enjoy the rights and privileges of American citizenship. We are not freemen in this land of freedom. We cannot be free men while our fathers and mothers, brothers and sisters are yet in bondage and slavery. We, the Irish in America, cannot consider ourselves freemen until the green flag shall float free in triumph over many a well-contested battle field in Ireland."[14]

Indeed it was a conundrum never understood by Irish rebels in Ireland, even now. The Irish loved being in America and being loyal Americans. They simply had a dual love of seeing Ireland free. O'Neill added, "I tell you the men who went to Canada would have infinitely preferred fighting upon an Irish hillside—I tell you John O'Neill would much prefer fighting upon the hills of Tyrone or Monaghan, to fighting upon the bleak hills of Canada."[15]

O'Neill was still living in Washington, D.C., trying hard to balance a claims office and the Brotherhood demands. To most it would be an easy decision, with family and business first, and the avocation of Irish freedom following. But John O'Neill's lifelong animus of England overlapped all sense and sensibility. He took a partner in the claims office, Joseph M. Dufour, a former Indiana soldier, but like the bookstore in Richmond, O'Neill would soon be gone. In March, he realized the presidency of the FB was consuming too much time, and he reached back to Nashville for help. It was a calamitous mistake, perhaps the first one since Utah. Newly installed Fenian President John O'Neill, whose perceived arrogance, impulsiveness, impetuosity, and love of Irish whiskey was enough for a brave, intelligent, and honorable man to overcome, didn't need secret vermin to make his life more laborious. Nonetheless, in walked Henri Le Caron to do just that; worse, O'Neill invited him in through the front door.

After Le Caron's letter to his father in 1866, it took a year for the British and Canadian governments to vet him and set up meetings, code names, and letter drops. But once Le Caron took the Fenian oath in Nashville, O'Neill reached out, made him his personal aide, and gave him the title of major. By April, O'Neill had wrangled an invitation to the White House for a meeting with President Andrew Johnson. The two Nashville friends had been on opposite sides politically since Ridgeway, but it was just politics. Johnson must have been pleased to see the ex–Indiana cavalry officer he so admired in the war reach the ultimate height of the Fenian Brotherhood, and his Nashville neighbor O'Neill may have reveled in it as well, and brought Le Caron with him to show off. The meeting was by all accounts cordial and soon the topic became the Brotherhood and its future aims. O'Neill raised his impression of Johnson's inaction, or lack of continued action, towards the Buffalo invasion. As only a friend could say, Johnson replied, "I want you to understand that my sympathies are entirely with you and anything that is in my power I am willing to do to assist you. But you must remember I gave you five full days before issuing any proclamation stopping you. What more did you want? If you could not get there in five days, you could never get there; and then, as President, I was compelled to enforce the neutrality Laws, or be denounced by every side."[16]

Whether the high-strung Fenian Brotherhood president smiled is unknown, but President Johnson shocked many, including Canada and Britain, when he agreed by meeting's end to return all the Fenian arms seized at Buffalo. The meeting was a Brotherhood success by any measure. The Irish regained their needed arms and O'Neill walked away with a renewed sense the President of the United States was still a Tennessee friend and desperate for the Irish in an election year. The indefatigable O'Neill soon embarked with James Gibbons on a nationwide tour to raise funds from Maine to Minnesota. His aide, Henri Le Caron, meanwhile, was busy writing letters to Canadian Prime Minister John A. MacDonald and his other handlers in England.

Four months into his presidency, O'Neill and the Fenians were again taken to task by worldwide press condemnations and serious setbacks. On April 7, Patrick Whelan, a known Fenian sympathizer (if not a member) living in Ottawa shot and killed Thomas D'Arcy McGee, the most famous

Irishman in Canada. McGee was only forty-three, but had crammed much into a short life. A native of County Louth, he emigrated as a teenager to Boston and became a published poet and popular editor of the *Pilot* by age twenty before returning to Ireland, where he was embroiled in the 1848 Young Irelander Rebellion with the likes of Meagher, John O'Mahony, James Stephens, and Michael Doheny. He escaped to America disguised as a priest, and eventually moved to Canada, where he became great friends with Prime Minister MacDonald. Sometimes called the "Father of Canadian Literature," McGee became a Canadian Minister, and denounced the Fenian Brotherhood and American political mentality as an obstacle to Canada. His murder shocked Canada, the U.S., and Ireland. When he was buried in Montreal, 80,000 of the city's 105,000 citizens turned out in his honor.[17]

But many Irish nationalists of the diaspora were enmeshed in the cause, and though O'Neill and McGee never met, their histories, goals, and approaches to Irish freedom found common ideals and ferocious disagreement. When John O'Neill was still a teenager in Elizabeth in 1855, Thomas D'Arcy McGee was a thirty-year-old firebrand urging Irish Catholics to leave the cities of the east to establish a colony in the American west, a concept General John O'Neill would adopt and work feverishly towards twenty years later. When this idea failed to gain traction (as many ideas would under O'Neill) D'Arcy McGee found his way to the north, settling in Montreal in 1857, the very year O'Neill went west to Mormon country.

McGee, finding Canada more comfortable to an Irish immigrant, began a campaign in newspapers decrying the United States' approach towards acquiring land they didn't own but nevertheless coveted, now called Manifest Destiny. The Canadians, with McGee leading the way, correctly assailed the Americans for their hard-handed acquisitions of Florida from the Spanish, Louisiana (cheaply) from the French, and California and Texas from Mexico. By 1865, the brilliant McGee, long a lightning rod among Irish north and south of the border, was effectively shepherding Irish Canadian Catholics away from Fenianism. By 1866, when John O'Neill chose to leave his family and become a full-fledged revolutionary, D'Arcy McGee had become the most outspoken enemy of Irish republican nationalism. McGee saw Canada in a completely different light than his Irish American Fenians, and his outspokenness was never thinly disguised. "I deny that [Fenians] represent Ireland, to whom Canada has done no wrong. I will add that a more wanton, immoral, unjustifiable assault has ever been made on a peaceful people, and the fate of pirates and free-booters is the only fate they can expect."[18]

Whelan was tried and convicted despite being defended by the best lawyers in Canada. The trial was a writer's dream and a defendant's nightmare. The jury was totally Protestant, and Prime Minister MacDonald astonishingly sat next to the judge. Whelan was certainly guilty but likely just one of several men involved in the non-sanctioned assassination. On February 11, 1869, five thousand people showed up in a snowstorm to be sure he would die. He was never once accused at trial of being a Fenian, though there is absolutely little doubt he should be counted a member. Whelan told a fellow prisoner he once served eighteen months in an English jail for Fenianism. His brother Joe was reportedly shot in the aborted uprising in Ireland in 1867, and another brother was in prison for similar experiences.[19]

The Brotherhood's public image was on its heels, and the murder strengthened the Irish Canadian conviction against any United States involvement in their future. The killing, trial, appeal, and hanging of Whelan made headlines worldwide for months, and every story contained four words: "Patrick Whelan, Fenian sympathizer"—or worse. The Fenian Brotherhood had absolutely nothing to do with the murder of McGee, and even Le Caron, in his constant quest for bonuses tied to Fenian news, never made the connection, and added to his handlers, "O'Neill repudiates that outrage."[20] The Canadian government spent weeks seeking information from spies and informers from New York to Montreal trying to link the Fenian Brotherhood to the McGee killing, but found none except the rogue Whelan and his unknown conspirators. All reports were convinced that General John O'Neill privately condemned the assassination, and just three days after it occurred, he told a packed house in Cincinnati, "We are not cowardly assassins, going about seeking plunder. We are honorable men, making way for the liberation of our oppressed countrymen."[21]

It also did nothing to help the Fenian Brotherhood's finances. O'Neill and Gibbons's national tour attracted enthusiastic crowds, but not much money, and the three years of squandering money on officials' salaries and expenses were wasteful to say the least. O'Neill kept working hard, but after six months was still facing criticism from some, especially in Chicago. The *Irish Republic* accused O'Neill in mid–June of chicanery, trying to influence the membership into voting for President Johnson in the upcoming election—which, of course, was very probable. The paper, now O'Neill's Irish American in-house enemy, went a bit far, saying, "O'Neill would disgrace the foulest character in Sing Sing Prison," but criticism always stung O'Neill more than it should, and he would attack the Chicago paper and its editors for years.[22]

Two weeks later, on June 29, O'Neill sent out a missive to the entire Fenian membership, warning them "to look out for spies."[23] There is no record of what forced this memo, but based on the timing he may have been referring to the *Irish Republic*. Unfortunately all the general had to do was look over his shoulder. Le Caron had begun his official work on behalf of England and Canada with O'Neill and would continue until 1889, when he testified against Charles Parnell in Ireland and the Clan na Gael in Chicago. The spy, who

Canadian Prime Minister John A. MacDonald called a draper boy and who everybody thought was odd, fooled every Irishman in America for more than two decades, with one exception. In late 1868, Fenian Patrick Roche of Troy, New York, a delegate to the November Convention, publicly accused the man born Thomas Beach as a spy. The result of the accusation was quick. Roche was himself reprimanded, and Le Caron was promoted.[24] The spy cared about one thing—money—and was paid by the Fenians, Canada, and Great Britain, all at the same time. O'Neill, who historically has paid the biggest price personally for Le Caron's perfidy, is often portrayed as a dupe for being taken by his old Nashville neighbor, but that is unfair. The bane of all Irish rebel organizations—the informer and men like him—are considered to deserve their own level in Dante's hell, and the "ugly little man" was exceptional at his work. After O'Neill's death, Le Caron spied successfully against the Clan na Gael, a much more secretive and dangerous Irish organization, for well over fifteen years. Still, it is hard to fathom how a man who would write to Robert Anderson, one of his English handlers, in 1868, "The Irish were a pack of low dirty foul mouthed beings—worse than niggers," could operate so well for so long.[25]

But he must have had something going for him. Later in life, Mary Ann O'Neill would tell her son John Hugh, "I met Le Caron many times and he was tall and handsome, very dark, with a brown mustache. He was brilliant in conversation and the life of the social event."[26] After the publication of his memoirs when he was outed in 1890, several Fenian historians have correctly pointed out the obvious exaggerations, distortions, and lies detailed in Le Caron's memoirs, but there can be no doubt he damaged both Irish organizations and was responsible in large measure for the sudden fall of John O'Neill and many other Irish for decades. As O'Neill worked feverishly his first year as president, every intimate word was relayed to the Brotherhood's enemies, and it would only get worse.

Good news awaited O'Neill in August. Mary Ann gave birth to a daughter, Mary Ellen, known forever as "Mamie," on the 28th in Washington. The general, still and always a dissociative individual, and perhaps still smarting from the betrayal of George Macklin, chose no family members as godparents. Instead, socialite Margaret Lackey, wife of District of Columbia Fenian Chief James Lackey, was the godmother, and P.J. Meehan, publisher of the *Irish-American*, was the godfather at baptism in St. Patrick's Church in Washington, D.C. The well-off Meehan, like all of O'Neill's family, was from New Jersey, making his home in Jersey City. Once again, John O'Neill bypassed his brother Bernard and numerous relatives from Elizabeth, fueling speculation that either the relationship between the now-famous General O'Neill and his family was strained with the memory of cousin George's perfidy, or celebrity status had changed the Fenian Brotherhood's chief.[27]

The November 1868 Fenian Convention in Philadelphia was important to O'Neill and the Brotherhood for a myriad of reasons. It had now been more than two years since Ridgeway and despite O'Neill's zealotry for a second invasion, money and membership were lessening as veterans of the Civil War were starting to find their place back in traditional civilian life. In addition, the Catholic Church provided another difficulty to future membership. Philadelphia Archbishop James Wood, along with other bishops, issued an episcopal circular condemning the Brotherhood. But despite the hierarchy's adamant opposition, many local clergy remained close to the Fenians. Father Patrick Moriarty, a pastor in Wood's own diocese and an ardent Irish nationalist, was forbidden to speak at a rally which posed the question, "What right has England to rule Ireland?" Moriarty defied Archbishop Wood and told a roaring crowd, "Britain is a tyrant, robber, murderer." Though there were many priests across the country like Moriarty, few challenged the hierarchy.[28]

Infighting between the Chicago and eastern circles was also taking a toll, and the Canadians were well aware of the intentions of O'Neill. The British vice-consul in New York, J.P. Edwards, remarked, "O'Neill appears to be thoroughly earnest in his intentions to undertake a hostile movement on as large a scale as possible."[29] Of course, anyone with knowledge of O'Neill would not be surprised at his intentions; the general wanted men, money, and commitment for an army, nothing less. Just prior to the convention, he sent out an earnest plea to all Irish Americans, urging them to redouble their efforts on behalf of their homeland now that the "sacred work"[30] was close. Remember, he had pledged, "Any sacrifice is not too great that will achieve the liberation of one's native land."[31] No one could accuse O'Neill of lacking effort for his $2,000 annual salary plus expenses. It was the first true election for Fenian President O'Neill, and he wished to prove his worth. He ostentatiously marched at the head of two thousand uniformed Fenian soldiers through the streets of Philadelphia to open the convention on November 24 in a great show of political force and importance. There were 108 circles represented, from Montana and Nebraska all the way to England, Scotland, Ireland, and places in between. Though some from Chicago were dissatisfied, no strong candidate emerged and John O'Neill was unanimously elected President again.

O'Neill's election speech was straight to the warrior's point: "The education we want is that which teaches our men to pull a trigger and push a bayonet at the right time, and in the right way, and to keep doing it.... We have advanced too far upon the road of revolution to turn back before we have crossed swords with the enemy and tried once more the cause of Irish freedom by the issue of battle."[32]

But when December closed, the money just wasn't there, with only $4,746 reported left in the treasury. The Brotherhood was forced to cancel any plans for a second invasion for another year. President John O'Neill must have been dejected, but there can be little question that General John O'Neill was bedeviled at the lack of action. This election would mark the zenith of O'Neill's Fenian career.

O'Neill moved to New York Fenian Headquarters on West 4th Street in Manhattan, ignoring the Moffat House extravaganza of 1865 while Mary Ann and the two children were welcomed by family in Elizabeth. Catherine and Mary O'Neill, John's mother and sister, were living on Price Street, a one-block area next to the Pennsylvania Railroad in downtown Elizabeth. There was no lack of room for Mary Ann and the two children and no doubt Catherine, now sixty-four, was thrilled to have Mary Ann and two grandchildren with her and daughter Mary, thirty-seven. Their next-door neighbors the Foxes, with their patriarch Laurence Fox, who was recognized as "a better neighbor I never had" and "one of the most respected common men" in the city of Elizabeth, were emigrant farmers from County Meath and would surely have provided a healthy and enjoyable haven for Mary Ann O'Neill.[33] Elizabeth was only twelve miles as the crow flies from Fenian Headquarters in downtown Manhattan, and O'Neill holed up in Manhattan, with the family at a safe distance just an hour away. It was the smart move, since anti–Irish and Canadian operatives were always looking for O'Neill's weaknesses and targeting the family of the Brotherhood president was surely a possibility.

John would have a total of twenty first-generation O'Neill and Macklin nephews, nieces, and cousins born in Elizabeth between 1849 and 1872. In spite of this large number, the well-mannered, charming national hero would be the godfather or best man of none. Though war and the Fenian Brotherhood were valid excuses, the detached O'Neill engaged with people other than his family, no doubt a direct result of his unfortunate abandonment as a child. John would later be criticized for his lack of compassion, with warmheartedness only toward Irish freedom, but it was of little surprise to his family; they had experienced his familial separation for years. Nonetheless, this first move to Elizabeth, besides his marriage, since his departure for Richmond in 1855 was met with joy by all, especially young John Hugh.

> My first memory is of Elizabethtown, New Jersey, [John Hugh was 5] where we were living with my father's people while he was engaged in another attempt to invade Canada. I remember my grandma, my father's mother, his sister Mary O'Neill, and also my father's brother Bernard O'Neill, who kept a grocery store at the crossroads of Elizabeth Avenue. Uncle Bernard had a large family. The two oldest sons being John J. and Thomas. It was at Elizabeth that I first attended school [St. Mary's], but I do not know how long we lived in Elizabeth, as my father was away most of the time. I think he was involved in politics.[34]

The New Year 1869 saw a resolute and dogged O'Neill determined to invade Canada, but once again, lack of money and resolution held the president back. Finances forced some salaried Fenian Brotherhood officers to be removed, including an early Fenian from Nashville, Rudolphus Fitzpatrick, who was at Ridgeway and, when released, became a Fenian assistant secretary of war. It would be years before the Brotherhood would discover Fitzpatrick was another of the many spies in the employ of the great Canadian leader MacDonald and his top agent, Dominion Police Commissioner Gilbert McMicken. At Brotherhood Headquarters in New York, the Fenians had another Canadian undercover agent, William McMichael, reporting to McMicken and MacDonald. O'Neill was doomed whatever direction he undertook. Le Caron, Fitzpatrick in Nashville, McMichael in New York, and his own ego were getting in the way.[35]

As the reality of a sunken treasury stared the FB in the face, the Brotherhood Senate now began to oppose the idea of a second invasion completely, an idea O'Neill could never accept. Ever the optimist, he desperately made a plea on March 17, St. Patrick's Day, for all Fenian members to contribute one dollar or more to help the cause. He inanely hoped for a million dollars, yet had to be shocked when a paltry $16,000 was taken in, the highest of the year. By April, funds available were about $4,000. Except for the hard men of Irish nationalism it was becoming more obvious each month that Irish Americans were war weary, and that the grand idea of a Canadian invasion in 1866 was a one-trick pony.

All in the know realized there was no chance at any future invasion, and thoughts were shared that indeed the Fenian Brotherhood itself was in real danger of disintegration, its time perhaps come and gone. O'Neill's biggest supporters, Gibbons of Philadelphia, Meehan of New York, and Gallagher of Buffalo, tried mightily to convince their young star of the political realities but each was met with denial and derision. For the first time in O'Neill's career, the word arrogant was used regularly as his first name. But, when challenged, John O'Neill would attack. From February 15 to March 15, he spoke in fifteen cities in twelve Midwestern and Eastern states. In May, he went on an extensive and exhausting tour attempting to rally the troops throughout the South. His travels were obsessive, spending two months in at least six states, turning down no invitations. In Georgia, Tennessee, Alabama, Louisiana, South Carolina, and Texas, he implored the membership to unite and fight. "His speech was practical and convincing," wrote one paper in Alabama. "He is eloquent, excellent, although still a young man."[36]

But no matter how much O'Neill worked, it was evident the country was changing. Fenian membership in 1865, though often exaggerated, was a minimum of 100,000 with money rolling in daily; in midsummer 1869 membership was less than half that, and the finances reflected the numbers. It was the fault of neither O'Neill nor the executive council of senators, just a change around the Irish world. The Fenian campaign in Ireland had failed; the Irish

Canadians were developing a love of their new confederation thanks in some measure to Ridgeway; the Irish in Australia, twenty-seven percent of the population, were now integrating with increasing freedom, many after beginning settlement as convicts, and more and more Irish in America were accepting their role as second to Americans. One of the minority in the Fenian Brotherhood hierarchy who didn't recognize this was President General John O'Neill, who, when backed into a corner, knew only one answer—deny the obvious mismatch and plunge forward with alacrity. It was a wonderful quality in a cavalry officer, but a weakness in a CEO. One hundred and twenty-five years later, the Irish Provisional Army would be faced with similar questions, and unlike O'Neill, Gerry Adams and Martin McGuiness chose the ballot over the bullet, for the most part.

In November 1869, O'Neill rounded up the wagons and prepared for a fight, hoping for 10,000 men and the money to support them. He gave his aide Henri Le Caron complete control of all arms and munitions caches throughout the country and raised the informer's salary to $100 a month. He made a complete split with James Gibbons and P.J. Meehan, his oldest and most trusted former mentors and allies. The general already was at odds with the Chicago circles. In February 1870, with the Brotherhood almost completely broke, he tried to surround himself with supporters by appointing a crony, Doctor Patrick Keenan of New York, to an executive position. Meehan, godparent to Mamie O'Neill, and others rejected the appointment, and shockingly, Keenan waited for Meehan in the street outside Fenian Headquarters and shot him in the back of the head, and though much can be traced to past and future problems, this foreshadowed the end of the Fenian Brotherhood, with the evolution of the Clan na Gael lurking in the shadows.[37]

The incident reverberated throughout the country, and O'Neill was always named, one way or another. The *San Francisco Chronicle,* headline read:

IRISH MATTERS
"The Shooting of Meehan"

Patrick J. Meehan, editor of the *Irish-American,* was shot in the back of the head and mortally wounded by Dr. Keenan, Secretary of the O'Neill branch of the Fenian organization, as the former was leaving the headquarters.... It appears that both these persons had been in attendance at a stormy meeting of the Fenian Senate, and that Meehan, as President of the Senate, took a prominent part in a serious misunderstanding, which had arisen between O'Neill and the Brotherhood. Among those who seemed most obnoxious to the Senatorial party was James Keenan, Secretary of the organization, and a warm adherent of O'Neill and his policy.

The shooting of Meehan gave proof to true discord in leadership, and was the worst possible scenario for John O'Neill. When Meehan was lying wounded outside FB Headquarters, he was taken unbelievably to a drug store, where his will was immediately made and a priest called in to give him the last rights of the Catholic Church. After this, Meehan, lying in a chair, called Frank Gallagher, Buffalo Fenian leader, to him and said, "Frank, I hope this will be a warning to the General not to surround himself with such men. Let the General retrace his steps and work with the Senate who are his best friends. If my death will unite all I will not have fallen in vain, and the cause will triumph in the end." Whether this ridiculous deathbed scenario was conjured up by Meehan's reporters or not, it spread throughout the country.

Opponents of O'Neill, though he was never directly accused of ordering Keenan to shoot his daughter's godfather, did not waste one second in blaming him anyway, desperately trying to stop O'Neill's wishes for a second Canadian invasion. The Canadians, English spies, and U.S. government just let it all play out between the Irish themselves. Philadelphia's *United Irishman* said in an editorial:

> It has been known for a long time that General O'Neill and the Senate have been at variance. Of the merits of the quarrel we have our opinions, but leave it to the coming Convention to decide who was right and who was wrong. This feeling has become wild and outrageous on the part of O'Neill, who has his partisans worked up to frenzy. So far had this gone that O'Neill had boasted that only for extreme control over his feelings he would have shot the editor of this journal long ago. Thus we have been carrying our life in our hands without knowing it.

This Philadelphia newspaper, now the official FB organ, aligned with New York's *Irish American*, now a full-fledged member of the anti–O'Neill Wing, and it added, "General O'Neill has become impressed with the idea that the Senate were thwarting him and holding him back for some time from moving on the enemy. O'Neill is a gallant soldier, but without a spark of judgment, and is only too anxious to meet the English foe, prepared or unprepared, to prove his devotion to Ireland. Of his courage and patriotism there can be no doubt. But that is about all we can say in his favor."

The duel to capture the membership continued. O'Neill, as was his lifelong response to criticism, attacked, this time verbally, and it was a mistake the non-savvy O'Neill never mastered. He assailed the editor of the above editorial, who O'Neill was convinced was nothing but a tool of James Gibbons's, one of the very men that placed O'Neill into the Fenian presidency. He thus addressed a response directly to Gibbons. The general castigated Gibbons's supposed entourage attacks, but defended himself and attempted to distance himself from the Meehan shooting.

"This [Meehan] is your friend—I once believed him to be mine and to the best of my ability I defended him against all assailants, even when he was preparing to plunge the assassin's dagger in my back." O'Neill continued, "If I were a fool, my injury would not be interrupted—conspirators do not blunt the edge of their own instruments. But I am no fool now, though there was a time when such a temptation might be cast upon me—that time is past."

But O'Neill, saying he has matured and will not be made a public fool, tried to redeem himself with Gibbons, though he must have known that that opportunity had come and gone. "With respect to the other work the Senate may be required to perform, I have nothing to say. The past meetings of that body speak emphatically enough. You, my dear friend, are the last link that binds me to that body. For my part, I would rather go hand in hand with you to the end, but I cannot influence your action. I shall never forget our personal friendships, and shall always regard you as one of the most honest and laborious workers in the Fenian cause."

But the Fenians could not let go of each other. Gibbons, the Senate president who had literally handed the FB presidency to O'Neill just two years prior, responded publicly, as all Brotherhood differences seemed to be handled, openly questioning O'Neill's mental stability. Feeling no doubt that he was winning the battle of public opinion, Gibbons wrote:

> Dear Sir: You are laboring under some terrible hallucination, or smarting under some imaginary wrong, which I firmly believe and know if not removed will prove injurious to yourself.... With regard to my being the last link that binds you to the Senate, I regret to know that you have come to that conclusion. But, my dear General, I will say now what I have said before: that I would follow you your fortunes to the bitter end in the right path, believing you to be an honest and brave man—but honest and brave men may be, and others have been, men of mistaken judgment, and I will not follow you or any other men in violation of my oath of office and the provisions of the Constitution.

But Gibbons definitely gets to the heart of the case, with time ticking down to the second invasion O'Neill is desperate to engage. "I warn you earnestly, and beg of you, in the name of the friendship you so warmly express for me, not to place yourself in a false position by the error of your judgment, or suspicions of 'being got rid of'" that leave no foundations in fact."

Gibbons, in fact, seemed to be taking a much more proper course, but of course O'Neill wanted to be not simply a general but a president, and he was in over his head. "Your letter is a sad commentary indeed on the President of a great organization, proving as it does that you are willing to imperil its holy purpose, and destroy the hopes and aspirations of millions, to gratify ambition or hate for supposed personal wrongs." Gibbons concluded with a plea.

> Dear General!—These are hours in the lives of men when friendships must give way to stern duty. Such an hour is now presented to me, and while I value your friendship, I value the cause of my bleeding country more. You may say our intercourse may cease. If so, that is your choice, but I deeply regret that you should avail yourself of the medium of a friendly letter to misrepresent and slander my friend—a man that I know to be as pure and dedicated a patriot as ever lived, whose labours and sacrifices are so well

known to me—and the only link of friendship that binds us together is the wrongs of our suffering country.

Trusting that God may open your eyes to your dangerous position, I am, my dear General, yours most respectfully,

James Gibbons
President of Senate, Fenian Brotherhood

Doctor Keenan was found guilty in a short trial for shooting Meehan, given ten years, and sentenced to Sing Sing Prison on the Hudson River, the notorious prison that gave rise to the American lexicon of "gone up the river." Even the *New York Herald*, a pro–Fenian paper, commented on the damage to the organization after Keenan was convicted. "Whatever there is of good in the Brotherhood has always been frittered away in personal rivalries and jealousies, which have on more occasions than one resulted in serious shooting matches. If the punishment meted out to Keenan serves to deter other jealous Fenians from shooting their rivals, so much the better for the Fenian Brotherhood and the general peace of the community."

Stunningly, P.J. Meehan would recover, and lead a motion for Keenan to be paroled, but the editor would never again be a major player in Irish nationalism, dying in 1906 at seventy-four with the bullet still in his head. O'Neill was completely innocent, but Keenan was without any question his protégé, and whispers are dangerous.

In February 1870, O'Neill issued a circular, which was printed in the *Irish People*: "Let me know if there are any men, and how many, in your neighborhood, who are ready and willing to enter the field as soldiers in the Irish Republican Army.... We mean fight—speedy fight—and nothing else."

O'Neill's enemies now smelled the wounded deer. On March 26, Brotherhood senators hurled charges of graft and corruption at their president and his associates, though not Le Caron. The charges, emanating predominately from the Chicago Brotherhood, said the man of steel from Monaghan was "trampling on principles of representative government by attempting to move on Canada." The second charge was of graft, charging O'Neill with spending $3 a day without Senate approval. Both charges, of course, were ludicrous.[38] O'Neill was elected to fight Canada and for two years exhausted himself physically on Fenian business, ignoring personal finances and family. The $3 graft charge is not worth consideration; especially considering Boss Tweed of Tammany Hall stole an estimated $200,000,000 during the same period. Tweed, who was a friend of the Irish Fenians and O'Neill for political purposes, surely would have advanced the president more than $3 had it been asked. Anti-Fenian newspapers, especially the *New York Times*, often used charges of financial chicanery to denigrate the Brotherhood, or in fact, any Irish movement. John O'Mahony, a founder of the FB, was often accused by the *Times* when raising money of taking advantage of the poorest Irish, including servant girls. O'Mahony, a simple scholar, was the most honest of men, and died without a dime, much like O'Neill would a decade later. The general retaliated, as always, by taking the offensive. He fired Richard McCloud, secretary of the treasury, for making the charges of graft.

But money was a problem in the Brotherhood, and it would remain a problem for several more years. A treasurer's report shows that the Senate had "expenses" of $44,400 per year (about $900,000 today). Higher salaries, of course, went to the individuals running operations, with perhaps fifteen individuals controlling the expenditures. Salary plus expenses were given an average of $4,800 per year ($95,000 today) to these dozen or so officials. Senators and ranking personnel would surely hesitate before accusing anyone of misappropriating funds or keeping finances from the general membership, the paupers paying the annual subscriptions. It did, and still does, take money to run a national organization. Money disagreements had been ever present in the Brotherhood since 1864, when the Roberts faction used it as an issue in its attempt to displace Stephens and O'Mahony.

On April 11, the senators called for a meeting in Chicago, but O'Neill chose not to walk into the lion's den. But he had to be careful, as he was still drawing a sizable salary and it was his only income. On April 19, the break became official. The senators wanted, under no conditions, a second Canadian fight. Under proper perspective, it was certainly the right call, but they were dealing with a man with an aversion to challenge, a man of earnest fanaticism whom they had wished, perhaps begged, two years prior to raise an army and attack Canada. The Chicago cabal sent three men to meet with O'Neill and reach some kind of compromised accommodation, a sane and practical move. John Finerty and two associates trained in from the Windy City to New York but were barred from entering the O'Neill meeting at Fenian Headquarters in New York by armed guards, not exactly the smoothest start to an accord. Finerty, who never believed O'Neill was anything but honest, angrily returned to Chicago with no pact at all. Despite O'Neill's apparent popularity with much of the general membership, leadership now openly questioned his compulsive confidence and his single-minded wish to fight, and saw his behavior as nothing more than manipulative arrogance.

O'Neill almost immediately called his own convention in Troy, New York, with what was left of his supporters, who predictably rejected any and all charges against O'Neill. Gibbons, an original O'Neill proponent, finally gave up, not just on O'Neill, but also on the entire Fenian Brotherhood. Wearied of it all, he wrote in a private letter, "I am now an old man. My business is ruined. I am too old to work and ashamed to beg. My hopes for Ireland blasted."[39]

8

Vermont and Imprisonment

But while he caught high ecstasies,
Life slipped between the bars.
—Patrick Kavanagh, *The Great Hunger*

Once the Fenian Senate rejected the general when he called for another attack on Canadian soil, O'Neill, openly desperate for both political and military victories, called his Fenian Military Officers Committee together in Troy, New York, and simply told them he was authorizing an invasion. O'Neill wanted to fight; he was elected to fight; he had left Ireland at age eleven determined to fight—end of discussion. Whatever chance of keeping the Fenian Brotherhood together exploded, and the Senate expelled O'Neill as their president. O'Neill, realizing all but one of his options had evaporated, compulsively formed another wing of the Brotherhood. Under his own banner, he launched a second invasion, frantic but always confident.

In late spring of 1870 bitterness ruled all factions of the Brotherhood, but victory is always the great equalizer, and should he be successful in Canada, John O'Neill, against all reason, convinced himself his place in history would be secure. Politics is a vicious team sport, but O'Neill was never an earnest or intuit politician, and while he could be a team player, he always had to be the captain and head coach. Perhaps if his mentor John Adams had been alive, O'Neill may have been more circumspect. But John O'Neill's imprudence remained deep in his DNA, and the older Brotherhood executives were wrong to think he could or would change. In truth, they never really knew the gambler in him.

In April, O'Neill and Le Caron went to Buffalo looking for help from Frank Gallagher, the last Fenian executive he believed to be in his camp, the man who initially was his first supporter in Buffalo following Ridgeway. Rebuffed completely by Gallagher, the two men left for Vermont on the 22nd to finalize an attack plan near the Vermont and Canadian border. O'Neill smartly shipped his arms north during winter to locations throughout the border, but he still had no idea Henri Le Caron was informing the Canadians of every deposit.

While O'Neill spent a week making plans and meeting with local supporters, Le Caron was able to sneak off to Montreal and reveal locations of all plans and arms dumps in the entire Northeast. The Canadians despised the spy. Premier MacDonald said, "A man who will engage to do what he offers to do, that is betray those with whom he acts, is not to be trusted," but proceeded to give him a $2,000 bonus.[1] The general and his perceived best friend returned to Manhattan with a firm date to invade Canada for the second time in four years on May 25, Queen Victoria's birthday—no surprise to England or Canada.

In mid–May, O'Neill's ground-level supporters convinced the general there were three thousand men pledged to fight, and Le Caron reported there were sufficient arms, including a cache hidden on the farm of former Union Cavalry General Judson Kilpatrick in Deckertown, Sussex County, New Jersey.[2] All told, Le Caron said there were twenty thousand rifles and a million rounds of ammunition in store. O'Neill was so pleased with the work of Le Caron he also gave him a $2,000 bonus. Even the most ardent O'Neill stalwarts denounced the move bitterly, not thinking Le Caron was a spy, but a tool of O'Neill's. The acting adjutant general was also collecting almost $200 a month as salary, half from the Fenians, the rest from Gilbert McMicken, his Canadian handler.

But the pressure was mounting on O'Neill and soon after, a secret meeting was held in New York City. The men, including command officers Sam Spear, Owen Starr, and J.J. Donnelly, all loyal O'Neill supporters from the Midwest, expected to receive orders for opening hostilities, and were disappointed when the general showed up "awfully drunk" and postponed the invasion for a few days. The Headquarters' spy, McMichael, might be accused of embellishing his own role and that of O'Neill's inebriety, but he had included a guest at the meeting—Father Patrick Loughran of County Armagh, who was in the country searching for funding to build a new church back home. McMichael quoted Loughran on the way out of the meeting, "I believe now what I never did before that there was a curse on the Fenians."[3]

The Canadians, meanwhile, had their own problems. Though Le Caron was their chief conduit because of his relationship with O'Neill, Prime Minister MacDonald and McMicken had dozens of men working for them for years, some of them delegates to Fenian conventions, spread from Minnesota to Massachusetts, including the top Fenian fundraiser from Missouri, Charles Clarke. The British were adamant that the Canadians allow the attack since they were aware of the time and place, thus crushing any future Fenian incursions. The Canadians were of a mind to just grab all the arms, but that would have meant exposing their agents, particularly Le Caron. In the end, the

British decision won out, and the trap was set. This was not President Andrew Johnson's 1866—the mind of the country had changed.

On May 24, President Grant, knowing full well what was planned from his own sources, issued a proclamation forbidding any breach of the Neutrality Act, and U.S. marshals and army officers were in place to enforce the order. With Grant's permission, Marshal George Foster even read the proclamation to O'Neill the evening before the proposed raid. But O'Neill pompously ignored the warning and, according to witnesses, expressed contempt for Grant. Foster, upset at O'Neill's behavior, simply crossed over the border and informed the Canadians of his inability to stop O'Neill. It wouldn't have mattered. Thanks to Le Caron and a dozen other Fenians in Canadian pockets, the Canadians were about to avenge Ridgeway.

John O'Neill was, however, now back in his element as a professional soldier. Though he had to realize that the invasion was a major personal gamble, O'Neill hoped to get lucky. The general certainly realized he wasn't going to conquer Canada, but he did need to cross onto Canadian soil and fight a worthy battle or even a skirmish—another Ridgeway—to regain relevancy. This might restore him to prominence within the Brotherhood and keep the O'Neill dream of Irish freedom alive. In Vermont his orders were simple and direct. Commanders of all regiments, companies, and detachments were told "to hold their respective commands in readiness.... Officers and men must avoid the use of uniforms or any insignia that would distinguish themselves... . Take no man who is a loafer or a habitual drunkard.... Take no men who had not seen service or who has not sufficient character to ensure his good behavior."[4] At noon on May 25, General John O'Neill was in Franklin, Vermont. Unknown to the general, Le Caron had done a superb job of undermining all Fenian plans. Thousands of Canadians (some said 13,000) were spread across the border just waiting in ambush; this would definitely not be another Ridgeway. On the American side, the anticipated three thousand men did not show up on time or at all, compounding O'Neill's plans. Fifty men got off the train from Boston, not the thousand expected. Vermont and northeastern New York combined for a total of one hundred men, not six hundred, as promised, and so it went, hopelessly, with about two hundred men.

It was over before it began. As the first group of Fenians approached the border at what would become known as the Battle of Eccles Hill, a Canadian volley sent them running, embarrassing O'Neill who was a few hundred yards back. He tried to rally them to no avail. "Men of Ireland, I am ashamed of you. You have acted disgracefully today, but you will have another chance."[5] Before O'Neill could act, United States Marshal George Foster and his assistant, Irishman Tom Failey, arrested the belligerent O'Neill. When O'Neill challenged Foster verbally, the marshal put a gun to his head and said he would shoot him. Failey and Foster then shoved the general into a coach and headed to the jail in St. Alban's, eighteen miles south. Along the way, the coach passed the newly-arrived Fenian contingent from New York, who didn't even recognize General John O'Neill, their late president and the hero of Ridgeway. The whole episode was over in less than an hour. No Canadians were even injured, while the Brotherhood soldiers suffered five killed and fifteen wounded. One O'Neill biographer would claim that O'Neill quarreled with his advisers and simply attempted a raid, and only a handful of Fenians joined him.[6]

This was a charitable view to O'Neill's problems. In fact, it was humiliating for a man who demanded unconditional loyalty and a reversal of 1866. This time the Brotherhood leadership received fair play in the media, and placed much blame on John O'Neill. President Grant was not Andrew Johnson; the American military was as prepared for the invasion as were the Canadians; and the War Department gave no free rides home, though Boss Tweed and Tammany Hall did the favor this time around for any Fenians short of funds. All but three Fenians received free fare home.

Criticism abounded, most of it directed at O'Neill. Even fellow Fenians fanned the flames. The local St. Alban's Brotherhood accused O'Neill of having arranged before the battle for his own arrest. The *Ottawa Citizen* said, "Most of the dupes have gone away ... and those who remain are making Fenianism stink in the nostrils of their American sympathizers."[7] In typical American fashion, there was talk among Buffalo Fenians, but no action, that the government should release O'Neill to the Canadians, who just might execute him—this coming from the people who most adored O'Neill, sang his praises, and carried him on their shoulders just four years prior.

A young John Boyle O'Reilly, a seminal figure in both Irish and Irish American history. He joined the fight at Eccles Hill, much to his regret (Library of Congress).

Even Fenians present at the

"battle" ripped into O'Neill. As he was being arrested, O'Neill turned to John Boyle O'Reilly, a true Irish hero who had recently arrived from Boston to join the fight. O'Reilly previously suffered imprisonment in Ireland, England, and Australia because of Fenian activities, and O'Neill turned command of the troops over to O'Reilly as he entered the coach with the federal marshals. O'Reilly had no idea what commands or troops O'Neill was referring to, and later said, "The men who framed and executed this last abortion of war-making have proved themselves criminally incompetent." And of O'Neill in particular, O'Reilly said, "That man ought to have been placed in a strait jacket."[8] It was a sad day for Irish nationalism, reminiscent of previous failures in Ireland, and the biggest personal defeat of the thirty-one-year-old leader, John Charles O'Neill.

But the resilient general still had friends, influential and not, including the Rev. James Quigley of California, famous pastor and author, as well as James Lackey of Washington, whose wife Margaret was Mamie O'Neill's godmother. The sheriff of Erie County, New York, which included Buffalo, was Grover Cleveland, who as a young lawyer helped Fenian prisoners avoid trial after the Ridgeway attack, and now arranged for O'Neill's defense pro bono. But as these and half a dozen other wealthy celebrities were all from out of state, the $20,000 bail was delayed, then lowered. Despite O'Neill's many socialite friends bail was never met and O'Neill stayed in jail with other prisoners until the trial started. Mary Ann and children John Hugh and Mamie hustled up to Vermont from Elizabeth on the largess of friends and rented a home to be close to the general. O'Neill was no doubt happy to have his family in Burlington, especially with Mary Ann pregnant again.

The July 24 issue of South Carolina's *Daily Phoenix* seemed content to leave O'Neill in jail. "The Fenian generalissimo has written a pathetic letter from his dungeon at Burlington, complaining of his utter destitution. He says he has not 'a dollar to fee a lawyer, or a cent to buy a newspaper, or postage stamp.'"[9]

Nonetheless, the ever-assured general portrayed a confidence many men would have shirked. The *Burlington Weekly Free Press* interviewed him in jail six weeks into his confinement, just a week before the trial.

Burlington rejoices in the possession of a "caged lion." The once proud monarch of the Fenian Brotherhood, and the General of the Fenian army, is behind the bars of the Burlington jail. Last Sunday evening I sought and obtained an interview with General O'Neill. The General was in good spirits, having been visited on that day by a prominent Fenian of the Savage branch of the organization. Taking a seat in a cozy parlor, the sheriff said he would be bringing the General down. In a few minutes there appeared at the door a medium sized, erect looking gentleman whom I was introduced to as General O'Neill. The General was dressed in a suit of grey, and did not seem all the worse for his confinement. He has a pleasant face, is frank and ready in conversation, and certainly impresses those who meet him very favorably. I told him I would be glad to have him tell me as much as he wanted with reference to the great fiasco. The General then gave me at some length, the full details of his plans and preparations. O'Neill said he expected to be released in a day or two, and that he felt the whole affair had been misrepresented.[10]

Even beyond the outrageous optimism O'Neill always showed, it is hard to understand how, after spending two months in jail awaiting trial, he thought he would walk free in a few days. The meeting of the Brotherhood Savage Wing buoyed him, and there were reports that President Grant was being pressured. The reporter and O'Neill were accompanied by the sheriff to his cell, a twenty-eight-foot by twelve-foot room with two other occupants, "a gentleman of African descent and a New Englander." When the reporter left, a "few other visitors were lined up to visit the prisoner."[11]

O'Neill was not released, and on July 30, he pleaded guilty to the breach of the Neutrality Act before his Vermont trial, and gave a spirited speech asking for leniency based on his past record as a soldier in the service of the United States. Excerpts reveal his deep-set and most sincere feelings, learned long ago while growing up in County Monaghan. After opening with his stellar Civil War record, O'Neill got to the crux of his soul.

> As one of a persecuted race—as one who had suffered at the hands of tyranny and oppression in my native land, I came to America like thousands of my countrymen because I had been oppressed. But while I have felt the duties of an American citizen, and while I felt that I was duty bound to respect the laws of the land of my adoption, I could not, I cannot, and I never shall forget the land of my birth. I could not, while fighting in the armies of the United States, forget that I was born in another land—a land oppressed and tyrannized over. I cannot forget it; I shall never forget it. No matter what my fate here—*I am still an Irishman*, and while I have tried to be a faithful citizen of America, *I am still an Irishman*, with all the instincts of an Irishman.

The third part of his defense was his blaming of the Fenian Brotherhood hierarchy who did not support him. "I was not the originator of the scheme of freeing Ireland by an invasion of Canada, though I have been one of its warmest supporters, and have advocated it from almost every platform from Maine to Minnesota. I am sorry to have to confess that the men who originated it, and who urged myself and others to take part in the endeavor, basely and deliberately deserted us at the critical moment, and left us to our fate." He continued, "Here I wish to be distinctly understood, that my love for Ireland remains the same, and my hatred of that flag which to the Irish people is the symbol of tyranny and oppression, can never be changed. That flag I desire to tear down. It is the English government that we hate—it is the English government that we desire to fight." In the middle of his explanation, O'Neill gets to the heart of the matter. "As the matter now stands, the invasion appears to have been a ridiculous farce. Had the attempt succeeded, it would have been otherwise." General John O'Neill, the Drumgallan boy raised to fight, continued, "I did believe that a successful attempt could have been made, and I have believed it for years, and for years have labored to bring it about—but I am now satisfied, however, that any further attempt would be highly criminal, because there is not the slightest chance to succeed. As far as my influence will go, I will use it to convince the Irish people in America that any further attempt would be futile."

In conclusion, O'Neill apologized for speaking for an hour, and added, "Perhaps the only legacy that I shall leave my children, the fact that their father fought and bled for this free land, which has offered a home and an asylum to so many thousands of the homeless and persecuted of Europe. It will always be my pride and pleasure as long as life remains, that I have fought and bled for this land of my adoption."[12] These were not hollow words to O'Neill. Prime Minister John MacDonald, his Canadian enemy, admiringly said, "His hatred of British institutions appears to have been so deep-seated he was willing to sacrifice not only his own liberty, but life itself."[13]

Judge Woodruff disagreed, seeing clearly that this was the second time the Fenians had violated American law, believing that just because they got away with it the first time didn't mean they could use the same defense. He argued that the only regret shown by O'Neill was the fact that the planned attack on Canada didn't work. "To the suggestion that you have been misled by others, and that you were deceived, we can give no interpretation save this: that you were disappointed; that instead of finding a force adequate to secure a large measure of success to this expedition, and a support in men and supplies, and needed material aid, you found the force insignificant or the supplies deficient." Woodruff stated, "The Court has listened to the history of your services in behalf of our own country, and the maintenance of its laws. But any real or supposed wrong of your country and countrymen furnishes no vindication, though it may in a sort explain the insane folly and wickedness of making that occasion of suffering and wrong to a people who are innocent, and it is idle to say that not indenting wrong to them you simply sought an injury to the government to which they owed allegiance." Woodruff, though not insensitive to O'Neill's past, was unforgiving, even hostile. "In some aspects of the case, the more you are exalted by the exhibition of courage, of military skill and successful achievements of the past, the greater is the crime when you prostitute that skill and courage and achievement by making it an instrument in the breast of others, and a stimulus to them under your leadership to engage in hostility towards a nation with which we are at peace. It thus becomes an aggravation." Woodruff finished, simply saying, "Especially since we are dealing with a repetition of this offence, I am constrained to make an example, and the sentence of the Court is that you be imprisoned in the state prison for a term of two years." Bizarrely, Woodruff also fined the former FB president $10.[14]

Two other Fenian officers also pleaded guilty with O'Neill on the advice of their collective counsel and, with the approval of future president Grover Cleveland, O'Neill's handpicked choice to defend O'Neill, E.J. Phelps. Colonel J.F. Brown was given nine months in the state prison and Captain J.J. Monahan received six months in the custody of the U.S. marshals. Many in the courtroom agreed that O'Neill's lengthy and self-serving speech was an effective one and a purse was begun for the relief of O'Neill's family, now prepared to stay longer in Vermont while the general served his term.

Grover Cleveland as a young lawyer in Buffalo was enamored by the Fenians and the local Irish vote. He was a silent Fenian supporter in 1866 and the prime attorney for O'Neill and others in Vermont in 1870 (Library of Congress).

The leadership of the Fenian Brotherhood quietly let O'Neill suffer the pangs of defeat, arrest, and humiliation, but there were still many rank-and-file Irish Americans who saw General John O'Neill as a quixotic Irish romantic who was fighting their own fight and who deserved a better fate. Donors from as far away as Wyoming raised money so that Mary Ann and the two children could remain in Vermont and be near the incarcerated general.

Back in New Jersey, the state's oldest newspaper, the *Elizabeth Daily Journal*, saw Eccles Hill much like Judge Woodruff, and the hometown paper's treatment of John O'Neill must have made the Macklins and O'Neills of that city cringe.

The Fenian Farce

The Fenian movement upon Canada has been the topic of conversation during the week. Small bodies of men have gathered on our northern frontier, and five hundred under command of General O'Neill, while advancing from Franklin, Vt., were fired upon by some Canadian militia. The fire was returned, and two Fenians were shot. After the skirmish, U.S. Marshall Foster arrested the Fenian commander O'Neill on the spot, and thrusting him into a carriage, drove him off to Burlington, a prisoner, leaving—as the telegrams say—his little army so demoralized that many of them eagerly turned their faces towards home and were sent home subsequently.

In England, the Fenian raid is generally commented on by the press. The promptitude of President Grant, in issuing the proclamation elicits praise, but the London Times eagerly calls on the Canadians to raise the Union Jack flag, and spare none of the marauders. In government circles in Washington the whole affair is looked upon as a device by the Fenian leaders to tickle more money of the rank and file of the Irish laboring population of the country, and we are inclined to look upon it in that light.[15]

Even while in prison, O'Neill recognized the need to get his side of the story to the Irish American public, and he resorted to going on the offensive—what he always did best—this time with pen. Helped by the New York publisher John J. Foster, O'Neill published a lengthy 62-page defense tract outlining all of his actions from Ridgeway to his release from jail. He attacked the entire Gibbons Wing of the Fenian Brotherhood and was especially vehemently bitter towards P.J. Meehan, his daughter's godfather, who was still in New York with a bullet in his head. O'Neill described the editor as "the evil genius who went to work in his own particular style to foil my efforts by seeking to destroy my influence with the Brotherhood and ruin my character."[16]

O'Neill also deflected any issue of monetary malfeasance, which had been whispered about but for which he had never been directly accused of, by saying, "It is a well known fact that since 1868, the greater portion of the funds of the Fenian Brotherhood had passed through the hands of Mr. Meehan, as he had entire control of the payments made for arms." O'Neill further accused Meehan specifically. "He has spent over sixty thousand of Fenian hard earned money and never been subjected to any examination." There is little doubt O'Neill was correct, but many believed O'Neill guilty of something. Meehan was never investigated.[17]

The "Official Report of Gen. John O'Neill, President of the Fenian Brotherhood on the Attempt to Invade Canada, May 25th, 1870" became a manifesto defending the idea of Fenianism, but in particular supported the life of John O'Neill. "Nearly five years ago I joined the Fenian Brotherhood with the simple wish of serving the cause of Irish liberty.... I hesitated not a moment to risk all.... The fight at Ridgeway was a success, though the movement proved a failure. You cheered and applauded; proclaimed me a hero, a great patriot, skillful commander etc.... I sought nothing so much as to go home, feeling I had done my duty to Ireland."

O'Neill made a fair point when he compared the 1866 invasion with Eccles Hill. "The movement of 1866, for two causes, either of which had been sufficient, resulted disastrously. The men failed to be on the ground in available numbers at the appointed time; and those who did arrive were unprovided with arms and ammunition. Various reasons were assigned for these two mishaps, nearly all reflecting on the management of the commanding general, T.W. Sweeny. The charges then made against General Sweeny have since been repeated, but with more bitterness, against myself. In a movement like ours, if unsuccessful, it seems inevitable that someone has to be made the victim." But the comparison begs one issue. In 1866, Sweeny was rushed by leadership to attack too soon against his wishes, while in 1870, it was O'Neill, as his own leader, who precipitously rushed into disaster.

After castigating almost every Fenian leader from Ridgeway in 1866 to Eccles Hill in 1870 and defending every slur he ever perceived or received, he concluded, "I now bid farewell.... I was an Irishman, a patriot, and a soldier for Ireland, before I was ever a Fenian. I am all three still. My connection with the Organization has neither made me a 'coward,' a 'traitor,' nor a 'dishonest man.'"[18]

The publication of O'Neill's "Official Report" met with mixed results. Horace Greeley, editor of the *New York Tribune*, one of the country's great papers, defended him privately and publicly, as did Erastus Wells, Missouri congressman and one of the most influential men in the country. The working-class Irish, not to be outdone, filled a double-spaced, ten-foot-long petition that was presented to the president seeking a pardon. Others were not so generous. The *Boston Herald* said, "General John O'Neill, who calls himself President of the Fenian Brotherhood, and who certainly was Commander-in-chief of the forces that attempted to invade Canada last May, has published an official report of that brief and inglorious campaign in a pamphlet of sixty pages. He attributes his failure mainly to the fact that instead of ten thousand men who were promised him, only two or three hundred arrived and intimates that it was neither his cowardice nor lack of military genius, which compelled a retreat. It hardly needed sixty pages. What is more to the purpose is that Gen. O'Neill has come to his senses, and declares himself opposed to any further Fenian attempts on the Queen's dominions."[19]

In the course of his detailed pamphlet, John O'Neill mentioned every person and organization who had pledged or given money for bail or family sustenance, even if they had contributed as little as five dollars. There was no mention, however, of anyone from Elizabeth, New Jersey, named Macklin or O'Neill. Either O'Neill was one of the most private men in the world when it came to family, or something was clearly amiss. Not a dime, apparently, went to their very own Drumgallan boy, John O'Neill, unless given very secretly. Just two years before, St Mary's Church in Elizabeth had their first major fundraiser. John Macklin gave $255 and Bernard O'Neill pledged $110, both in the top ten of the city and a lot of money for the immigrant Irish community. The list remains today prominently displayed in the rectory office in Elizabeth, 150 years later.[20]

Meanwhile Thomas Beach, alias Henri Le Caron, quickly and quietly absented himself from Vermont and returned to his family in Illinois, nobody the wiser. With an election looming, President Grant, though considered an anti–Catholic, acquiesced while on summer vacation in Long Branch, New

Jersey, and pardoned O'Neill and the remaining prisoners, knowing the Irish vote still counted, and so still did John O'Neill. A few months later on February 22, 1871, Grant greeted many freed Irish revolutionaries at the White House with a "Glad to see you," but not O'Neill.[21] The man who may have understood the best and worst of John O'Neill was Prime Minister John MacDonald, who, like President Grant, was a serious lover of Irish whiskey. MacDonald was so displeased by the proposed pardon he wrote to his British counterparts, "You should be aware that Canada is not a consenting party to the cause proposed to be pursued by the pardoning. On the contrary it views it with regret and apprehension." Politically the Canadian understood Grant's motives but felt, if allowed, O'Neill would do it again. MacDonald knew his man.[22]

U.S. Grant, a great American so very underrated, pardoned O'Neill from a Vermont prison after six months, primarily for the Irish vote, not because he cared much for O'Neill or the Irish (Library of Congress).

O'Neill was finally released on October 12, but there were no serenades this time in Nashville, and nobody played "Hail to the Chief." After the pardon, John O'Neill remained in Vermont for the winter and spring, as there was no need to rush back to New York without a job. Mary Ann delivered a boy on Christmas Day, 1870, whom they named Eugene after John's brother who died in infancy in Ireland. Sadly, this Eugene O'Neill would soon suffer the same fate in Nebraska. Nonetheless, the interlude was one of peace and quiet after two years of warring with the Brotherhood. He had promised Judge Woodruff and all of Irish America he would desist from any future thoughts of military action against Canada, "as any further attempt would be criminal."[23] John O'Neill seemed finished with the Fenian movement; he was neither the first nor the last, but the question Mary Ann must have asked herself was what the future might hold. John O'Neill was only thirty-one years old and had been in the spotlight for almost a decade—and liked it. Many years later in California, in direct contrast to his father's situation, an aging John Hugh O'Neill recalled the year-long stay in Vermont as the happiest of his childhood. "I remember perfectly the barrels of apples in every cellar, and the maple sugar from our own trees. In the Spring I watched the tapping of the maple trees that grew nearby, and when summer came friends of our father who lived in the country would take us on visits. It was there I first learned what the country looked like and the beauty of a farm. I can picture those trips over the Green Mountains and through the little valleys with the stone houses, the air full of fragrance from the wild honeysuckles that grew all over the mountainsides. The best day was Sunday when we drove together fifteen miles to Mass in Burlington."[24]

In June 1871, the O'Neill family of five returned briefly to Elizabeth, where John would magically pull another rabbit out of his hat.

9

I Promise Until I Don't

The Irish have memories, imagination, a passionate involvement in history, traditions of rebellion, of sympathy for desperate causes, of a human, illogical respect for martyrdom. —Thomas Flanagan

Many perceived that an embarrassed and repentant O'Neill would return from Vermont with his leadership of the larger Fenian Brotherhood stripped and his income dissipated, though still the leader of his own newly created O'Neill Wing; other observers may have expected the proud and egotistical O'Neill to crawl into a historical hole, never to be seen or heard from again. In fact, he did not even leave the Brotherhood. Even before the publication of his manifesto, the minority Fenian Brotherhood wing led by John Savage, always in severe opposition to O'Neill, saw a strategic opening and acted quickly on O'Neill's predicament. For years O'Neill had been in competition to the Savage Wing, but now, having sat in a cold Vermont prison and finally understanding how hazardous his position in official Irish circles had become, O'Neill was visited in Windsor, Vermont, a full month before his pardon by a committee led by John O'Mahony of New York, Edward Counihan of Boston, and Edward McSweeny of St. Louis. It would be a coup for the Savage Wing to enlist O'Neill, no matter his current predicament. He was still John O'Neill, handsome, eloquent, defiant, and the hero of Ridgeway. The resultant meeting would bring O'Neill back into the game, and he switched sides in a New York minute.

Windsor Prison, Sept. 7th 1870
   Agreement made between Gen John O'Neil on behalf of self and the Fenian Organization of which he is President—and Col John A. O'Mahony, Edward McSweeny and Edward Counihan—a committee appointed by the Ninth National Convention FB on behalf of the organization presided over by Chief Executive John Savage.
   1st—That the said Gen John O'Neil accepts the constitution of the FB presided over by C.E. John Savage as the constitution of the United Fenian Brotherhood.
   2nd—That the said Gen O'Neil agrees that on the part of the organization of which

he controls, he may nominate two members of the council—one of whom shall be an auditor; the other a position on the council for himself.

3rd—That this agreement between the parties above named is made with the honest hope that it will tend to the union of all Irish Nationalists for the common cause of Ireland's independence.[1]

The general clung to his Fenian membership by his fingernails. Joined by his most loyal followers, the irrepressible O'Neill confidently switched allegiances and alliances, and retained a place in the minority John Savage Wing of the Brotherhood, which for years he had been in open dispute. The majority Fenian leadership led by Gallagher and the recovering Meehan were glad to see him go, but the minority Savage Wing simply could not ignore O'Neill's continued appeal throughout Irish America, where he remained extremely popular, and the general was again placed in the ruling hierarchy and given a paycheck. It should have been enough.

Now only thirty-two years old, a career change was in order for the twice defeated but still widely admired O'Neill, even if he stayed involved in Irish nationalism. When William Roberts left the Fenians, he retired to Long Island and lived comfortably off his contacts in politics and business for much of his life. Former General Tom Sweeny resigned from the Fenians to keep his army benefits and pension, and also enjoyed a post–Brotherhood senior life. John O'Mahony, the oldest Fenian, returned to New York and lived a quiet life until he died at age sixty-one in 1877.

Fenians of all ranks found careers after 1870 in American politics. John Egan, Ridgeway veteran from O'Neill's hometown of Elizabeth, New Jersey, who stored arms in his cellar in Elizabethport, turned to politics and became the speaker of the New Jersey Assembly and a powerful politician in Elizabeth and the Garden State. Victor Vifquain went home to Nebraska and became a Democratic Party leader. Patrick Collins, another young Fenian from Boston, became the first Irish-born mayor of Boston. O'Neill's staunch compatriot, P.W. Dunne, became a prosperous citizen of Sioux City, Iowa, and his son Edward Fitzsimmons Dunne became both Mayor of Chicago and then Governor of Illinois. There were dozens of others who could have helped place him in a well-paid position. Even the abominable Henri Le Caron could be found living a family life of sorts in the Chicago suburbs as a doctor of all things, mistakenly thinking his harried five-year spying career was over. Soon he would return to spying, this time on the Brotherhood's successor, the Clan na Gael, and when he was outed in 1889, it would send shock waves throughout Irish nationalism.

It should have been an easy transition for the devout Catholic O'Neill. He was still young, younger than anyone knew, and had a growing family as well as a successful and large extended family only fifteen miles away in Elizabeth, New Jersey, that was not dependent upon him. Despite the misguided defeat at Eccles Hill, John O'Neill was still revered by a sizable portion of the Irish population, and numerous well-connected patrons throughout the country were in position to ease him through his early middle age. Only one thing seemed certain—John O'Neill's military career was over.

Like many ex-soldiers, O'Neill could and would carry his rank until death, and in fact, insisted on it; but this country and Ireland would not need his military services. The United States would now be at peace for more than forty years, still reeling from the bloody Civil War; the Fenian Rising of 1867 in Ireland (like the one in America) ended any future thought of serious armed rebellion until 1916; and most importantly, O'Neill himself had publicly told Judge Woodruff in Vermont, "Any further [military] attempt would be criminal, and as far as my influence goes, I will use it to convince the Irish people in America that any further attempt would be futile."[2] Finally, the general told his own Fenian Brotherhood upon his return from prison he would have nothing to do with any Canadian invasion attempts when he published the above statement in his manifesto. O'Neill promised everybody, and, up to now, he was always a man of his word.

But out of the far West came a lone shadowy rider with similar exaggerated dreams of Irish freedom. Though rejected by every sensible government and Fenian official in Washington and New York, the Sligo-born William Bernard O'Donoghue would capture the soul of John Charles O'Neill, just as the Fenian Brotherhood oath had six years before. As a result all promises to Judge Woodruff, the Brotherhood, Mary Ann, and the children were turned to dust. Any hope Catherine may have had for her youngest child— the one she so unfortunately had left in Ireland the longest—to return to a life of normalcy disappeared when John O'Neill and W.B. O'Donoghue shared their first drink, with O'Neill looking for redemption.[3]

The story of this third Fenian invasion of Canada is the one least covered by historians, but it may reveal the most about John O'Neill. Unlike 1866 or 1870, it was never a Fenian fight, though it has often been depicted as such.

Irish-born W.B. O'Donoghue burst into the North American scene as a twenty-five-year-old in the Red River area of present-day Manitoba after studying briefly for the priesthood at St. Boniface College in Winnipeg. In 1868, as John O'Neill was preparing for a second term as Fenian Brotherhood president, O'Donoghue became entranced by Louis Riel's Red River Independence Movement. The Metis, a mixed race of European and Native American people (including some Irish but mostly French), were seeking independence or at least self-determination from the majority English-speaking Canadian Dominion. Riel was their unquestioned spiritual and political leader. Riel's ultimate goal was for the Canadian government to recognize ancient Manitoba Metis land, territory legally granted in the seventeenth century by the Hudson Bay Company. O'Donoghue found his way into heavily Catholic Metis land when introduced by Bishop Giroux, a Metis favorite, in 1868. Starting as a mathematics teacher, he soon joined Riel in his quest for self-determination. Tall and handsome, O'Donoghue soon became a member of Riel's inner circle.

Historian Roy Johnson portrayed O'Donoghue in terms that could have made him O'Neill's twin. "O'Donoghue," said Johnson, "was an eloquent speaker [in French and English] and an able organizer. He was fiery-tempered, proud, and egotistical." Though not a Fenian himself, he was attracted to the Brotherhood's principles. Like O'Neill, the good-looking O'Donoghue easily won loyal followers among the people of the west. The most troubling attribute the two men shared, however, was a "characteristic propensity for impulsive action."[4]

In September 1870, with O'Neill in a Vermont prison, Riel had dispatched O'Donoghue to Washington with one singular charge. It was a logical assignment, Riel being aware O'Donoghue had acquaintances with some prominent local Americans. The Irishman was to ask President Grant if he would appeal to the Queen to intercede in the dispute between the Canadian government and the Metis. Riel was not looking to join the United States, and distrusted the Americans as much as he did the Canadians under John MacDonald.

The strange ex-math teacher from the Northwest arrived in Washington in early December, but was not able to see President Grant until January 29, when he was finally granted a private meeting. O'Donoghue met with the president accompanied by Senator Alexander Ramsey of Minnesota, Chairman of the Foreign Relations Committee General N.P. Banks, and Michigan Senator Zachariah Chandler, all no doubt eager for American involvement in the West and possessing their own alliances and allegiances. O'Donoghue may have done as directed by Riel, but he also added an unauthorized plea of his own for United States annexation of the western Canadian province, which Riel had specifically told him not to bring up. Grant rejected both the Metis petition and the O'Donoghue addendum without discussion, though by all accounts was "very kindly and listened attentively."[5] Even Charles Sumner, the powerful chairman of the Foreign Relations Committee who approved of almost any revolt and annexation that would harm Great Britain, believed correctly that Canada now wanted nothing but independence or annexation. In February, O'Donoghue left the capital empty-handed, unaware that back in Manitoba, Riel, with good cause, was turning on him in his absence. Riel began to suspect (correctly) that O'Donoghue was also working with Americans south of the Dakota border, eager to capitalize on the burgeoning situation.

Undeterred, before returning to Maintoba, O'Donoghue traveled north and pitched his idea of annexation twice to the financier Jay Cooke, one of the richest men in America, once in New York and again in Philadelphia. Cooke, who was the primary financier of the northern effort in the Civil War, refused the irrepressible visitor, citing his business interests in England might be jeopardized. The ex-seminarian then desperately turned to the Fenian Senate, asking for arms, men, and military assistance—in effect, an army. With the memory of Eccles Hill only months old, the Irishman from the northwest was turned down flat, the Fenians immovable, forever finished with invasion plans in North America and on last rites themselves as an organization of any kind. The red-headed messenger from Manitoba was rejected at every stop—with one singular exception. John O'Neill, only four months removed from a Vermont prison, was mesmerized by O'Donoghue's eloquence, persistence, and promises of glory. Now even the minority Savage Wing of the Brotherhood was shocked. The Brotherhood had just concluded their Tenth Annual Convention in late March where two O'Neill representatives were invited to the floor, and O'Neill himself was escorted to the floor. At the conclusion of the convention O'Neill, as promised by the prison agreement of September 7, 1870, was appointed to the Executive Council along with his choice, W.J. Davis of Brooklyn. After a year-long bitter dispute with the Brotherhood, a disastrous military move on Canada, and arrest, trial, and imprisonment, O'Neill was back in the good graces of at least a sizable percentage of his fellow Irish nationalists, but not for long.

Just weeks later, the entire Fenian organization appallingly realized that O'Neill was in the O'Donoghue camp, where he was joined by O'Neill's most loyal compatriot, F.B. General J.J. Donnelly. O'Neill arranged for O'Donoghue to place his complete plans to assist the downtrodden people of Manitoba before the Brotherhood. O'Neill, once more on the FB's council, pleaded with all his power to be granted "arms, men and money to form a brigade in the northwest."[6] The council, and every other thinking Irishman privy to the meeting, was aghast. But John O'Neill made the mistake of dealing with a man more dreamy-eyed than himself, and would pay for it.

The general resigned completely—one report said "in violent passion," another said "in a towering rage"[7]—from the Brotherhood he had sworn allegiance to six years before in Nashville, and less than five months after his contract with the Savage Wing and release from prison. A deal was quickly struck absolving the FB from any blame forthcoming between the two simpatico dreamers, though the Brotherhood did make good on a promise to O'Neill that they would not denounce the movement.

One historian says John O'Neill apparently saw this as a final opportunity to strike a blow against Great Britain. But this is oversimplified, and O'Neill did not behave like a sound military commander when he boasted that he could conduct the entire campaign alone. In truth, General John O'Neill had finally done to himself what the leadership of the Fenian Brotherhood could never do—rid themselves of the man who was once their brightest star. Compounding the situation, O'Neill had no idea he was attempting to fight the Canadians on behalf of Riel and the Metis when in fact the French-speaking Metis people of Manitoba wanted nothing to do with him. It is also unlikely O'Neill, now a lone ranger, would have honestly attempted this alone, without his new Tonto, W.B. O'Donoghue.

The two Irishmen headed west, O'Neill with much to accomplish for their planned attack against Manitoba, just south of the Red River. The sainted Mary Ann packed up the three children, John (seven), Mamie (five), and Eugene (seven months), and the general rented a home in East St. Louis, Illinois, while he conducted his newest excursion, this time in the west.[8] The prospects for success were slim and none. Riel, sensing trouble, had turned on O'Donoghue while the ex-seminarian was courting O'Neill. Riel notified his English-speaking Canadian enemies and said he would remain loyal to the government, which he did, at least temporarily, hoping that this information would lead to leniency for himself and his fellow Metis, all wanted for real and imagined crimes in the far west of Manitoba.

Despite the odds both Irish dreamers, now joined by Donnelly, were convinced they would be successful, "like dogs barking at the moon."[9] The Canadians, despite their success defending the borders against the Fenians, were taking no chances, especially when they discovered O'Donoghue had roped O'Neill into the scheme.

O'Neill had never been to the high plains of the northwest, and O'Donoghue had no experience as a soldier. Compounding the situation, O'Neill stopped in Lockport, Illinois, and visited his most loyal and supportive friend, Henri Le Caron. Now raising a family and living as a doctor, even the heinous British spy was incredulous when O'Neill arrived and explained his mission. O'Neill asked for Le Caron's help in acquiring arms. The odd little man, thinking his nefarious career over but always on the lookout for cash, agreed to give O'Neill four hundred modern breechloaders plus ammunition the former inspector general had stashed away in a Fenian secret cache in Port Huron, Michigan. The spy then wrote immediately to the Canadians, expecting, and receiving, a check for the information provided.

Le Caron sent the following to his old handler McMicken on June 16. "I received a telegram from O'N wishing to meet him ... he came here yesterday from Detroit.... I learned something of interest to you.... O'Neill talked and an invitation to take part in an expedition to [Red River].... He left the city this morning for St. Paul, Minnesota, where he will meet O'Donohue to make arrangements with him about the affair.... He says he has been to Buffalo, Dunkirk, and Detroit to look up assistance.... Donnelly is in with him and will be here next week ... what shall I do.... I have no desire to leave my practice—but if it pays well I am in."[10] This new escapade of O'Neill's was so bizarre even Le Caron turned down an invitation to participate (though he would be paid), so O'Neill and O'Donoghue continued northwest.

Unaware the Canadians were now alerted, O'Neill and O'Donoghue headed for Saint Paul, Minnesota, to raise money and men. A local priest, Father Richot, reported that O'Neill visited him and asked how the Fenians would be received by the Metis. Richot told them they would be welcomed as settlers but resisted as raiders. Ignoring his advice, two idealists gave impassioned speeches for several months, passed around the collection plate, and used the prestige of O'Neill's name to attract recruits. In what should have been an eye-opening omen, General John O'Neill left Minnesota and headed for Canada at the end of September with thirty-five men. He had expected two thousand, but he was always exaggerating. O'Neill was now in the midst of an impossible dream, as twenty-eight of the men were simply seasonal sawmill workers from MacCauleyville, Minnesota. By October 4, this force of untrained men was just south of the border near Pembina, North Dakota.[11]

Before deciding to invade Canada for the third time in five years with less of a stellar force and more of a laughingstock, did O'Neill realize that American law enforcement and Canadian troops were prepared for them, and worse, that both the United States and Canada had agreed to let American soldiers seize any troublemakers? If so, it did not stop the man once called a military genius and a star of Irish nationalist pride in America. O'Neill should also have realized the quest was failing when there was no communication between O'Donoghue and Riel. In fact, just days before the "attack," Louis Riel had conveyed to the Canadian government: "Be assured that there is not the least danger that I or any of my friends will join with the Fenians. We detest the Fenians, for they are condemned by the [Catholic] Church, and we shall have nothing to do with them."[12]

The U.S. consul in Winnipeg apprised General William T. Sherman of the upcoming raid. "There are danger of inroads into Manitoba for pillage under pretext of Fenian invasion. I urge patrol on the frontier." Sherman alerted Captain Lloyd Wheaton, the local colonel, and thus both American and Canadian forces were prepared for both Irish Don Quixotes.[13]

The result of the raid was sadly predictable and ludicrous, though it would eventually assist in small measure the Canadians wishing to forge Manitoba into a province a bit sooner rather than later. O'Neill's men captured a Hudson Bay Trading Post plus two deserted log buildings, only to discover much later in court they were still in the United States, and not in Canada. The "invasion" force led by O'Neill was operating with a survey map completed in 1823, while Captain Wheaton possessed the survey of the international boundary completed in the summer of 1870 by Captain D.P. Heap of the U.S. Army Corps of Engineers.

The approaching U.S. army under Wheaton promptly dispersed the invaders from Fort Pembina. A dozen men were arrested plus O'Neill for illegal possession of the trading post, while another two dozen freedom fighters scattered hither and yon, leaving three hundred stands of arms and seven thousand rounds of ammunition.

The Metis that O'Donoghue expected to rise up by the hundreds never materialized, but four did grab the ex-seminarian and turn him over to the Canadian authorities, where he was promptly jailed. When the "battle" was over, there had been no shots fired by the O'Neill forces, no fatalities, and no injuries except the military and personal reputation of General John O'Neill. O'Neill's "forces" immediately abandoned the four hundred arms they had carried with them 1,100 miles from Port Huron, Michigan.

In what turned out to be typical frontier justice of the American far west, the men arrested with O'Neill were soon simply released as "simple dupes" of the two Irish leaders,[14] except for O'Neill's loyal officers, J.J. Donnelly and Tom Curley. After the initial embarrassment of surrendering his magnificent sword when arrested, and despite all that had led him to this lonely place, the unconquerable spirit of John O'Neill remained unchanged. In an interview he granted the day after his arrest, O'Neill's overconfidence, arrogance, and denial was still quite apparent. "The General looks to be in splendid condition physically, and so far as recent events are concerned, they do not seem to wear very greatly upon his elastic and hopeful mind," wrote the reporter.

"I desire to state that if I had not been interfered with by the United States authorities, I would have had fully one thousand men with me," said O'Neill. "They would have been subject to my command for whatever I chose to do. I had enough men to resist Colonel Wheaton had I desired to fight United States soldiers. I had fought too long under the Stars and Stripes to want to fight United States troops, whether they had crossed the line legally or illegally." O'Neill was then unaware he had never crossed over into Canadian territory, and he then verbally attacked Wheaton, who had done his job simply and effectively. "Instead of wearing the United States uniform, Wheaton would act with more propriety if he should wear the British uniform. As a prosecuting attorney, though, he made a perfect ass of himself, and showed a complete ignorance of the law. I believe the action of Colonel [Captain] Wheaton to be entirely unauthorized, in crossing into British territory and arresting anyone. Nor do I believe his conduct will be sanctioned either by the department commander, or at Washington...."

Wheaton went into British territory and ordered his men to fire, and they did fire several volleys. It is surprising no one was killed. It was no fault of his that there was no one killed. Had there been any killed, I have no doubt he would have been guilty of murder." One might wonder exactly what O'Neill expected with thirty-five unemployed armed men (or the expected thousands) when he attacked. He concluded the interview with the following. "I do not fear any arrest. I have fought and bled for the United States government. I am not aware that I have violated any law of the United States."[15] The one question O'Neill was never asked about the North Dakota raid was what helping the Metis rise up against the Canadian government had to do with Irish Freedom.

The disaster was complete when O'Neill, who wholeheartedly believed he was in Canada at the time of the raid, was released after his lawyers explained he could not be convicted of attacking Canada when, in truth, he never got there. Even the arrest and trials, or lack of them, were comical. The Dakota Commissioner didn't want to prosecute O'Neill, Donnelly, and Curley because he was afraid a jury composed of western backwoodsmen who were anti-government would never convict the popular Irishmen or anybody else. He was correct, but after their release, anti–Irish government officials, in particular Hamilton Fish of New York, protested and the three men were arrested again in St. Paul, Minnesota. The Minnesota Attorney General released them on "lack of evidence" and no trial was held. Canada, for the third and final time, was saved from the Irish and General John O'Neill. The hero of Ridgeway, the flaming star of Irish nationalism in the United States, was reduced to a minuscule fallen meteor.

But O'Neill was lucky he did not get to Canada. W.B. O'Donoghue was quickly convicted by the Canadian court and sent to prison, where he stayed for six years before being pardoned in 1877 and evicted from the country. He moved to St. Paul and taught school for one year before ignominiously dying of tuberculosis on March 26, 1878, aged thirty-five, two months after John O'Neill.

O'Neill's instability was nevertheless again offset by his energy and fierce hatred of England, which enabled him to garner loyal supporters as brave and intelligent as Donnelly and Curley. Tom Curley, a native of Roscommon, had fought in the Civil War and risen to the rank of Major after immigrating to St. Louis in 1851. Curley was, like O'Neill, a minor Civil War legend. Fighting with an Irish regiment, the 7th Missouri Infantry, Tom saw action at Vicksburg, Lookout Mountain, Missionary Ridge, and was part of Sherman's March to the Sea. He was a brevet brigadier general for meritorious service and went home to Missouri at war's end until the Fenians called. He joined the Pembina attack because of friendship with O'Neill, and when he was released, became a revered assemblyman in Wisconsin, following the post–Brotherhood careers of many successful ex-Fenians across the country. When he died in 1904 at age seventy-nine, he was the last of the O'Neill military entourage.[16]

Donnelly was born in Rhode Island of Irish emigrants and was the same age as O'Neill. After attending Holy Cross College, he studied law, joined the

Union Army, and served with distinction. Donnelly was at Ridgeway, was wounded in the second attack in Vermont, and after Pembina fought Chief Joseph and the Nez Perce. Perhaps the most loyal of all Fenians to O'Neill, he was, like his friend, a man of triumph and tragedy. Popular and capable, Donnelly later turned to politics, becoming a member of the Montana Assembly in 1881 and chosen Speaker of the House of Representatives.

A dozen years after the disaster at Pembina, Donnelly and Louis Riel spent time together when Riel was in exile in Montana. But he also suffered from some of the same demons as his mentor, General John O'Neill. In 1889, Donnelly's drinking problem caused this brave, loyal, proud Irishman to fill his pockets with stones, cut his own throat, and drown in the Missouri River, not far from the fate suffered twenty-two years earlier by Thomas Francis Meagher.[17]

The Fenian Brotherhood, despite its complete innocence in the Pembina affair, was as finished as John O'Neill in its quest for Irish freedom. A rival organization, the Clan na Gael, was founded by another Irishman determined to free the country of his birth, Jerome J. Collins of County Cork. Collins joined the Fenians on his arrival in New York, but by 1870 realized the Brotherhood was rife with informers and the Fenians were airing their open laundry to every newspaper on the east coast. After the debacle in Vermont, many Fenians crossed over to the Clan, whose "chambers" replaced the Fenian circles and became the dominant Irish nationalistic force in the country, with one primary rule—secrecy. Its goal was the same as O'Neill's, a free Ireland by any means necessary. J. J. Collins, however, realized that the flamboyancy of O'Neill would not fit the new organization, and thus did not open its arms to the general.

But the Fenians did not give up easy. After John Savage recruited O'Neill in prison, placed him on the executive board, and then lost him to O'Donoghue and Manitoba, the Brotherhood was struggling to stay relevant. When O'Neill went to prison, Savage traveled west to California to gauge Brotherhood commitment. Now in his early 50s, the green-eyed, pleasant Savage tried desperately to disassociate the Fenian Brotherhood from O'Neill, without once mentioning his name. Savage, a great patriot who served with Corcoran in the Fighting 69th Brigade and whose Irish father was arrested in 1798 with the United Irishmen, was treated royally and used conciliatory messages to large gatherings, with no words of war.

"I want men who can exercise their heads in this organization." In another setting, he said to thousands, "For if the strong head does not check the impulsive heart, day after day, the time will arrive when the body will be dragged after it also." In every California gathering he repeated, "In America the Fenian Brotherhood stands today in a prouder, better, more practical position than it has ever occupied."[18] None of it worked. John O'Neill was off to Pembina and the Fenians were withering on the vine as the Clan na Gael slowly became the voice of Irish American nationalism. The Brotherhood, which had boasted of more than 150,000 members in 1865, held its last convention in 1885 with 132 in attendance. But no matter how much the Brotherhood executives attempted to distance themselves from John O'Neill, it couldn't stop the Irish from loving the hero of Ridgeway.

O'Neill headed back from St. Paul to Mary Ann and the children in East St. Louis after almost six months away, but stopped, beyond belief, to pay a return visit to Le Caron in Lockport, Illinois, never imagining that twenty years later his loyal friend and aide would pen a bestselling memoir of his decades as a spy. In it Le Caron called General John O'Neill "the most egotistical soul I ever met in my life. In [O'Neill's] belief the Irish cause lived, breathed, moved and had its being in John O'Neill."[19] What more can you ask of a friend?

10

A Second Career

He could not walk the easy way to his destiny.—Patrick Kavanagh, *The Great Hunger*

General John O'Neill fought for a decade—against Mormons, Indian cattle thieves, the Confederacy; for the Fenians; against Canada; against the Fenians; and for himself. He was during that interval a military hero, a celebrity of Irish nationalism in America, a rash and raw politico, and at the end, at least temporarily, a grandiose lost patriotic soul. But perhaps the small *New York Star* most correctly summarized it on October 24, 1871, in an article that was reprinted nationwide:

Gen O'Neill's Last Farce

The news that General O'Neill, the once popular President of the Fenian Brotherhood, had attempted to perpetrate another foolish fiasco on the Canadians of British North American frontier, has greatly incensed many of his former friends against him. It is extremely doubtful if there be a dozen persons in this city who do not regard him as an unauthorized, irresponsible and reckless character, who has no character to lose, and who is ready to engage in any adventure that may present itself. Having lost the hold he once had upon the affections and support of the great mass of his countrymen, and forfeited their confidence to that extent that he will never again be permitted to occupy any position of trust or honor in their ranks, he seeks to revenge his fall upon the heads of Irish nationalists in general. That this supplies us with key to his reckless career, there can be no reasonable doubt, for he is known to have repeatedly boasted that he would "rule or ruin" the Irish national cause, and it is believed that this latest move was designed by him to induce the President of the United States to suppress every Irish revolutionary body in the country.[1]

One wonders if, on the return trip from North Dakota to his family in East St. Louis, O'Neill realized his first career, a once shining star that crashed and burned, was truly over. Americans love a second chance more than most countries, and after all, John O'Neill was still just thirty-three. But who indeed was the real John O'Neill? Until 1872, all biographical information came from a singular source—O'Neill himself. He gave up nothing of his family. He mentioned his mother once in a Civil War request for leave, but only by the term "my mother"—never by her name. He never mentioned his sister, brother, or uncle publicly in print by name at any time, ever. For decades, commentators wrote his mother's name as "Elizabeth," but she was Catherine and as Catherine, or Kate, O'Neill, she lived a full adult life in Elizabeth, New Jersey. The O'Neill grandchildren, who up to the present time methodically and lovingly saved hundreds of records about their famous grandfather, never knew his mother's name. And in the voluminous papers given to the author, including searches done by numerous family members both in the United States and Ireland, there is no mention of Catherine, Bernard, or Mary O'Neill, with one exception—Mary Ann's Civil War pension request from 1896.

Yet Mary Ann and the children lived on and off in Elizabeth for more than two and a half years, and two of O'Neill's nephews and a cousin, all from Elizabeth, would figure prominently in John's future, so there had to be considerable interaction with his estranged family. But there is no record, except John Hugh's great childhood memory of family in Elizabeth, thoughts he still remembered fondly at age seventy in 1936. Some historians have downplayed O'Neill's 1858–60 desertion from Utah, for example, saying he was fighting Indians for three years from Kansas to California, but that was never true, as his own diary affirms. During two short occasions at Fort Crook, he performed admirably as a sergeant, helping to track Indian cattle rustlers on the Oregon border before heading east to fight Confederates.

O'Neill has been portrayed by many, but seldom accurately. One biographer had him in President Andrew Johnson's office with a "shock of facial red hair that made the wild beard of Karl Marx look groomed and effeminate by comparison."[2] O'Neill was always described since childhood as dark haired, well groomed, neat with a simple moustache, even when in active military service. By 1872 he was 5'9" and with his frenetic work habits, always trim. In the ten years ending with Pembina, there is one direct mention of alcohol abuse. By comparison presidents Johnson and Grant and Canadian Prime Minister John MacDonald were all publicly fond of a drop, especially MacDonald. By 1872, O'Neill had spoken in almost every state except Florida and California on behalf of the Brotherhood, but without exception newspapers mentioned him consistently as eloquent, with nary a single mention of being under the weather. Even the papers that were anti–Irish were never accusatory about his early alcohol abuse, despite nineteenth century papers' great latitude to do as they wished. Most importantly, neither his chief aide nor any Canadian spy, of whom there were a multitude, accused him of substance abuse before 1872.

But at the age of thirty-three, and not the thirty-seven the nation believed him to be, and despite the gargantuan failures including arrest and imprisonment, O'Neill still counted famous and powerful friendships, and could easily have found a respectable job in a comfortable lifestyle. There were certainly aspects to be cleaned up. In those forty-eight months, he was gone a great deal—away from his wife, children, and family—fighting in a strange "war," touring and leading the Fenian Brotherhood, spending months in jail, and spending six months of the utmost folly on the North Dakota scheme. There can be little doubt that during his Brotherhood presidency, his ego, hubris, and arrogance grew to a point of creating unneeded enemies and inflamed allies, though many still saw his single-minded desire for Irish freedom a rare and wonderful quality.

O'Neill was a confirmed soldier, a religious conservative of deep faith (except when it came to trying to fight against British rule in Ireland), and a man with an ingrained sense of propriety. Despite his weaknesses, and with spies watching his every move, not one ever accused him of being a philandering husband, though for sure he was often an absent one. Le Caron, with his penchant for absolute lies and exaggerations, never mentioned anything of the sort, though he excoriated the general in other ways, even twenty years after John was long in the grave.

From 1862 until 1872, O'Neill was accused once by the Fenian Brotherhood of a $3 per day graft for a year, and several commentators have added similar charges, saying he was "loose" or "absconded" with Brotherhood funds.[3] In truth, O'Neill may have lived over his head while serving as FB president, with an extravagant $2,000 yearly salary plus expenses, but McMichael, the Fenian Brotherhood spy in Fenian Headquarters who oversaw all paperwork, never issued an accusation to his Canadian paymasters regarding financial misappropriations and John O'Neill. Even so, General John O'Neill, the name he would answer to and insist on for the rest of his life, came off a train in St. Louis just after Christmas 1871 and had life decisions to remake.

Arriving in Illinois, however, he found sycophants unfortunately still praising him, and he remained the darling of a percentage of the Irish American community. Many Irish Americans read the press stories on the botched invasions not with regret or apology but as attacks motivated as prejudice against their race. In this contrary way, O'Neill was thus further exalted, especially by the poor and downtrodden. Some press accounts of the Dakota raid incredulously praised O'Neill's bearing, personality, and his unrelenting nationalist persuasion. After he was released from arrest with all charges dropped, many were even convinced of the general's public invincibility. John O'Neill, the outstanding soldier, had by now become a brilliant self-promoter, but he had no job, no income, and owned no property. In a life somewhat reminiscent of his own earlier childhood, General John O'Neill was the father of three children under the age of six who barely knew him.

The general finally took the advice of some, including former Civil War General Judson Kilpatrick, and attempted to make a living as a public speaker, a lucrative undertaking for many after the war. He would not be unique, as many GAR ex-officers did the same. It was a good living, at least for a while. Fellow New Jerseyan Kilpatrick, an ex-cavalry officer, friend of O'Neill's, and whose farm near the Delaware Water Gap had been a hidden cache of Fenian arms in 1870, made a very fine life traveling the country in 1871 and 1872 with a speech titled "Sherman's March to the Sea" (in which he had played only a minor role) and then later another lecture series called "Incidents and Battle Scenes of the Rebellion." The success of the lecherous, unattractive little Kilpatrick, who was earning thousands of dollars for just a few talks, may have inspired the more appealing O'Neill, who had now been a polished speaker for years.[4] The general opened an office across the river from his family at the St. Nicholas Hotel in St. Louis and hired his nephew John Joseph O'Neill of Elizabeth as his secretary and agent. It was a job, and O'Neill surely enjoyed the travel, public adulation of an audience, and income. One item his lecturing did not include was Irish settlement in the West.

Irish-born John C. O'Neill, heroic Civil War lieutenant, Fenian general, Nebraska colonizer, ca. early 1870s (O'Neill family collection).

Most reports on O'Neill's life have him abandoning his military persona and starting a new life as a colonizer of the downtrodden eastern Irish for the beauty of the West, in particular, Nebraska, but that is inaccurate. One 1919 commentator said, "O'Neill turned his attention to the material welfare of his race, guiding them from the squalor of the mining zones of Scranton and Calumet to the broad fertile prairies of Nebraska."[5] Another added, "O'Neill shifted his attention to the founding of Irish colonies in the American Midwest."[6] Even a third has claimed the general "conceived the idea of establishing the Irish resettlement while a prisoner in Vermont."[7] In truth, John O'Neill had not yet changed, and he certainly never conceived of the idea in prison. Buoyed by his old reputation, the general decided to earn his living on the lecture circuit.

O'Neill traveled all over the Midwest with appearances beginning as early as April 1872. His loyal nephew, John Joseph O'Neill, was just nineteen, brother Bernard O'Neill's oldest son, and the general would employ him in various capacities for the next six years. During the next year and a half, from February 1872 until November 1873, General John O'Neill lectured extensively, but without a single mention of colonization in Nebraska or anywhere else. If nothing else, he was consistent. The lecture title, which was usually advertised for a week prior to appearance, read[8]:

> Ireland—Past and Present
> With An Account of the
> Attempted Invasion of Canada
> In 1866 and 1870
> And the Causes of the Failure, also
> The Object of Going to Manitoba, British
> North America in 1871
> A LECTURE
> Upon the Above Subject will
> Be Delivered by
> Gen. John O'Neill
> Admission 35c Gentleman and Lady 50c
> 8 o'clock

Kilpatrick was paid $3,000 to make twelve appearances in California during the same time period that John O'Neill spoke more than thirty times. O'Neill, unquestionably urged on by his extravagant Irish nationalism, found a way to feed his family while still maintaining a high public profile.[9]

The general spoke in more than eight states throughout the Midwest, avoiding for the most part the Northeast, where his greatest critics, the *New York Times* and P.J. Meehan's *Irish-American*, were found. Audiences in Minnesota, Wisconsin, Iowa, Illinois, Nebraska, Indiana, and Missouri flocked to hear the hero of Ridgeway.

A lecture in St. Joseph, Missouri, in June 1872 illustrates the typical magnetic pull John O'Neill still possessed on the Irish in America. In the *Daily Gazette*:

> **Ireland—Her History and the Cause**
> **of Her Present State—the Fenians and their Efforts**
> *Lecture by General John O'Neill*
>
> A very respectable audience assembled in Elridge Hall last evening, for the purpose of hearing General John O'Neill's promised lecture. The General was greeted by warm demonstrations of favor as he stepped upon the platform. He announced "Ireland, Past, Present, and Future" as his subject. It was an able and eloquent effort.
>
> O'Neill spoke for an hour and a half to an enthusiastic audience, explained all the

successes and failures of the Fenians and Irish history. He ended with a personal touch, no doubt shared wherever he spoke. As for himself, he was a ruined man financially and broken down in health. He gave his means and whatever soldierly ability he possessed to the cause of his native land, and he did not regret it. He still hoped to see Ireland rescued and made free and independent.

There was enthusiastic applause as the General sat down, and for some he was obliged to give quite a reception, so many were the people who pressed about him to make his acquaintance.[10]

But a major roadblock occurred a year into his professional speaking career, as the country became mired in a serious economic depression, and O'Neill realized his lectures would not be sufficient to support his lifestyle. While many Americans are constantly reminded of the Great Depression of the 1930s, few realize the equal panic the Long Depression of 1873–1879 had on American life. Following an economic surge after the Civil War, the economy of both America and Europe went sour.

In New York City, home to O'Neill for several years, there were 5,000 people in relief in 1873. In 1874, the number was 24,000. The New York Stock Exchange closed for ten days and of the country's 364 railroads, eighty-nine went bankrupt within a month. In the next two years, 18,000 businesses failed, and unemployment nationwide was over twenty percent in both 1873 and '74; there were soup kitchens all over the East, reminiscent of the hated Famine soup kitchens in Ireland. Union membership in New York City alone fell from 45,000 to 5,000 and thousands upon thousands of people slept outdoors after being evicted from their homes. For the most part, the government did nothing. William Roberts, the one-time Fenian Brotherhood president, lost his huge fortune as a result of bank collapses. Even Ireland discovered America was no longer nirvana. Only 15,000 emigrants arrived in 1877, compared to 221,000 in 1851.[11] What may have begun as a lucrative income for General John O'Neill dried up quickly, timing and luck being a known commodity to all successful people. Though the O'Neill lectures were in demand among the Irish of the mines and factories, the income was insufficient, and John O'Neill was beginning to suffer financially yet again. Though the O'Neills lived well until 1870, they hadn't owned a home since leaving Nashville in 1864, and the Fenian Brotherhood salary had dried up in 1870, with even that income often dissipated by travel, entertainment, and lawyers.

Indeed, there are ominous signs that O'Neill was struggling. After a fine lecture in Mankato, Minnesota, the *Evening Press* of Muscantine, Iowa, mentioned for the first time publicly on June 25, 1872, just five months after he began his new job, that O'Neill was in ill health and financially deprived, and he was then only thirty-four. "When he embraced Fenianism, General O'Neill was possessed of a fine competency, which he spent in the cause, and now, though broken in health and property, he still is sanguine of better days for

Ireland and Irishmen."[12] Just months later, on September 12, 1872, the *Missouri Democrat* ran a small article that said, "The breastplate worn by General O'Neill is now for sale. It fits mostly under his coat-tails and is laced in front."[13] There is no mention ever again of his magnificent sword, an heirloom he undoubtedly cherished, that may have suffered a similar fate.

Since their marriage in November 1864, John and Mary Ann O'Neill had lived in seven homes in six states (there would be three more in Nebraska), but the loyal Mary Ann had somehow maintained a correspondence with her father, Patrick Crow, in Australia since she found him in 1862. How consistently Mary Ann and Patrick stayed in touch is unknown, but Patrick's knowledge of the O'Neill family hints at at least some regular correspondence. In January 1873 she received a reply to one of her letters, sent months prior, and it is the only one since the first discovery in 1862 to survive. Patrick wrote to his daughter from the very rough-and-tumble Harp of Erin Hotel on Queen Street in Melbourne. Unfortunately key lines of the letter have been removed and are lost, perhaps for good reason. Why Patrick of all people was astonished at John O'Neill's behavior is unknown, and the address of James O'Brien is also lost.

> My Dear Daughter I received your recent letters—I am sorry for your troubles but it seems it cannot be helped I am also sorry that I cannot do something for you but I will do all is in my power & that is not mutch [*sic*]. At the present I was troubled enough before I came along way down the country to get your letters & when I got them they caused me to fret lonely for you but there is nothing but fret & trouble on this earth but i hope we will meet to gether again in a Holier place where we will have none. I am astonished at your husband and his friends....
>
> I have wrote to James Obrien by this mail as I had a letter from him stating that he had 75 dollars belong to me so I have wrote to him to send it to you. So as soon as you get this letter you can write to him for it—I told him to send what ever he had belong to me to you. His address is as follows....
>
> Direct your letters to me to Mr. Stapleton, Harp of Erin Hotel, 114 Queen Street. For if I am not there Mr. Stapleton will answer them to you as he knows all particulars and I might be up the country.
>
> I am sending Mary Ellen one pair of gold earrings as a present from her grandfather by this mail. Please tell little John i will not forget him the next time. I hope what ever your troubles may be that you will keep your spirits up & do not be fretting. I must now conclude but my fond love to you and your two dear children.
>
> Your loving father Patrick Crow.[14]

According to son John Hugh in his 1936 notebook, Mary Ann received a letter from Stapleton stating Patrick left soon after and was never heard from again.

A year later General John O'Neill was still struggling, and he reached back to settle some old scores. William Joseph Hynes, known as W.J., was a Fenian veteran who O'Neill had mentored. Hynes was born in Kilkee, County

Clare, in 1843 and immigrated in 1854. Upon his mother's death, he found himself at age twenty-one in Nashville in 1864, where he met the popular and famous war hero John O'Neill. Hynes joined the Brotherhood and took part in the 1866 Canadian invasion, but saw no action.[15] O'Neill then let the youngster live gratis in his Nashville home for months while Hynes studied law at O'Neill's popular claim agency. When the general relocated to Washington, D.C., Hynes followed and passed the bar, still chasing O'Neill's coat-tails. The general, always too trusting, gave Hynes a loan of $200 in 1868 (almost $2,000 today) in order to marry Miss Delia Kenny of New York. But the wedding never came off, and Hynes married socialite Jennie Way in 1871 in the District of Columbia. With the new Fenian Brotherhood President O'Neill's blessing, Hynes became one of fifteen Fenian senators in 1868, but like so many others, distanced himself quickly from the general after the Vermont mistake at Eccles Hill.

While in jail in Burlington, O'Neill desperately reached out to Hynes for repayment of the loan, now over two years old, but Hynes never responded. After Pembina, O'Neill discovered Hynes had become a congressman in Little Rock, Arkansas, and sent him a letter again demanding repayment. It was apparent to O'Neill that Hynes had written him off as a fallen angel of Irish nationalism and could be ignored, but that was a mistake. It was now summer of 1873, and the general wrote to Hynes in Little Rock.

> Sir: Over five and half years ago you asked me to loan you two hundred dollars so you could marry Miss Delia Kenny.... You obtained this money under <u>false pretenses</u>.... I now want this money with interest to date. I telegraphed you for it but received no reply. I am lying sick in bed, otherwise I would not write but go myself. Do not treat this letter with <u>distinguished silence</u> as you did when I wrote to you from Burlington jail, and do not tell any more lies about this money for you have done enough of this already.
>
> I have the letter of gratitude you sent when you received the money and the receipt when I was the only man in America who would grant you such a favor. You ignored me when I was in prison and my wife and children were suffering for the necessities of life. I need not remind you of what I did for you when you arrived in Washington, D.C.
>
> Do not force me to go after this money, for it will not add to your credit. You have <u>trifled with me long enough</u>.
>
> John O'Neill[16]

There is no notice of whether Hynes paid the loan, but it may explain how the O'Neills were able to afford the move to Nebraska. Hynes lasted only one term as a congressman. In the second election, he was accused of bribery and fraud and, while not found guilty, left Arkansas and moved to Chicago, where he became a lawyer for the Clan na Gael. Two decades later Hynes would become one of the most celebrated lawyers in Chicago, but when the Clan na Gael assassinated Dr. Patrick Cronin in May of 1889 in Chicago after the good doctor became a whistleblower on Clan financial mismanagement, Hynes turned on his fellow Irish nationalists. Hynes testified for the prosecution of Alexander Sullivan for the murder of Cronin, reportedly when he discovered he himself was next on the list to be eliminated. Hynes later retired to Los Angeles, where he died in 1915, a non-player amongst the Irish community.

But the unbending general could not be swayed by his own past. A year after Pembina, he still defended the Manitoba affair, the least credible of his actions on Canada. "The wealthy Irish ... who had proclaimed on many a St. Patrick's Day festival their willingness to spend their last dollar and shed their last drop of blood in the course of Ireland's liberation were found timid when their opportunity to do for their country came, and they withheld aid until the granting of it was too late."[17]

11
Nebraska

That is no country for old men.—William Butler Yeats, *Sailing to Byzantium*

Finally in November 1873 in Lincoln, Nebraska, O'Neill changed gears. He had just moved the family again, this time because of rampant fever in St. Louis, and the doctors recommended Omaha for the health of the children. The general arrived with Mary Ann, John Hugh, Mary, and Eugene. The family settled briefly into the Donovan House and the children's health improved, but O'Neill's finances did not. Amidst national and personal depression, O'Neill, now a fading national figure, met another Irishman, like Gibbons, Meehan, Savage, O'Mahony, O'Donoghue, and Devoy, who he hoped could lead him to a promised land. Unlike the others, Patrick Fahy cared not a whit about Irish patriotism or freedom, just money, and this time around that was enough for John Charles O'Neill, who had been struggling for two years.[1]

In Lincoln, he met the twenty-nine-year-old County Mayo–born Fahy, a land speculator interested in a town site in Holt County, Nebraska, 180 miles northwest of Omaha.[2] Until this meeting, there is no public record that shows General John O'Neill had any interest in Irish resettlement, only in Irish freedom fighting. It was known in Nebraska that the general had little income and needed money, and he eagerly agreed to work as a land agent for Fahy and his partner S.M. Boyd of Lincoln, who had purchased 160 acres in the newly proposed Holt County, 200 miles away in northwest Nebraska. Fahy and Boyd agreed to pay O'Neill a salary of $600 on condition the general would work on migration among the Irish. O'Neill's job was to tour the East and North, promoting settlement in Holt for four months at $150 per month. Fahy, for his part, agreed that the town would be platted and ready for the first colony the following spring.[3]

After coming to terms, O'Neill, with his customary energy, immediately visited the northern Nebraska location and the site met with his approval, whereupon he would soon set off for the East to fulfill his contract. Ever the optimist, O'Neill may have thought this would be a temporary and quick job, but with his accustomed zeal and dedication to a cause, he would work at it for six years. It would eventually kill him, and would be the longest and most difficult mission in his short life.

Within a week of accepting his first paid job in years, the general was reported in the *St. Joseph Daily Gazette*, a place that always welcomed him: "General O'Neill is in this city for the purpose of obtaining statistical and personal information about the city and the surrounding country. He will soon leave for the East where he intends to spend the winter in the interests of the West, making faithful representations of the advantages of the various states and inducing immigration."[4]

O'Neill continued his speaking tours predominately in Pennsylvania, Michigan, Indiana, and Illinois, but turned down no invitation anywhere. From December 1 until May, he visited fifteen states and the District of Columbia. He generally spoke for free, typical of his poor business acumen. The indefatigable thirty-six-year-old was still (and always) an Irish nationalist first, and everything else second. From December 1874 until his stroke three years later, O'Neill is said to have spoken to well over a hundred audiences, from New Jersey to Wisconsin. His new lectures, however, were exactly like the old ones, with an important addendum. O'Neill opened with a history of his time with the Fenians, discussed each "invasion" of Canada, defended his strategies and honesty, castigated his cowardly enemies, and vowed to continue the fight to free Ireland. During the conclusion of an hour-long talk O'Neill would argue for migration "from the overcrowded cities and states of the east to settle upon the cheap and free lands of the west." General O'Neill added to his stump speech that once the Irish have moved west, "their improved circumstances can assist the cause of Irish liberty."[5] O'Neill's personal appearance added to the lectures, especially to these downtrodden miners and victims of economic depression. Le Caron, his perceived friend but most incipient enemy, and never one to praise the general, admitted, "In personal appearance O'Neill was a very fine looking man. Nature had dealt with him kindly. Within a couple inches of six feet, he combined an undoubtedly military bearing, which lent a persuasive charm."[6]

O'Neill's lectures on migration took a back seat to the one true passion of his life, but there was now absolutely no doubt that the general was truly pushing for emigration. For perhaps the first time in his life, he had dual agendas, and for O'Neill, that was a hugely prodigious step. "I shall continue to furnish information on the subject of immigration and organize colonies. I shall travel throughout the country, and attend meetings and deliver lectures on Irish immigration and Irish Revolution, for I propose to have both these noble objects go hand in hand."[7] For the first time in his life, John Charles O'Neill was discovering that more than one thing can be true to a man.

But John O'Neill was not a lone Quixote tilting at windmills as he had at Pembina. Bishop John Ireland of St. Paul, Minnesota, was long convinced, like O'Neill, that immigrants, especially the Irish, should settle in the West. Like O'Neill, Bishop Ireland came to this position unclearly. John O'Neill came to his realization when he needed a job and was looking for redemption as a national figure. Bishop Ireland took his position on Irish emigration on personal grounds, having been born Irish in Minnesota. Yet he was ignored and shunned by most Catholic clergy on this issue alone. John Ireland, long a favorite son of the Vatican, became a dominant leader of the Church not only in the United States, but worldwide. As a young prelate in 1865, years before O'Neill became active in colonization, Bishop Ireland said, "The cities have blighted our people. What had immigrant labor on the railroads, the canals, led to, except broken homes, lost faith, and perverted morals."[8]

Ireland founded the Minnesota Emigration Society in 1865, and, following a banquet, a committee was formed, which never again met. Ireland was faced with the same stubbornness O'Neill would meet a decade later by fellow churchmen. The Catholic Church in the Eastern Seaboard, led by Bishop "Dagger John" Hughes of New York, crushed any move by fellow clergy, no matter their standing. Years later, after Hughes's death, Bishop Ireland was severely critical of Hughes. "Colonization was often met with strong opposition on the part of men whose position and intelligence should have known better."[9] The Catholic Church, then and now, is sometimes overly focused on consolidating power.

Despite John Ireland's best efforts, the fact remains that no colonization plan ever gained support of the Catholic Church hierarchy, and John Ireland never sponsored any Catholic colonies beyond the limits of western Minnesota. If western migration was thwarted against powerful prelates like Ireland, one can only imagine the obstacles faced by layman John O'Neill.

There is no record that General John O'Neill and Bishop Ireland ever met, but in 1876, when O'Neill was beginning his quest to fill the Nebraskan plains, Bishop Ireland tried twice to bring the Irish to Minnesota, once with the aid of the railroads. Like O'Neill, John Ireland was smart, full of ideas, and eager to populate the prairies with Catholics, especially Irish. The bishop had ambitions that complemented the railroad's desire to build towns and markets for its transportation services. Between January 1876 and June 1880, Bishop Ireland bought 379,000 acres of Minnesotan railroad lands, in effect becoming a powerful landlord. As did O'Neill with Nebraska, Ireland defended the Minnesotan climate, noting that the winter's short days are "clear with bracing air" and "the dryness of its atmosphere is healthy."[10] For such exaggerations, many of the early Minnesota settlers felt they had been abused and shortchanged, and they were correct. Both Bishop Ireland and O'Neill had difficulty with handling finances, and both overextended themselves in land speculating. John Ireland, however, who would be castigated as harshly by his few colonists as O'Neill, had the Church at his back in hard times. John O'Neill did not.

Both Minnesota efforts suffered for much the same reasons as O'Neill's, with the depression of 1873 the major factor and the quiet antagonism of the eastern Church a serious contributor. Bishop Ireland and General O'Neill had one common premise: The promise of future success in the east would make all present sacrifices worthwhile. Both would receive major criticism for their vision. Surprisingly, only the work of John O'Neill would bear fruit.

In 1879, a year after the general's death, a national convention in Chicago formed the Irish Catholic Colonization Association. Bishop Ireland made one last attempt, and, like O'Neill, toured the Northeast seeking support, but his fellow Catholic administrators gave lukewarm support at best, and by 1880 the leading Catholic prelate of the United States gave it up and moved on to other issues.

O'Neill worked his colonization plans foremost in the Pennsylvania mining districts in and around Scranton and Pottstown and the copper fields of Hancock and Red Jacket, Michigan, where economic depression, combined with awful working conditions, saw hunger and poverty reach astounding levels. One report showed fully one third of Pennsylvania workers "idle" and O'Neill's pitch surely made sense to many. He asked in one questionnaire published in various newspapers, "Why are you content to work on the public projects and at coal mining when you might in a few years own farms of your own and become wealthy and influential people?"[11] But despite the promise of a better life with almost no down payment, relocation cost money. O'Neill, like Bishop Ireland, admitted that a family should not go west without $500 in capital, single men less, a considerable if not impossible task in the midst of a deep national depression.

But while O'Neill was feverishly traveling the country throughout the winter of 1874, Patrick Fahy, who had earned a small fortune in the lumber business, was doing nothing except promoting a fraud. Nebraskan law needed 200 residents to form a county. Fahy told the state government there were more than enough, but in truth there were barely forty residents in all the proposed Holt County, and none yet in Holt City, the original name for the Fahy and O'Neill settlement. In addition, bonds amounting to thousands of dollars at six percent were issued and sold to eastern investors and banks. O'Neill never mentioned this in any lectures for one simple reason—he didn't know. The general offered Civil War veterans wonderful legal terms of a free title of "eighty acres within twenty miles of a railroad, or one hundred sixty acres if outside for only $18,"[12] provided it be settled for five years, unaware that Fahy was working both sides against the middle. In March, O'Neill was in Pennsylvania and Vermont, and at the end of the month he had his first small group prepared to go west. Fahy had not yet paid him anything, though O'Neill regularly blistered him in writing, almost begging to be paid. Friends of the general, and there were many who never forgot his zealous love of the mother country, thankfully carried him on credit throughout the winter. This despite the letter Fahy had sent to O'Neill.

> The country for several miles around the town is now thickly settled, and my brother James [Fahy], who has just returned from there informs me that settlers are coming in rapidly, even at this season of the year, and undoubtedly by next summer there will not be a claim untaken within eight miles of the town. When you return in the Spring [1875] we will have the county organized, with O'Neill City as the County seat, and there will be a large hotel and a number of business houses and other buildings put up in town in the spring and summer. Lots will become valuable and command a ready sale.[13]

Buoyed by the letter and trusting Fahy, O'Neill pushed forward like the ex-cavalry officer he was, and on April 29 the first colony arrived in Omaha. After speaking to thousands, only fifteen men, two women, and three children came by train from Chicago with O'Neill. Leaving Omaha, the all–Irish group took a railroad thirty miles to Blair, then the Sioux and Pacific line to Fremont, then an Elkhorn R.R. line to Wisner, Nebraska. A stagecoach took them sixty miles northwest to Neligh, and finally, they arrived forty miles later in Holt City on May 12, 1874.

These original settlers were primarily from Pennsylvania. Ralph Sullivan, Neil Brennan, Pat Hughes, Tim O'Connor, Tom Connolly, Tom Kelly, Henry Carey, Tom Cain, Pat Brennan, Henry Curry, Mike McGrath, Thomas N.J. Hynes, Mike Dempsey, Bob Alworth, and Pat McCarney were no doubt exhausted by the extended journey, but the party led personally by O'Neill was met with shock instead of Fahy.[14]

There was no railroad and there were no trees, no structures, no streets, no plans—just miles and miles of tall grass in the middle of a vast prairie. Within a week, out of desperate necessity, they constructed a sod house four feet deep, thirty-six feet long, and eighteen feet wide—for all of them. The men were in their twenties or younger and came from seven different states. It was hard not to be discouraged, and resentment and anger would come later. None were farmers by trade, food had to be hunted or transported from the nearest railroad a hundred miles away, Indians were always feared though never appeared, and grasshoppers plagued the entire area for decades. As Gregory Passewitz pointed out in *O'Neill, Nebraska: The First Quarter Century*, "The town of O'Neill had no special drawing card to lure settlers. There were no valuable mineral deposits, the land was hard to farm and suffered from soil erosion and drought, and access to the region was by ox-drawn wagons over the virgin prairie. In short, there was no easy road to success except the lure of cheap land and the idea of a new fresh start in life."[15] These original settlers of what came to be O'Neill were one hundred miles away from civilization; fifty miles from a post office, and a hundred and three miles from the nearest railroad at Wisner.

By October, only five men were left. Donegal-born Neil Brennan, a Fenian from Buffalo; Vermonter Tom Connolly, with wife and two children; Patrick Kearney (McCarney); Pat Hughes; Tom O'Connor; and Tom Cain. Three miners from Pennsylvania—Roddy Hayes, James Ryan, and John Reddy—joined them. One historian has blamed the early flight from O'Neill on grasshoppers, but the grasshopper scourge was still a few years away. The five original men (the women and children were never mentioned, except for Connolly's family) and the three later arrivals survived the winter in a 36-foot by 18-foot sod house with no windows christened "The Grand Hotel." The settlers also soon discovered that Fahy was either behind the fraud or was complicit with the bankers involved. They were right on both counts.

General John O'Neill finally was paid the $600 salary owed, much of it not with needed cash but with plots of land in O'Neill, and given a $100 bonus. It was hardly enough to provide for a family after eight months of work, cross-country traveling, and paying off creditors. But it was in the fall of 1874 that John O'Neill reversed course and became a hero again in Irish America, though not in his lifetime. In previous years the general had followed his usual course when he felt slighted, ignored, or criticized. He made immoderate rash decisions, constantly changing direction. When the bookstore failed, he joined the Army. When there was no action or excitement, he deserted. After a stellar career in the Civil War, he quit twice when denied promotion. When told not to invade Canada a second time, he attacked anyway against all reason. After Pembina he discovered he never reached Canada, so he railed against Colonel Wheaton and the government. After spending eight months on the recruitment of Irish to Nebraska, and uprooting his family halfway across the country into an unknown territory, O'Neill brought eighteen fellow Irish into a miserable early existence. His funding completed, he could easily have quit and just walked away, having fulfilled his contract. But O'Neill stayed the course for the first time in his life. It would not be easy, and criticism would come, much of it justified. In the end, however, it would be his finest legacy. He finally seemed to understand, in the words of Irish balladeer Christy Moore, "some high ground is not worth taking, and some connections are not worth making."[16] Indeed, the general seemed to finally realize his old military mission was over. "I have tried to do the best I could to give the Irish people their freedom at home, and for the time being at least, I have failed. I have now engaged in doing what I believe to be the next best thing."[17]

In July, Mary Ann gave birth to a second daughter, Katherine Lillian O'Neill, known as Kitty, in Omaha, the Aussie's fourth child born in four different states.[18] O'Neill soon moved the family to West Point, Nebraska, about eighty miles northwest of Omaha on the Elkhorn River. There was no way the general would take his family to O'Neill just yet, despite his optimism for others. West Point also provided O'Neill with contacts, as it was "a town of considerable importance," at least by frontier definition.[19] Prominent men lived there, mostly politicians, and the O'Neills settled into the Neligh House Hotel, home to governors, congressmen, bankers, and their families. The general then went to work; first he had to deal with Fahy, and then find finances to support another colony in 1875. He was successful at both. During his recruitment, O'Neill had promised prospective settlers they would be able to harvest 250 to 300 bushels per acre, and could plow up to December. When they discovered that this was impossible, they turned on the general, accusing him of intentionally deceiving them. Indeed O'Neill did make such promises, but they were not intentional. Not a native Midwesterner, he relied on others familiar with the landscape, and he trusted Fahy, his biggest mistake since trusting Le Caron and O'Donoghue.

The editor of the *Oakdale Journal* visited O'Neill in the summer of 1874 after the tiny colony had arrived, and reported, "The area is rich in agriculture and mineral wealth and it shall stand without a peer in the catalogue of the best counties in the state." Worse, a government surveyor, Chauncey Wiltse, told an assembled public meeting in Omaha on December 21, 1874, "The land around the Elkhorn River [Holt County] is conceded to be as rich in fertility and as attractive in other respects, as any land in the state, and the particular portion selected by the General is not inferior to any.... We venture the assertion and do it without any fear of contradiction, that the place has the finest tract of agricultural lands ... of any town in the state.... This is a broad assertion, but we make it in candor, and believe it to be true."[20] Neither Wiltse nor the editor had to spend the winter, however, trying to survive in the "Grand Hotel" sod house. Wiltse, a one-man chamber of commerce, may have been more of an optimist than O'Neill, and not very objective. He was not only a government surveyor, but his father owned the local paper in West Point, and young Chauncey later became president of the Fullerton, Nebraska, bank, no doubt just as anxious in those early days to put a good light on colonization while gaining future customers.

Some of the settlers were still not content. They complained that the overzealous general had betrayed them and accused O'Neill of gross opportunism. They had a point, as O'Neill and most Fenians of the era had a serious tendency towards exaggeration. In more than one newspaper interview the general told reporters he had already received assurances that over 5,000 emigrants will settle in Nebraska in the spring. In a pamphlet O'Neill had published promoting the Holt County scheme, O'Neill stated, "If a man comes west in the spring he builds himself a small house of sods or cottonwood timber. He then plows a few acres, plants corn or potatoes in the sod. His cow is staked in a rich bottom, his patch of green vegetables grows in the front of his door, and four months after he arrived at his new home he is home indeed."[21]

O'Neill went to great lengths to promote himself and the colony. Still trusting in Fahy and people like Wiltse, Patrick Ford gave a large op-ed to O'Neill in the August 1874 edition of the *Irish World* looking not just for the poor Irish to move west, but for the rich to invest as well. Keeping in mind that there were now just eight men currently living in the settlement of O'Neill, the report is nothing short of outlandish.

The People Aroused
Increasing Interest of Irish-Americans in Colonization Schemes—
A Plan for a Town Site—General O'Neill Seeking to Show Rich
Irish-Americans a Way they can Invest Their Money Profitably

Editor, judging by the letters I have received in the last three months.... I am forced to the conclusion that our people, all over the country, are at last beginning to be thoroughly aroused to the necessity of getting a hold of at least a portion of the "Land of the Country" before it is all taken up by others.... I believe I have done something, and if it were not that I have been hampered and delayed for want of money, I could have done a great deal more. Last fall, while at Lincoln, I happened to meet Mr. Patrick Fahy, an astonishingly intelligent Irishman who said Holt County contained some of the finest land in the State ... and I have made arrangements for locating.

I now ask my friends to buy lots in this proposed town site immediately, so as to enable me to complete my arrangements.... I believe every lot offered will be worth twice if not thrice the amount asked for it in less than a year.... I do not want a single man to buy a lot, who has not the utmost confidence in my honesty and integrity, and who, in case the whole thing should fall through (which of course I do not anticipate) would not denounce it as a swindle, but would be willing to lose the amount in making the experiment.[22]

All three claims were preposterous, and out of necessity the settlers looked at the short term survival, while O'Neill, to be gracious, had a long-term vision in mind. Though often angry and dissatisfied, the tiny few became the fulcrum of future Irish American citizens of northern Nebraska.

O'Neill, however, had not been president of the Fenian Brotherhood because he was a rube. The general, no longer paid by Fahy, still recognized the speculator owned the initial 160 acres that formed O'Neill. The hero of Ridgeway, now back on his feet a bit, reached back to three Irish friends from his days leading the Brotherhood. The first was Ford, owner and editor of the *Irish World*. The Galway-born Ford served in the Union Army at Fredericksburg and Northern Virginia before coming to New York in 1870. He began the *Irish World,* which soon became the principal paper for all of Irish American nationalism.[23]

During his first decade of success, Ford was a radical supporter of Irish independence, though he would change direction drastically after 1880. His paper, with a circulation of 125,000 in America and another 20,000 in Ireland, preached militant republicanism and hatred of England, and it was thus inevitable he and the general would become friends. They had more in common: both left school at age twelve, neither ever returned to Ireland, and each was a vociferous voice in Irish America with friends and enemies galore. Both O'Neill and Ford were adamant that the destruction of British domination by force was imperative to the advancement of the Irish worldwide.

When the 1873 depression struck America, Ford was convinced the time was ripe for land reform and, true to his word, from 1874 until his death Ford promoted Irish expansion in the west, always praising John O'Neill.

The Galway-born Patrick Ford fought in the Civil War as a young man before becoming the premier Irish American journalist in the country. Ford backed O'Neill politically and economically, especially during the effort to colonize Nebraska (Library of Congress).

When the general began his colonization plans, there were two million Irish in America, and forty percent of them were laborers. Patrick Ford thought it would be beneficial for many of them to escape west. The *Irish World* generously enabled O'Neill to put food on the table for his growing family, and with Ford on board, the general soon connected with Colonel John Atkinson of Detroit and Lieutenant John Kelly of Washington, D.C.

Atkinson, one of ten children born to County Mayo Irish emigrants, graduated from the University of Michigan Law School in 1862 and joined the 35th Michigan Infantry, finally being discharged after a stellar career as a colonel in 1865. Atkinson had no known ties to the Fenians, but his hometown of Port Huron, Michigan, was filled with members of the Brotherhood. Colonel Atkinson spent his adult life in Detroit, where he became an advisor to several governors and one of the most influential lawyers in the country. A man who had great friends in all walks of life, Atkinson was drawn to O'Neill's history as a military man as well as the general's plea for the plight of the depressed Irish in Michigan. Atkinson took an active part in the

Nebraska settlements publicly and financially, and O'Neill would soon name a town after the Detroit mover and shaker. Many new settlers would come from the Port Huron area where Atkinson was raised.[24]

O'Neill also was able to count on another friendship, this time in Washington, D.C. John Kelly was a police lieutenant in the capital city for thirty years, and more than likely knew the general from his time living in Washington.

O'Neill was thus financially able to push for a second group of colonists who arrived in May 1875, among them Patrick Hagerty of Scranton, John Cantlan, Mike Ryan, Mike Costello, D.P. O'Sullivan, Herman Strasburg, and Will Sullivan. Almost immediately, the attitude of the new and old settlers became one of rampant disaffection, and though their anger was taken out on O'Neill, he held Patrick Fahy responsible. A year after the first group arrived, there was still not a single building constructed.

Two-dozen men were included in this second group, arriving from more than eight states, though the majority was from Michigan and Pennsylvania, a trend that would continue for years. But the numbers were deceiving, proving that General John O'Neill was on the right track. In 1874 two women and three children made the initial trek; sixteen wives, a sister, and a mother-in-law, plus an astounding four dozen children accompanied the twenty-two men in 1875. The average age of the mostly single O'Neill colonists in 1874 was twenty-four, but the second group averaged thirty-four years old and consisted of almost all married men.[25] Included in this number were Mary Ann O'Neill and children John Hugh, Mamie, and baby Kitty O'Neill, now in their eighth domicile in eight years, ranging from Tennessee, Washington, D.C, Vermont, New Jersey, Illinois, and three places in Nebraska.

Because O'Neill again personally delivered the second group, he was again the target of the immediate dissatisfaction, and it was questioned whether the entire colonization was just O'Neill's personal El Dorado. Years later, a descendant of these settlers still remembered "the expectant new people had intense disappointment and disgust, which often found expression in the most emphatic manner."[26] The general responded by showing the people a letter he sent to Fahy, which was published in the *Irish World*.

> One of the arguments used by our enemies to discourage people from settling in O'Neill was that you were not making any improvements in the town, and did not intend to, and that all you cared for was to sell lots in the town and make all the money you could out of it, and that it was a swindling operation, etc., and as a proof of what they said they would point to the town site which had not the sign of a house on it. In order to put a stop to all this, I urged upon you the necessity of putting up some kind of a building, no matter how small or cheap it might be; but although you repeatedly promised to do this, yet you did not do it.[27]

The fact that the general had brought his own family from the comforts of civilization seemed to assuage some, and in addition, O'Neill gave up on the idea of Fahy platting the town, still undone. He hired his nephew John J. O'Neill, the engineer from Elizabeth, to do the job, and John J.'s teenage brother Tommy O'Neill left New Jersey to help. According to son John Hugh O'Neill, the family made the 100-mile trip from West Point in two days on a wagon with "a team of horses that seemed to run the whole way."[28] A ten-year-old John Hugh may have remembered it as a lark, but the move from Omaha and West Point had not come without a price. Eugene, not quite three, had died, and Mary Ann suffered while there, possibly of typhoid, which often ran rampant. The West Point papers recalled Mary Ann "convalescing at home," but make no mention of the death of Eugene, not uncommon in the rural west. The youngest often were the most easily stricken, and there were reports of families burying four or five children, though the older ones generally fared better. Some small towns were reluctant to report typhoid deaths, as few could afford to lose residents, and the rumors of typhoid could easily scare colonists away. Devout Catholics, the O'Neills purchased eight plots in the new Omaha Catholic Cemetery, Holy Sepulchre. Eugene would be the first O'Neill buried west of Elizabeth, New Jersey.

O'Neill knew that some of these hard and courageous folks were adamantly angry about the fraudulent bond sale, and played his ace card in the open letter to Fahy, which was distributed to all residents in O'Neill. The general felt forced to publish the letter in the *Irish World*, now the leading Irish American paper in the country. It was typical John O'Neill. The letter was 2,500 words long and castigated Fahy to the bone.

> Mr. Fahy, both yourself and Mr. Boyd were fully aware of my financial circumstances, for I very candidly told you and you knew I could not travel, or do anything unless you furnished the money as you had agreed to do. And yet to my utter astonishment, when you got me compromised in the business and started on the road, you treated me shamefully, allowing me to remain for weeks at a time, at Pittsburg, Philadelphia, and New York, under expense, without a cent of money to travel and meet the engagements I had made for attending meetings, etc. and would not even answer my letters or telegrams, but simply trifled with my time so that I was unable to do anything worth speaking of. Had it not been for the kindness of Mr. Ford, of the *Irish World*, who, when I explained to him the situation I was in, very kindly allowed me the use of his columns to write the matter up, my first effort to organize a colony would have been a complete failure. Although the money which you agreed to pay me has all now been paid, yet it was paid in such a way that it was of very little use to me.
>
> I have heard that you accused me of ingratitude, which I am not willing to admit is part of my character. I was also more anxious to make arrangements with you because you are an Irishman, and as my mission is entirely in behalf of the Irish people, I preferred dealing with one of my countrymen. But your subsequent conduct, which has been a very serious drawback to me and highly injurious to the colony I have worked so hard to build up, forces me to make some things public, which I would much rather not be compelled to do.[29]

O'Neill explains the lack of planning, including the fraudulent scheme with the eastern banks, and, finally, attacks Fahy and his family.

> To crown your conduct toward me I learn that you have been going around like an old woman telling people I took advantage of your brother being absent sick to "jump" his claim. I should think that respect for the memory of your dead brother who I hope is in heaven, would prevent you from thus lying about me. You know your brother had no claim at or near O'Neill City, had never entered a claim, or taken out papers on one.
>
> Being satisfied that I could no longer depend on you for doing anything, and feeling heartily ashamed of not having a single house in O'Neill City, notwithstanding that there was a good settlement around it, which was constantly increasing, and feeling that in justice to myself and my family, I no longer had any right to continue working and spending money in enhancing the value of **your** property.

The general, with advice from the brilliant lawyer Atkinson or just his street smarts learned in Brotherhood backrooms, continued to hit Fahy hard.

> I have joined with Mr. Patrick Hagerty in locating a soldier's additional eighty acres as an addition to O'Neill City, which we intend building up or having it built up as the principal part of the town. This of course was a bank movement which you did not expect for you seemed to have acted all along as if I was completely at your mercy, and that I must continue to work for and build up O'Neill City, because my name happened to be connected to it. Well, I shall continue to build up O'Neill and Hagerty's addition to O'Neill City, and I shall give to every man who bought of me in O'Neill City a deed of an equal number of lots in this addition.[30]

The community responded with a long vote of confidence in General O'Neill, signed and published in Ford's *Irish World*. The resolution ended with the statement, "We return our warmest thanks to Gen O'Neill and shall be ever grateful for the untiring zeal manifested, and the self-sacrifice endured for the welfare of the colonists." It was signed by a majority of the men, eighteen in all, but not everyone. What the women felt is not recorded. Mary Ann and the children were lucky enough to have the first wooden-frame home in the colony, with timber, said young John Hugh years later, "hauled by oxen from Sioux City, Iowa, a hundred and twenty miles away."[31]

Buoyed by the response, in August 1875, the general published "Northern Nebraska as a Home for Immigrants" in Sioux City, Iowa, a pamphlet urging further Irish to join the exodus. In October, Patrick Fahy finally erected a frame building. It was for use as a much-needed general store, and rented to Patrick Hagerty, no doubt an arrangement between Hagerty, Fahy, and O'Neill.

John O'Neill was beginning to get the hang of the expansion mentality. His biggest initial mistake was recruiting colonists on a paltry salary, which he did simply out of economic necessity. But even after his second group of colonists arrived, O'Neill never made the settlers pay a surcharge, and relied on his friends for support. Every other land speculator in the West charged

The O'Neill home in O'Neill, Nebraska, was the first wooden structure in town, though O'Neill was deep in debt to Edward Johnson for its construction (O'Neill family collection).

each male colonist an organizers commission, a reasonable tactic. The O'Neill family survived these Nebraska years almost totally on the selling of lots in O'Neill and nearby Atkinson and Greeley, lots given as gifts or purchased from friends throughout the country. But the general soon was willing and eager to look for consignments from railroads, legislatures, the Catholic Church, and even the rush to the Black Hills for gold. In early June 1875, O'Neill created headlines as far away as Pittsburg when he held a large meeting in Wisner, Nebraska. It made headlines in Chicago:

The Black Hills

General O'Neill, the Fenian Leader, will head an Expedition to the Gold Region

General O'Neill, was the only great Fenian leader who came out of that remarkable campaign poorer than when he began. No one has ever doubted that he was wise, brave, and had he not been deceived by his trusted friends, Britain would have felt his power. Such is the man who is organizing the most formidable Black Hills expedition yet proposed. For months he has been in correspondence with hundreds of adventurous spirits all over the country from Florida to Maine.... No man in the United States is so well adapted for gathering an immense army of fortune seekers as General O'Neill.

Irishmen everywhere have an ardent admiration for the hero of Ridgeway, and are willing to follow his leadership, as hundreds of letters received by the General is ample proof; but not by the Irish alone—a great number of Americans and many Germans are going with O'Neill to the land of gold.

How much O'Neill paid this "correspondent" is unknown, but it achieved its purpose, which was to make money for local Nebraskans, entice the railroads, and certainly help bring the general out of debt, all with well-known enticement of gold fever. It certainly gave the general some much needed ego boosting as well.

> Last night, for the first time, this project was made known to us. Bankers, merchants and capitalists were the invited parties. After speeches by leading businessmen, O'Neill stated that he wished to ascertain if supplies could be furnished for 1,000 men for six months. O'Neill then stated he did not know the exact time he could begin, but said, "I will go just as soon as government protection is withdrawn from the Indians," and owing to their refusal to make a treaty, he considers this a short time.[32]

The expedition never got beyond the meeting in Wisner. The Army kept out the miners, and the majority who snuck into the Black Hills were evacuated or killed by Indians, and thus another O'Neill project was unable to get off the ground. On November 3 President Grant lifted the embargo on Army protection, but it was too late for O'Neill and the northern Nebraskan businessmen to capitalize on the gold rush, and the following year Custer did his own part in keeping out gold seekers.

At one point the general persuaded a priest to begin his own town. The Rev. John Fanning, the Irish-born pastor in Fairbury, Illinois, originally bought 260 acres of land from O'Neill in 1874, and shortly thereafter, an article appeared in the *West Point Republican* with an interesting oxymoron:

> We learn that Gen. O'Neill has made arrangements with a wealthy Catholic priest of Illinois named O'Flannigan [Fanning], who is to invest $50,000 in Holt, and in consideration thereof the town is to be called O'Flanniganville [Fanningville]. He is also to bring a large emigration from his former home to Holt County this spring. This no doubt will add greatly to the financial and material wealth of the town and county, and much credit is due to the enterprising zeal and work of Gen. O'Neill in the face of hard times and financial depression to attain good results in his efforts to people in Northern Nebraska. We wish the Gen. all success of which he is so much deserving.[33]

Whatever the reason, Fanningville never happened. The Reverend Fanning, the pastor in the poor town of Fairbury, sold the two lots he bought for $250 for a profit of $50 the next year, not quite the huge amount reported. Where the Reverend Fanning, another refugee from the Famine, planned to accumulate $50,000 (a little over a million dollars today) as a pastor in a town of 1,300 people is unknown. But failures such as this never even slowed down John O'Neill. Judge Atkinson bought out Fanning along with John Kelly of Washington, D.C., and Pat Ryan of Chicago, and the town was then officially named Atkinson, to this day a prosperous town of 1,300.

Now committed totally, the general, ever the pioneer optimist, spent the fall and winter preparing to bring in a third colony for the spring of 1876, telling anyone who would listen that he expected 550 families. O'Neill's pamphlet helped him financially secure the purchase of lots in O'Neill and two other town sites he had begun just west of O'Neill. The other town site was in Greeley County sixty miles south of O'Neill ("Go West, young man!") and later became Spalding. Both Atkinson and Spalding, named after local Catholic Bishop John Spalding, were just the beginnings of O'Neill's future plans of a string of Irish settlements throughout Nebraska.

There could be little doubt O'Neill was now completely pledged to resettlement. Though constantly absent from O'Neill City personally, he arranged for a permanent home for his family. At one point during his winter walkabouts in the North, O'Neill made a business arrangement with Edward Johnson of Marinette, Wisconsin. Johnson owned a successful mill boarding business, and agreed to provide the wood and more for O'Neill City homes. The financial arrangements are unknown, but Johnson, a fellow Irishman, wanted in on the future of Nebraska settlement, and his goal was to build a hotel in O'Neill, an idea the general originally encouraged. But it seems nothing was easy for O'Neill when it came to money during the depression, and he was becoming the proverbial man rich in land, poor in cash. He wrote to Johnson from Chicago just after Christmas, 1875. "Enclosed please find statement of the cost of putting up the house, as near as I can get it at present. You will confer a favor by remitting the balance due me, according to our agreement, if possible, as soon as you get this letter. I have quite a number of little bills to meet about the first of January." Ever the entrepreneur and perhaps realizing he had in Johnson a fortune hunter, O'Neill wished his home to be the center of attention for newcomers, and he wished to be in total control of the colony. "Let me know if you will be able to get to the settlement in the Spring; if not, I must get an addition to the house, so as to have it form an 'L,' as it is of the utmost importance to have a place large enough, where people can stop for a short time when they go out there, and if I cannot accommodate them someone else will be sure to start some kind of a hotel, and this of course I want to prevent."[34]

In 1936, at age seventy, John Hugh recalled the early years vividly, still with eyes of a young boy. "Father returned to the East again, and the next two years it was not all lonesome around our place. With new arrivals every few days, most of the newcomers stayed at our home it being the only place available. Mother worked and fed them and in the long winter nights entertained them and us by reading aloud. Mrs. Reilly held the first school in our front room. The general store was run by Mr. Hagerty, who was a bugler in the civil war and played the flute."[35]

The general's absence from his family and O'Neill in the winter is amplified again. "When I last wrote, I expected to go home to spend the holidays with my family, but I find that I could not spare either the time or the money necessary. I have been a little slow in getting things in proper shape here, but this is an insecure field, and well worth working up properly.... Give my kind regards to Mrs. Johnson and Lilly [Johnson's daughter]—my health is exceedingly good."[36] Johnson replied quickly and O'Neill wrote back in early January, again from Chicago at Burke's European Hotel, lodging much better than the abodes in O'Neill City.

> My Dear Mr. Johnson,
> Your very kind letter of the 1st reached me this morning. You have certainly been very kind in letting me have money when I needed it, and I assure you I feel very grateful. Do not send any more money than is perfectly convenient, for although I need considerable money right now, yet I can always manage to get along. I raised considerable money since coming to Chicago, but I have a good many old debts to pay, and never kept a cent in my own pocket. I have just sent a bag of things to my wife, which she needed for herself and the children, and which cost me $37.85.

The ever optimistic old Fenian added, "It is expected that Congress will open the Black Hills this winter, but of course we have nothing positive just yet. In addition, everything looks favorable for a large immigration to Holt County this spring."[37]

O'Neill was still traveling throughout the country and kept up his friendship with the extremely well-known and respected John Atkinson. The following was reported in Detroit:

General O'Neill

> Gen. John O'Neill, who is well known in this city and State, especially among Irishmen in consequence of his connection with the Fenian raid into Canada some eight years ago, is the guest of Col. Atkinson. The General is on his way to New York and other eastern cities, being engaged in an endeavor to colonize some of the rich fertile lands of Nebraska with Irish settlers.... His idea is to have them settle in communities, so they can establish schools and churches at once.... A year ago he took a colony of 150 families out there, the place being called O'Neill's settlement.... At once they put in their crops and obtained a plentiful harvest in four months.... The country is prairie land and will produce a crop the first year.... Gen. O'Neill hopes and expects to take out 400 and 500 families this spring.... He will remain in the city for a few days and can be reached at Col. Atkinson's office.[38]

O'Neill's idealistic tours did bring in his largest group, but his promising statements about the settlement's current status would continue to haunt him. By April 9, 1876, O'Neill sent letters to third-group colonists detailing all costs, including train schedules and meeting places. On April 20, 102 people (no longer just men) left Chicago and arrived at O'Neill early in May. An *Omaha Herald* reporter visited O'Neill a week later and reported, "The General takes great pride in the results of his exertions to build up this part of Nebraska, and well he may for he has succeeded in establishing his colony with a very fine and intelligent people that any country might well feel proud of. They are mostly all young, or in the prime of life, industrious and sober. They are all well pleased with their new home."[39]

The residents, new and old, may have been well pleased until July, when

the first great grasshopper tragedy put a serious dent in their life and economy. Fifty percent of all crops were destroyed within hours, and caused much
consternation in O'Neill, as many homesteaders left as quickly as the
grasshoppers. One resident years later still remembered the carnage he saw
as a young man.

> As I passed south of the home I saw a field of corn on second breaking, of the most
> luxuriant growth that I have ever seen. I may have been in the house ten or fifteen min-
> utes when all of a sudden everything became dark. When we rushed out the door, we
> were ankle deep in a mess of grasshoppers and they were still alighting. We were all
> awed and dumbstruck when we cast our eyes in the direction of the beautiful and
> healthy field of maize, which I had just passed a few minutes before. Not a vestige of
> green growth, not even a stalk was left…. The hoppers continued to alight for hours
> till the ground was covered to a depth of four to six inches. The aerial flight of the
> insects was about one and a half miles to two miles wide and lasted for two days.[40]

It was the only serious grasshopper scourge for more than a decade, but the
timing was disastrous. The first two groups of colonists had spent a year or
two clearing the land and living in sod homes, and finally had a beautiful
crop, only to see it disappear within hours. The third group had only been
in O'Neill for two months, and the shock only added to what many felt as
disappointment. True, the platting was done by O'Neill's nephew and a school
was run by Mrs. O'Reilly, but there was no church or priest for these Irish
Catholics, no post office except in Wisner, sixty miles away, and most importantly, no homegrown crops.

The general surged forward with the same unbridled enthusiasm he
showed with the Fenians, but left angry colonists in his wake. The Neligh
newspaper published a letter to the editor where an O'Neill settler called the
general "a fraud for many reasons."[41] The paper responded the following week
with an editorial stating, "We cannot agree and regard fraud as a pretty harsh
term." Then the paper washed their hands of the matter, saying, "We are willing to give all sides a hearing. We are not the champions of either side in this
faction fight now in progress in Holt County. We believe both sides are more
or less to blame for the state of affairs that exist there today."[42]

The general announced that any newcomer to O'Neill could choose land
in any of the three Irish colonies, O'Neill, Atkinson, or the area soon to be
called Spalding. It was a smart move, as all three places would provide freedom of choice and kept the almost exclusively Irish localities tied to each
other for decades. John O'Neill was carving out a national reputation on a
second front and it was being noticed, at least in Nebraska. The colonists
were busy nonetheless, breaking up the land and building houses mostly of
sod or logs hauled from the Niobara River, twenty-five miles to the north.

The renewal of energy in John O'Neill's second career showed in his lectures. In St. Joseph, Missouri, the *Daily Morning Herald* observed:

General O'Neill

The Irish Orator at Brady's Hall Last Night

It is vain for us to attempt to describe the eloquent address that those present in Brady's Hall last night, had the privilege of listening to. There is something about Irish eloquence, distinctive and characteristic, that defies description, and which shows its effects by claiming the breathless attention of an audience, rather than by noisy demonstration or boisterous applause. Such was the effect of General O'Neill's address last evening, and for an hour and a half the audience listened without the least sign of weariness.

After describing in detail the problems of Ireland, England, and colonization of Nebraska, the article concluded with: "No words can portray his earnestness and impassioned eloquence. Those who failed to hear him lost a treat which will not come again. He is evidently a friend of his country and his countrymen, and is laboring earnestly for the welfare of both, and who does not wish him God speed."[43] It seemed like all the dominos were beginning to fall into place, for the general and the future of Nebraska.

Chauncey Wiltse, the government surveyor, banker, businessman, and ultimate cheerleader for Nebraskan settlement, was always impressed with O'Neill.

General O'Neill is a stranger to me, I had met him but once previously to his present visit to Omaha, at O'Neill City. I found him at work making himself thoroughly acquainted with that entire section of the country. He has traveled over it in person, slept on the ground with no cover but for the wagon box, eating such food as campers-out are compelled to eat, often going hungry, enduring anything, no matter how great the hardship, so that he might become perfectly familiar with the country, and able to represent it from personal observation. I admire his course, and approve his undertaking. My sympathies and hopes are strongly in favor of General O'Neill.[44]

Wiltse may not have been entirely truthful about meeting the general for the first time. He lived in West Point during the same time period as the O'Neill family in 1874 and early 1875 at the Neligh House. His father and the general were acquaintances and young Chauncey worked for the railroad and later became a friend of John Hugh when they both lived in West Point. In addition, Wiltse had purchased two lots in O'Neill City from O'Neill as early as September 25, 1875, for $50.

O'Neill then left at summer's end and renewed his proselytizing throughout the East and North. He was especially successful in Michigan and northeastern Pennsylvania, but traveled anywhere he was asked. He wrote to Bishop O'Connor in Omaha asking for both political and financial assistance for the coming years. The bishop praised O'Neill's efforts and plans, but was not able to provide any finances. The diocese was too large and the economy still unstable enough to be able to pass out money, even for good ideas.

It had been five years since the attack at Pembina, and ten years since

Ridgeway. O'Neill's spirit no doubt rejuvenated by time and his burgeoning new success in Nebraska, the general set out to remind the Irish in America that though he was encouraging his countrymen to resettle in the west, his heart was still on Irish freedom and hatred of England. He just couldn't let it go, and old wounds opened again. He established for the first time head-quarters on North 12th Street in Philadelphia, the O'Neill Home of Irish American Colonies. Most O'Neill historians have him laboring with the Irish in the eastern ghettos, but for the most part, he avoided the large cities and found the vast majority of his success in the mining areas of the country. The choice of Philadelphia was a mistake, as he had spent years operating out of the Midwest, ever since the move to East St. Louis in 1872. From Philadelphia, he produced on December 8, 1876, a 3,500-word epistle addressed to "Fellow Countrymen." It was, unfortunately, the old John O'Neill. "It is now over eleven years since I first joined the Fenian Brotherhood. I then believed and have had no reason to change my opinion that there was a splendid oppor-tunity for the Irish people in America to strike a fatal blow at our ancient enemy England. But unfortunately for Ireland the ancient curse of our race, disunion, followed us across the Atlantic." The general defended his actions in 1866, but blamed "some" of the Fenian Brotherhood "too willing to aban-don the cause." O'Neill then goes on much like he did in his prison defense in 1870, "I had every assurance and as full promises as any man can ever have that I would be supported," and again blamed senators, their friends, and false statements and letters for the failure at Eccles Hill. "Now so far as I am personally concerned I have never admitted and don't now admit that I failed in anything I undertook in connection with the Fenian organization."[45]

The general stated that "immediately after getting out of prison" he began making arrangements for the attack in North Dakota, and that the fail-ure in the Red River Country "was caused by a mere accident."[46] O'Neill, almost two-thirds of the way through, poses a question many Irish Americans and historians have asked about the Irish nationalist boy wonder. "Perhaps it ought to be thought strange if, after participating in three different failures inside of five years and after being vilified and slandered with a persistent villainy by men who very unjustly blamed me for their own shortcomings, and feeling keenly the injustice done me, I had abandoned the cause, but no such thought ever entered my mind."[47]

The general said he had "avoided active work" on behalf of Irish nation-alism to regain his health and his finances, but now, "I come before the Irish people of America to say I am prepared to continue the work commenced of June 1866 at Ridgeway, where a few hundred Irish soldiers met the English enemy on his own territory and whipped him."[48]

Colonization, for which he had sacrificed time, money, health, and fam-ily, is thrown into the background, despite the fact he is on the cusp of distinction with a new career. "I now ask you, fellow countrymen, to stand by me and assist me in striking another blow for Mother Ireland.... I am ready to risk it again. Yes, and sacrifice it if necessary, on the altar of Irish liberty."[49]

Towards the end of his return to militarism, he mentions Nebraska. "For the last three years I have devoted most of my time to organizing and locating colonies in Nebraska. This of itself I regard as a noble work.... But I had a double object in encouraging our people to emigrate from the overcrowded cities and states of the east. The first was that they might better their own condition and that of their families, and the second, that they might be in a position ... to assist the cause of Irish liberty."[50]

It is difficult to believe that O'Neill's new old strategy had been planned all along. It is even more difficult to believe that the colonists in Nebraska, who had so courageously relocated and raised families on the prairie, would be willing to follow O'Neill's next statement. "I think I can safely promise from the colonies which I have already established at least some of the young men to assist on the battlefield while the older ones raise corn, flour, and potatoes to help sustain them."[51]

The general finished his address with the ominous. "I beg you to give me one more chance untrammeled and my word for it, you will never regret it. The governing passion of my life, apart from my duty to my God, is to be at the head of an Irish army battling against England for Ireland's rights; for this I live, and for this, if necessary, I am willing to die."[52]

What was his motivation for such a thoroughly defensive polemic, just when his immigration plans were beginning to show positive results? Philadelphia had not been a friendly place for the general since his election in 1868 as Fenian Brotherhood president. Enemies, real and imagined, may have gotten under the infamous O'Neill's thin skin while in the city. The general endured years of whispers after 1870 and didn't handle it well. For sure, the new publication of Sir John Rutherford's *The Fenian Conspiracy,* hurt O'Neill deeply. The English book of 646 pages held as many lies and distortions as pages, including a line that the Fenian Brotherhood "admitted that $100,000 dollars had been received by the O'Neill wing in 1868, and of this sum not $20,000 dollars was spent on war material. The rest was appropriated by officials" (meaning O'Neill).[53] Though the general had lived with that gossip for some time, it was never on a printed page, nor with so much money mentioned. But worse for the rehabilitated O'Neill was the salacious accusation regarding the murder of Thomas D'Arcy McGee in 1867. This time Rutherford did not simply imply an O'Neill misdeed. "One of O'Neill's preparations was the murder of Thomas D'Arcy McGee, which was deliberately planned and executed."[54] O'Neill had forever rejected assassination as an Irish weapon, insisting on "fair and honorable fight forever."[55]

Even Le Caron defended O'Neill on this issue, but it was too late, and the lies cut O'Neill to the bone, and gave his enemies more reason to castigate him. In a list of John O'Neill's lifelong consistencies, at the top of the list was a high moral code in combat, which even his most serious detractors acknowledged.

Perhaps it was a combination of insults and accusations. Much of the Catholic hierarchy in the East had quietly fought any colonization work of O'Neill's for years, anxious not to lose a single parishioner, and this may have been an additional factor, as it was for Bishop John Ireland in Minnesota. O'Neill did receive a fine accolade from the *Irish Catholic Benevolent Union Journal,* an independent religious publication out of Dayton, Illinois, but the eastern bishops followed party lines, more concerned about their own fiefdoms, and quietly ignored the general and his plans, much to their shame.

> Gen. John O'Neill has been doing good colonizing work in Luzerne County, Pa., in gathering in colonies all that desire to go to the land he has secured in Nebraska.... The General is entitled to high praise for his work in colonizing his countrymen.
>
> We know how difficult the work he had then in hand. We know of some of the difficulties he had to encounter. As a pioneer in the work of colonizing the Irish people he merits the gratitude of all who have desired the welfare of the people. When others talked of the good to be done by colonization, General O'Neill selected a portion of Nebraska for the settlement of such as were willing to follow him. He has been maligned and his efforts condemned, but no man, lay or ecclesiastic, can engage in this work without being censured. General O'Neill has stood the assaults on his motives, character and efforts as unflinchingly as he has borne still more dangerous, though with more deadly attacks on his person. He has sought no endorsements from any one. He has relied on his own efforts and these alone have been the basis of his success.[56]

For sure, something, or somebody, spooked him into publishing this miniature defense, a smaller version of his 1870 Vermont manifesto written in jail. It wasn't necessary or productive, but it is an absolute microcosm of John O'Neill's dreams and temperament since his arrival in the United States as a young boy, and a final defense of his career as a Fenian. One year to the day of this address General John O'Neill would be on his deathbed in Omaha.

O'Neill's apparent depression and change in focus were perhaps exacerbated two weeks later when his mother died at age seventy-one in Elizabeth, New Jersey. Catherine O'Neill died the day after Christmas of edema brought on by congestive heart failure. She had been living on Price Street in Elizabeth for years with her daughter Mary and nieces from Ireland. Both her brother John Macklin and Catherine's son Bernard were successful merchants and had large families. Catherine, a widow for almost forty years, was held in high esteem for decades and her funeral filled St. Mary's Catholic Church, the same church she had helped defend a quarter century before against the Know Nothing mob. The *Elizabeth Daily Journal* reported that the service, held on Thursday, December 29, was well attended and listed as survivors "daughter Mary and son Bernard." There was no mention of a General John O'Neill, or shockingly, even just a son John. Catherine died after "a lingering illness," and so the general may or may not have visited his mother and been present at the funeral. For sure, he was within eighty miles when his mother died. Catherine's nephews John J. and Tom O'Neill were in Nebraska with Mary Ann, and with still no post office or telegraph lines, the news of Catherine's death would be some time in coming to her grandchildren.[57]

January 1877 saw O'Neill still in eastern Pennsylvania. He lectured in Wilkes-Barre, Archbald, Pittston, Mill Creek, and Parsons. O'Neill gave a glowing description of Nebraska, and spoke on the "fertile soil, the richness of its vegetation, the good supply of water, and of the climate."[58] It was reasons like this that future colonists would denigrate the general, especially when he added at every stop, "the stories in regard to the devastation by the grasshoppers had been greatly exaggerated. There has not been a single failure of the crops for the twenty years intervening the settlement of the state between 1854 and 1874."[59] He conveniently failed to mention that grasshoppers had destroyed the entire crop just the year before, including his wife's own loss, and that he himself knew nothing about Nebraska grasshoppers in 1854. But it was not an easy time to recruit in eastern Pennsylvania. Employees of the four largest eastern railways had gone on strike—one third of them Irish— when wages were cut by 10 percent. In the Pennsylvania mining regions, O'Neill was faced by opposition to the Irish Molly Maguires, where ten railroad men were murdered and ten Irish hanged in retaliation.[60] A month after Catherine O'Neill died, John O'Mahony passed away in New York City of Bright's disease at 61. O'Neill was in the area, though it is unknown if he attended the funeral of the man many called the "Father of Fenianism."

Back in O'Neill, young John Hugh, with his father gone, remembered the kindness of neighbors in O'Neill. "One day a party of settlers came to our house and announced they were going to have a plowing and broke up ten acres of land for mother so she could plant a garden and raise some wheat and corn. There was quite a number of them and they finished in two days."[61]

Perhaps this was out of kindness for all the help Mary Ann did for newcomers and children, perhaps because they also knew that Mary Ann— despite her courage in following the general seemingly all over the continent—needed help with an absent husband. Again, John Hugh gives the child's view of innocence. "Well time passes and we all grew in the wisdom of many things. Mother had never done any cooking until she moved up on the prairies. But she learned from a small settlement of Yankee women that had been raised on the frontier and knew all the tricks of how to get along and make a good meal of whatever was at hand."[62]

Two months later, on March 11, 1877, O'Neill was still on the East coast. He wrote a letter to his thirteen-year-old son John Hugh from Hazelton,

Pennsylvania, more than two months after the youngster wrote to him the day after Christmas. Once again, he missed the holidays with his family, John Hugh's birthday, and the death of his mother, none of which he mentioned at all. It is difficult to imagine the devout O'Neill ignoring news of the death of the young boy's only surviving grandmother, though he may have mentioned it in previous letters to Mary Ann.

My Dear little son,

Your very nice letter of December 26th, reached me in due time, and I would have answered it before, only I have been very busy. I have written to your Mama often. My health has been very good for some time back; only when I get cold do I get the attack of asthma.

I was very sorry to be so situated that I could not go home at Christmas, for I too, was very lonesome in Philadelphia. I was glad to hear that you had so much good corn. It was very kind of Mr. Conlon to build a corn crib for you. I also feel very grateful to Mr. Cronin and Mr. Barrett for putting up a barn for the cow and calf. I sent Mama some money for you to buy hay for the cow. There has been considerable cold weather out here but the winter has been generally very pleasant, much more so than usual.

I was very sorry to hear that your vegetable garden was destroyed by the grasshoppers but they will not trouble you for some time to come and I will bring some seeds with me when I come. I was very glad to hear from Mama's letter that you were going to school. It was very kind of Mrs. Reilly to open school. Give my kind regards to Mrs. Reilly and her children.

I have been in this town and vicinity, for ten days, and will leave for Scranton tomorrow, but will stop over at a town called White Haven, to lecture. May God bless you and make you a good boy. Your papa received Holy Communion this morning and remembered Mama and all her dear little children. Give my kind regards to all my friends in the settlement. Your affectionate father,

John O'Neill[63]

The general, in a more politic mood, printed another circular, this time spelling out to every member of the Nebraska State Legislature his colonization plans and with it a personal appeal for financial backing, all written from Pennsylvania. His plea, like the one to Bishop O'Connor, was rejected politely by the Legislature, and O'Neill sent a gracious letter to Governor Silas Garber acknowledging the rejection but asking to be remembered in the future. The general and O'Neill City homesteaders Mike McCarthy, Pat Hynes, and the Rev. John Curtis, representing the Omaha diocese, would soon choose further plots in Greeley County. McCarthy and Hynes loved the area so much they stayed and sent for their families in O'Neill. The town, originally called Halifax, would soon come to be known as Spalding. Towns founded by O'Neill would soon spread all over northern Nebraska, according to the general.

By the end of March, John O'Neill was still in Pennsylvania, gathering up the last of his four groups of colonists. On April 24, 1877, he wrote to Edward Johnson, who was likely his largest creditor. "Your letter reached me in Omaha. Pardon the delay in answering. I sent you a copy of the enclosed circular, from Omaha, but did not have time to write. I have entirely too much to do for the last two months. I have no fears but what the railroad will go through our settlements. I did not have time to go home [again] while in Nebraska, but wrote to my wife."[64]

Seventy-one people once again met in Chicago before heading to Nebraska, where they arrived the last week in April. As had been the case the previous two years, the majority of settlers were from eastern Pennsylvania and northern Michigan. The newcomers chose sites close together, so that O'Neill City soon had a Michigan settlement and a Pennsylvania settlement. With Patrick Hynes working hard in Spalding, some of these last seventy-one colonists soon migrated south to Spalding, others northwest to Atkinson.

For the first time, the general spent the summer and early fall in O'Neill, in his home built or financed by Edward Johnson of Michigan. In June, the Catholic Immigration Bureau, in Washington, D.C., in recognition of O'Neill's work in Nebraska, awarded him $1,000, giving him temporary financial stability.[65] It would never be enough, as the O'Neills were always a step away from poverty, especially in these last few years. At least there were no public mentions of the Philadelphia December manifesto, no calls to Le Caron for hidden arms or munitions, no secret meetings with Canadian strangers, no overt egotism, and no more calls to arm. He had accepted this second calling of Irish freedom. The O'Neill family spent the majority of the spring and summer in O'Neill, no doubt helped by the presence of twenty-two-year-old nephew Tom O'Neill from Elizabeth. But even when present, there were struggles, as the general was sick with asthma much of the time. Nephew John J. O'Neill, after completing the platting of O'Neill, Atkinson, and Spalding, removed to Omaha, where the young architect had his own new office. The general was still only thirty-nine years old. But fate goes as fate must, and General John O'Neill was running out of time.

12

Death in Omaha

War battered dogs are we, fighters in every clime;
Fillers of trench and of grave, mockers bemocked by time.
—Emily Lawless, *With the Wild Geese*

As the summer ended in 1877, the colony of O'Neill was finally growing into a town, and Irish settlers sent by the general were populating new sites at Atkinson, Spalding, and Greeley, eventually cementing John Charles O'Neill's future reputation in Nebraskan history. The general, with his three annual groups, had brought in almost three hundred people, though some left quickly and others moved on to Atkinson and other sites. There were still obstacles, with no post office or church, but that would be rectified by 1880. Though John O'Neill would never bring in another colonist, the 1900 census would show the area had over a thousand Irish residents, hundreds of them women and children. Its future was secure.

But O'Neill's personal efforts were taking a heavy toll both economically and emotionally, and both contributed to physical ailments. For a dozen years he had traveled the railroads like a man outrunning a posse, speaking in every state of the Union east of the Mississippi except Maine, Florida, and Delaware. By mid–1877, the general's health deteriorated rapidly, in part due to severe asthma he had long suffered, the pace he kept, and, just perhaps, the alcohol he reportedly abused for years.

From Omaha, on September 17, 1877, the general wrote a letter to Edward Johnson, with whom he had not been in contact since April. From his always prolific pen, O'Neill explained much of his economic situation; the letter is defensive, apologetic, yet always optimistic, and concerned about his legacy. It is the most telling and honest document of General John O'Neill's struggles. The first sign of the general's physical condition is the communication itself. Research of O'Neill has produced dozens of documents and letters. Since his youth, all correspondence had been handsomely written, with polished grammar, spelling, and thoughtfulness. Even when angry, his letters show poise and his speeches were artfully written, remarkable for a man who left school at eleven. In this letter to his creditor, Edward Johnson, there are some crossed out words, run-on sentences, words written out of order, and occasionally repetitive ideas. John Charles O'Neill was suffering, though characteristics of the cavalryman are still present.

My Dear Mr. Johnson,

Pardon my long delay in writing to you at length; I assure you it was not because I had forgotten you and your extreme kindness to me. About the fifth or sixth of July, while I was getting ready to go to the settlement [O'Neill], I was taken sick with pleurisy and was under charge of a doctor for some time—This weakened me very much and disqualified me for attending to business of any kind. I have not yet entirely recovered my usual strength, but am improving rapidly. In addition to the attack of pleurisy, about the first of August I got a severe cold, which brought on an attack of asthma, and both combined made me so nervous that I could hardly use a pen. While at the settlement, last month, I never slept a whole night in bed, but had to sit up in a chair most of the time, though I am now fast recovering.

This however, is not my only excuse for not writing, but I was waiting from day to day, expecting to get my business affairs in such shape that I would be able to send you some money and have a satisfactory settlement with you, but it was not until the present that I could do it.

Money Matters

As I have been unable to carry out what I proposed to you myself, I deem it but just that I should explain to you some of my financial difficulties, which is the true cause of my failure to do what I had agreed to—to commence with, I will state that I should never have undertaken to organize and locate a colony on government land, where I had no interest in the land, without charging the settlers from ten to twenty five dollars each, for my time and trouble as every other man who undertook to organize a colony has done. But I was in hopes that long before this I would have enough of people around O'Neill City and Atkinson, to build up both places, and I depended on selling enough of lots to pay my expenses and support my family, but in this I was mistaken—grasshoppers first, second and third years, were serious drawbacks, and retarded my work very much, but could not stand still, I had to keep on, under the most trying circumstances. I always had, and have now, the most implicit confidence in the future, and today, would not take twenty thousand dollars for my chances of making money during the next three years.

O'Neill now confirms that from the beginning, he was not prepared for this venture he started with Patrick Fahy in 1873, and though he worked incessantly, he may not have worked correctly. There is little doubt O'Neill trusted too many people too easily his entire adult life. An argument can be made his only true friend was Captain, later General, John Adams, whom he met in Baltimore in 1857 and died at the Battle of Franklin in 1864.

I had been promised assistance at various times, but in almost every instance I was disappointed with the exception of the assistance I received from yourself, and a few other friends. I had to struggle alone, with poverty staring me in the face at almost every step. Last winter, soon after I went to the coal mines of Pa., I made arrangements with some good men there, to locate a colony near the line of the Union Pacific Railroad, where every alternate section of land belonged to the road and where I would have a good commission for selling it.

These parties were to furnish me about two thousand dollars to pay all expenses, and were to have an interest in a townsite which I was to locate in the center of the colony. I worked very hard all winter, and had on my list about six hundred names, mostly heads of families, who intended coming on with me. Thousands of others were ready to follow after, if the first parties were satisfied. I expected to send a large number of these men to Holt County; but while I was out here, last April, selecting a place for the colony, a few parties came as far as Omaha, and fell in with some lying loafers who discouraged them and they returned and gave an awful account of the country, which completely demoralized and discouraged those who intended on coming. So when I returned to bring out some six hundred, all I could get was forty-six; some went to Holt County, and others to Greeley County, the county which I had selected for the new colony.

I secured the land for the townsite in Greeley County, and have called it O'Connor, after Right Rev. Bishop O'Connor, as you will see from the map which I enclose. The parties who came out in April reported back favorably but owing to the strike, and trouble they have had back there all summer, I only got $225 of the two thousand, up to the present, but it is all good and I will get it before long.

No one ever accused John O'Neill of being a lounge lizard, from his days leaving Elizabeth, as a seventeen-year-old in the Army, or leading Fenians, even when he failed in Vermont and Pembina. A less driven man would have cut and run from the Nebraskan colonization almost immediately. The undertaking began in the fall of 1873, just when the Panic of '73 started, and continued even as he wrote the letter to Johnson.

Another source from whence I expected money, was the Covington Columbus Black Hills Railroad company who had promised me $2,500 for services rendered and to enable me to work at settling up Northern Nebraska, which will be tributary to their road, but owing to some trouble about the Bonds, which had been voted by the Counties through which the road is to run, the company is embarrassed and I did not yet get a dollar from them yet.

In 1875 O'Neill had contacted this railroad, whose goal was to reach the Black Hills. Citizens throughout the Dakotas and northern Nebraska were thrilled, and bonds were bought in every county within a hundred miles of O'Neill. But the railroad was mismanaged and the people revolted over their money being misused. The Covington Columbus Black Hills Railroad sued and lost in the Supreme Court in 1877, and once again, a good idea by O'Neill ran aground.

Still another source from which I expected money long before this. The prominent Irishmen and Catholics of this place, with Bishop O'Connor at their head, had promised to assist me, as they are all interested in my work. But owing to the absence of the Bishop, nearly all summer, visiting the different parts of his extensive diocese, it was delayed.

Besides this, I have every assurance from the governor and members of the Legislature whom I have seen, that when the Legislature meets, they will appropriate a few thousand dollars for me—so that after a few months I expect to have plenty of money, at least enough to settle up with everybody to whom I owe a dollar, and have enough left to carry me through the winter—while working up an extensive immigration both for Holt and Greeley Counties. This year's crop has given me a solid footing to stand on.

On both these points the general was being a bit disingenuous. As shown prior, O'Neill did indeed lobby both the Catholic Church in Omaha and the Nebraska Legislature. Both were favorably inclined, but strapped for funds, and Bishop O'Connor told O'Neill, as did the governor, that no money would be forthcoming. O'Neill was simply buying time.

The House

With regard to the house, as you desired in your letter of September 1876, I decided to retain it and pay you back the money you had advanced, to enable you to build a good hotel in the town. When I wrote you to this effect, on the 29th of December last, I fully expected to pay the money, with interest, before now, but for the reasons stated above, I have been unable to do so until the present.

Vacating the house

When I wrote to you proposing to vacate the house for a time, I had made the necessary arrangements for returning about the middle of March, proving up on my claim, and taking my family away for a few months, or as long as you might want to occupy it, while building your hotel. But as your brother-in-law could not get on so soon, I did not want to return to the settlement before I could take my family away with me. Before Mr. Sparks [Darwin Sparks, Johnson's brother-in-law] got there the disappointments in money matters before referred to, had taken place, and it was impossible for me to do in May, what I had proposed and could have done in March. This I regret exceeding on your account, and on account of Mr. and Mrs. Sparks being disappointed in not having the house to move into, for I know that it has inconvenienced them very much, but I assure you that it was unavoidable on my part.

Whatever financial agreement had been happily agreed upon between O'Neill and Edward Johnson, it is clear the general was in default, and had been for some time. The letter clearly suggests that upon failure, Johnson would take possession of the house, and had indeed sent his brother-in-law Darwin Sparks to O'Neill in anticipation of such a move. O'Neill had been prepared to leave the home and relocate his family, but changed his mind, relying on, or discovering, new Nebraskan law regarding homestead rights. Basically, the general could assign Johnson (or Sparks) another part of his homestead claim on land not contiguous to the first homestead. It was a win for O'Neill, but an ugly one.

Proposition

I now make the following proposition. If satisfactory to you, you can send me a statement of what money you paid me, with interest, up to the first of next month, October, and I will pay you one half the amount at that time, and the balance on the first of January. This I think, under the circumstances, will be the most satisfactory way of disposing of the matter. It has been talked of all over the settlement, and in fact through the valley, and has been published in several newspapers, that I have sold the house and place, which precludes the possibility of me even proving up on my claim at the present.

I send you by this mail, a circular from the General Land Office, at Washington, and by referring to page 23, you will see the form of affidavit I must make in proving up. The claim being a preemption, I cannot remove my family from it until I have proved up, without relinquishing my right to it. I would now prefer not moving at all, as there has been some rather unpleasant talk about the matter, by outside parties who are ever ready to devote more attention to other peoples' business than to their own, and on this account my wife would not be willing to leave the house unless I insisted on it.

If this proposition is not satisfactory, and you desire the house, I will have it finished and fired up as at first agreed, and will build a small house, on another part of the claim for myself. I presume that Mr. Sparks has or will build a house on his own claim.

The general was still ill, but he never did take criticism well, and responded to obvious negative rumors no doubt spread by Sparks and other enemies of the general in O'Neill with his old fire. He defended himself, his mission, and his legacy in Nebraska.

Prouty's House

With regard to your joining Mr. Sparks in purchasing Mr. Prouty's house for a hotel, I don't think it would be advisable at all. I know that the present appearance of the town is not calculated to impress Mr. Sparks, or anybody else, very favorably, and the numerous Solomons in Holt County who profess so much wisdom, and who modestly claim to know so much about the future of the place, and my own business, are well calculated to deceive him, but I shall have something to say and to do in this matter. I have spent thousands of dollars, and nearly four years of hard work in organizing and building up this colony, contending against the most adverse circumstances and before I get through, it will be one of the most flourishing and prosperous colonies in the West and O'Neill City will be a town of considerable importance.

Heretofore, I have been working alone, and struggling with poverty, and have been unable to pay my way, from the fact that I never tried to sell any land, and charged the immigrants nothing for my services. But I am through with this sort of business, and for the time to come, I shall make it pay as I go. It appears that no matter what a man tries to do for others, if he neglects himself, and is unable to pay his debts, he is a "fraud," a "humbug," and a "swindler."

John O'Neill was sick, apologetic, and humbled by his poverty and ill luck. But he would not take kindly to a dust up of Mary Ann and Mrs. Bridget Sparks, a newcomer to O'Neill, and more than likely co-habiting the house with the O'Neills temporarily. Mary Ann, it seems, was also tired of constantly moving, total subservience to the Irish dream, and living with the Sparks in the same home. The general got the message. Mary Ann, after a 7,000-mile trip to California at age five; living in a tent in San Francisco before being abandoned by her father; losing her mother to tetanus; living in an orphanage;

and marrying a mercurial Irishman who traversed the country like it was a cross country run, finally put her foot down.

The Crop

With regard to the crop raised on the place this season, my wife had the acres of wheat planted, on shares, before Mr. Sparks got there. The balance of the plowed land he planted in corn, and my wife expects a portion of this, as is customary. But if this is not satisfactory to Mr. Sparks, I will pay him for it, and will also pay him for whatever expenses he may have incurred on account of my family, while stopping at the house, for I do not wish that there should be any hard feelings about the matter. Now, with regard to anything that may have passed, of an unpleasant nature between my wife and Mrs. Sparks, I desire to make this explanation. I have never told my wife anything about my business with you and she knew nothing of it except what idle rumor had brought it to her ears; and having been knocked around

Mary Ann O'Neill circa 1880-85, age about 36-41 (O'Neill family collection).

so much with the children for some ten years since we left our home in Tennessee, which she regarded as her own, through my foolishness in engaging in the Canadian movement in 1866, and being told that she was again about to be turned adrift upon the world, she may have said some things to Mrs. Sparks which she would not have said had she understood the circumstances.

I assume all blame in this matter, and apologize to Mrs. Sparks. The fault is altogether mine, for not speaking to my wife about our business. I shall send a copy of this letter to Mr. Sparks by tomorrows mail.

Give my kind regards to Mrs. Johnson and Lilly. Hoping to hear from you soon, and that you will overlook any apparent neglect in not writing before.

I remain,
Your friend,
John O'Neill[1]

In November, with Johnson, Sparks, and illness hopefully behind him, O'Neill resumed his frenetic annual pattern of lecturing, securing land in Greeley County, and preparing for a fifth group of colonists. Before he left O'Neill around November 10, he placed the following in papers throughout the Midwest:

Real Estate and Land Office

Improved Farms for Sale in all parts of the State on reasonable terms
Address Omaha, Nov. 1877
Gen John O'Neill
Omaha, Neb.

A week later in Little Rock, Arkansas, eight hundred miles southeast of O'Neill, he aggravated what was thought to be a severe cold, and headed home to Mary Ann.[2] The general arrived home to his wife and children five days later, after numerous rail and stage trips, a very sick man. The next night, November 20, he had what was called "a slight stroke."[3] Mary Ann immediately took him to Omaha, a 180-mile trip south, none of it easy. Her soldier boy was in trouble.

> My dear Son,
>   Your Papa and myself arrived in Omaha last Tuesday evening. Papa had the Asthma real bad at Norfolk, and he is now at the Hospital and Dr. Coffman is attending him. Papa is getting along pretty well at present. Write or get Mr. Daley to write and let us know how yourself and Sister Mamie are getting along, also how everything is around the house. You can get something for yourself and Mamie with this change. I will send some more when I write again. You can write a few lines every mail to me. Mr. Strickler [?] is well. Papa and Mama and Kitty send much love to you and Mamie. Be good little children till I get back. I can't tell you yet when I can get home. Goodbye for the present and God bless you both.
>   Your affectionate mother[4]

Mary Ann stayed a month nursing the general in St. Joseph's Hospital. She had loved the dashing soldier boy since she was fifteen, but left him at the hospital after a month and returned to her children in O'Neill for Christmas. No one expected the general would take a turn for the worse. He was still young and had fought asthma his whole life. O'Neill was not without family. Twenty-four-year-old John J. O'Neill, the general's closest relative and most energetic follower since 1872, had a home and office in Omaha and could monitor his health and recovery.

History is a bit cloudy about the general's turn for the worst, but the most prevailing version is that after the 1878 new year and six weeks at the hospital, O'Neill tried to get up and fell from his bed, where nurses found him on a cold stone floor in January. Pneumonia developed and rapidly spread through O'Neill's body, aided by his severe asthma. On January 7, 1878, John J. O'Neill wrote sorrowfully to Mary Ann from his home in Omaha.

> Dear Aunt, I drop you these few lines to let you know that Uncle John is in a very low state. He has not been able to speak since Saturday morning [the letter was written on a Monday] and the doctors have given him up. His death is expected hourly. Mr. Donovan and his friend here think it would be useless for you to come down as he may be buried before you could get here, but still you can use your own judgment in the matter.
>   I have sat up with him the last two nights. If he should die, I shall have him buried from my house. If there is any request you have to make, please write by mail.[5]

The following day, Tuesday, January 8, 1878, the general received the last rites of the Catholic Church and died in his sleep at 11p.m. without a word. The hero of Ridgeway, his wife and family 180 miles away, was just months short of turning forty years old.

There were many conflicting reports about the general after his death, all perfectly consistent with his idiorythmic life. Henri Le Caron was despised by many, and echoed disparaging sentiments of his old neighbor from Nashville. Le Caron always looked out for himself first, but few unfortunately knew O'Neill better. Fourteen years after the general's death, Le Caron wrote in his bestselling memoir, "He took to drink and went entirely to the dogs, bringing to the verge of starvation an affectionate but broken-hearted wife. Drifting slowly downward through disgrace and drink, O'Neill, the once brilliant if egotistical Irishman, met a lone and miserable death."[6] Sir Charles Russell, the British Lord Chief Justice and no friend of the Irish, was one of many British high officials to pay Le Caron for decades. He told anybody who listened that Le Caron "is a living lie."[7] John Finerty, the Chicago Fenian leader who knew both O'Neill and Le Caron intimately, learning of the spy's death in 1892, added, "The world is rid of a moral monster."[8]

Captain John MacDonald, O'Neill's enemy and contemporary at Ridgeway, though no relation to the Prime Minister of the same name, wrote thirty years after O'Neill's death in 1910, "Becoming disheartened and discouraged by his failures, he began drinking heavily, and soon became a wreck, subsequently dying alone and miserable as the result of his excesses, unwept, unhonoured, and unsung."[9] MacDonald always tried to justify his actions as a leader of the British forces at Ridgeway and Fort Erie, even though he elevated his own importance in the affair, where he did very little. McDonald had never met O'Neill, but when he wrote a self-serving memoir of the invasion, *Troublous Times in Canada: A History of the Fenian Raids, 1866 and 1870,* he was without question relying on Le Caron's written disparagement of 1892, and thus like Le Caron cannot be trusted in his evaluation of the general's demise, even if some truth accrued in his self-seeking narrative. Both men's comments have been carried down through history with no certification.

In contrast to the viewpoints of the scurrilous spy and Canadian enemy, in the 1882 *History of Holt County*, William Cutler said, "O'Neill was buried, highly honored and sincerely mourned. It is not possible in a few words to give a just estimate of his character. His self-sacrificing spirit, his boundless generosity and his untiring zeal worked wonders."[10]

The *Niobrara Tribune* wrote the following:

Death of General O'Neill

The Founder of O'Neill City, Holt County, is stricken with Paralysis and Dies from its Effects. Mr. John Brennan's Tribute to Deceased.

Gen John O'Neill, the founder of our neighboring town O'Neill City, died at Omaha of paralysis, aged about 40 years. General O'Neill was the leader of the famous Fenian raid on Canada in 1866, where he made a gallant though unsuccessful record. For the past four years he has been laboring in colonizing Holt County with his countrymen, and has been quite successful, save in a financial point.... In character John O'Neill was essentially a soldier—the beau ideal Christian soldier. He was a devout Catholic, and while he saw no reason for conflict between religion and patriotism, the voice of mother church was the voice of God.... He was an Irish gentleman in speech and manner, but not Quixotic. The highest hope of his heart was to die fighting for Ireland.[11]

The *Irish Tribune* reported the most complete report of the death of O'Neill, and was much more sanguine about the general.

General John O'Neill died at St. Joseph Hospital after nearly three months' illness. About ten weeks ago, while at his home in O'Neill City, he suffered an attack of paralysis and came to Omaha for treatment. Under the direction of the most skilled physicians of Omaha he received Turkish baths for six weeks, his wife being in constant attendance. About a month ago he was removed to the Sisters Hospital where, under the kind and attentive care of the good sisters, he improved gradually. Business requiring the attention of Mrs. O'Neill at her home she left him about a month before he died, feeling confident of his speedy recovery. Last Friday night he suffered a second attack, his right side, tongue, and the muscles of his throat being paralyzed. He lingered until eleven o'clock when he peacefully passed away. During his sickness he was continually visited by the Irishmen of Omaha, and particularly by his nephew John J. O'Neill, who has lately moved to Omaha.

The Emmett Monument Association of Omaha immediately took charge of the remains, and had them promptly attended to and removed to St. Philomena's Church, where they lay in state until after High Mass Wednesday morning.

Rev. Father O'Brien delivered the funeral oration in a masterly and soul stirring manner. After giving a description of General O'Neill's former life and service to the country in the U.S. Army, where he won laurels for himself, Father O'Brien remarked that he well remembered the morning he saw General O'Neill in 1866 in Buffalo, with his green tunic on, a brave, dashing, bold officer, as he came fresh from the field of battle, where he had risked his life for his adopted country.

Now giving up home and fortune for the country that gave him birth, and crossing the foaming Niagara, he met the army of a tyrant government, and before the sun set on Canadian soil, the proud Union Jack was dipped in the mud, and the Emerald Green rose once more. He tried it again at Eccles Hill, but if he failed, blame him not; he did his best. In after years he turned his attention to removing his countrymen from the slums and the alleys, and rum-holes of the crowded cities, to the fertile prairies of Nebraska, and making them independent farmers; but now he has died by the borders of the Missouri River, a penniless man.

The Reverend father stated that the E.M.A. met his hearty approval, and deserved the thanks of all Irishmen. The congregation was moved to tears during the discourse.[12]

There has never been any report stated whether Mary Ann and the children were able to get to Omaha for the well-attended funeral, though it is hard to believe they could—another 180-mile journey back to Omaha with or without three small children in the midst of a Nebraskan winter might well have been impossible.

All the pallbearers were Irishmen from Omaha, and none of the citizens of O'Neill were mentioned, perhaps for the same reasons. More telling, Bernard O'Neill made no effort to bring his brother's body home to rest in New Jersey in the family plot at St. Mary's Church, a silent and harsh statement on family relations. Surely Bernard would have had no difficulty, since his oldest son, John Joseph, had done all preparations for the general's passing. The respected O'Neills and Macklins had flourished for forty years in Elizabeth yet no obituary appeared in the *Elizabeth Daily Journal.*

O'Neill's death created headlines in the New York *Irish American,* the paper that was for years his champion and later less than friendly to the old Brotherhood president. Though editorially in total opposition to the old Fenian since 1868, the paper recognized the vast appeal O'Neill still possessed in the Irish American community. Perhaps, as well, the editors recognized the passing of a most unique Irish American, unlikely to be seen again soon.

A telegraphic dispatch from Omaha announces that General John O'Neill, while well known, both here and across the Atlantic, in connection with the Fenian movement against English domination in Ireland, died from the effects of a stroke. His career, though brief, was eventful. His figure will be a conspicuous one in the history of the times in which he lived; and it is only fitting that the truth regarding the part he played in the events by which he was surrounded should be put on the record.

O'Neill ... in the future history of the Irish race, will be as inseparably linked with the struggles of the present generation for national independence as those of his ancestors with the efforts made by our people in the past against English tyranny and usurpation.... It is impossible to do adequate justice of a man like General O'Neill; we can only assume to glance at the many attestations of his bravery and gentlemanly bearing which should have a public record, as they are from men of high positions, and are of importance in illustrating the estimation in which he has always been held by his superior and brother officers.... No man can produce a more unsullied life, or one better calculated to confirm his equality to the high positions in which his countrymen have placed him.

The reporter, possibly editor P.J. Meehan himself, an old friend but older enemy, then faithfully recorded O'Neill's early life, before mentioning the split prior to the second invasion at Eccles Hill. "He began to show restiveness and impatience with the prudent and cautious policy which the Fenian Senate, warned by the experience of former failure, had adopted. O'Neill fell into the error of Stephens, and set a date beyond which he would wait no longer, and the expedition resulted even more disastrously than he had been warned it would."

The front-page article, with a huge drawing of the general's profile, continued with some thoughts on his passing. "It was a sad end to what might, under proper guidance, have been a glorious career; but it was a conclusion of which he had been forewarned, but disregarded the warning. The effects of this second raid upon the Fenian organization in America was ruinous, but upon O'Neill himself the result told the most heavily—his prestige and following [in the FB] were gone, and he sunk out of sight."

After mentioning O'Neill's foray into colonization, the paper ended with kinder words.

> In that service so different from that which the ardent soldier had hoped for—he died. In our short sighted human judgement we cannot help wishing rather that before errors of head, not of heart, diverted him from the path of true patriotism, General O'Neill had fallen in the flush of victory at Ridgeway, like so many of his race, with the old flag overhead, and the cry of "Ireland" ringing in his ear. But He who orders all things ordained a different ending; and while we bow with submission to the ruling of an all wise Providence, we close the charitable portals of the grave over the failings of the dead and remembering only the good fight he fought in the cause of the Old Land, pray that Heaven in its mercy may receive the soul of the brave soldier John O'Neill.
>
> We understand that General O'Neill is left with a widow and three orphan children. May God in his mercy pity and protect them in their sad bereavement.[13]

John Charles O'Neill, of Drumgallan townland, Clontibret Parish, County Monaghan, Ireland, thirty-nine years old, was buried at Holy Sepulchre Cemetery in Omaha with his young son Eugene. There was no headstone.

13

Legacy

Our Irish Blunders are never Blunders of the Heart."—Maria Edgeworth

News of O'Neill's death was soon known throughout the country, picked up by newspapers in Los Angeles, Chicago, New York, Philadelphia, and Montreal, and small towns from Montana to Alabama. His death brought back intense memories for old Fenians, those who had abandoned the fight for Irish freedom for an American way of life, and those who longed to continue the fight in the Fenian Brotherhood's successor, the Clan Na Gael.

From the United Irish Rebellion of 1798, there followed a succession of hardened Irish patriot revolutionary confederacies, societies, and conspiracies all with one honest aim—Irish independence. Some were treated with disdain, some caused their own problems and demise, but they were all among the building blocks of the Easter Rising of 1916. The formation of a modern Ireland, these groups were found on both sides of the Atlantic and beyond. The Young Irelander Rebellion of 1848 led to the Emmett Monument Association, then the Fenians, which gave birth to the Clan Na Gael, and finally, the Easter Rising of 1916. It is fair to say that Patrick Pearse, James Connolly, and the other martyrs of 1916 stand on the shoulders of men like John Devoy, John O'Neill, Tom Sweeny, J.J. Donnelly, Jerome J. Collins, and hundreds of others. Indeed, Pearse was primarily a poet and theorizer, and Connolly's ultimate sacrifice included not just a firing squad propped up forcibly in a chair, but hard work years before, organizing the laboring Irish at the Singer Manufacturing plant in O'Neill's hometown of Elizabeth, New Jersey.

Though the news of O'Neill's death reached Ireland, Great Britain, Canada, and the U.S., sometimes legends linger. The *Des Moines Register* of May 15, 1878, reported: "It is published in the eastern papers that General John O'Neill, who commanded the last Fenian raid, is at the head of the alleged movement to raise an Irish legion for Russia."[1] The general, John Charles O'Neill, four months in the grave, would have approved.

Irish freedom, of course, continued its inexorable destiny towards its own rule, none of it easy. Following an Irish civil war in 1922–23 that Sweeny, O'Neill, Collins, and Devoy could never have envisioned in their lifetimes, nor the Ulster civil rights movement decades later which led to 3,665 violent deaths from 1966–2001, one only the Irish could call 'Troubles.' Twenty-first century Ireland now finds itself part of the European Union and, despite its ancient divisions, one of the most popular democracies in the world.[2]

Today Tom Sweeny, in particular, is well regarded by American historians with righteous cause. After the collapse of the 1866 invasion, Sweeny rejoined the Army and was stationed in Georgia during Reconstruction, but like O'Neill, his protégé, he never handled peacetime well. His wife died, he drank a bit, and was charged in 1867 with interfering with the local Southern government he was protecting during Reconstruction. Worse, he was charged with drunkenness and public urination on, of all days, St. Patrick's Day. In the end, he was suspended with pay and married an Atlanta girl half his age. The marriage to young Eugenia Reagan was a wonderful success and Sweeny retired to his home on Long Island, New York, dying in 1892 at seventy-two with five children. The *Army and Navy Journal* called him "as gallant, warm-hearted, and impulsive an officer as ever wore a uniform."[3]

Jerome J. Collins succeeded O'Neill as the titular head of the Clan na Gael. Collins was the force in the Clan na Gael, until, like O'Neill, he met an early death. Collins became one of America's first legitimate weathermen and, in addition to his duties with the Clan na Gael, was the science editor of the *New York Herald.* Collins believed the open conventions of the Fenians were contrary to freeing Ireland, stating, in words O'Neill would have echoed, "a debating society will never free Ireland."[4] In 1879, one year after O'Neill's death, he eagerly joined a doomed expedition to the Artic as a reporter. The Jeannette expedition was an abject failure, and Collins and Captain George DeLong died of cold and exposure. Collins was just forty years old, one year older than O'Neill, when he died. His body was eventually returned from the Siberian Artic a year later, and Collins was given a monumental service in New York then a burial in Cork, which is now known as the longest funeral in the world.

John Devoy was the best-known member of the Fenian Brotherhood and Clan Na Gael, and in a long life would be one of the few Irish nationalists to be present for the 1916 uprising. Devoy spent almost sixty years fighting for Irish freedom in Ireland and America, and truly deserves status among the Irish American freedom fighters. Younger than O'Neill, Devoy was a compatriot in the Brotherhood until he moved towards the Clan na Gael. He died in Atlantic City, New Jersey, and was given a grand funeral and large memorial in Dublin's Glasnevin Cemetery.

Sweeny and Devoy had the public image advantage of dying old, and the Collins story was a headline for William Randolph Hearst's newspaper for years. All have been, and deserve to be, counted among the Irish American nationalistic pantheon of heroes. John Charles O'Neill died young, suspected of many things, but is the only one of these four Fenians who is lost a bit to history. His Fenian career, however, was superior to each of the others'. By age thirty-two, O'Neill was an acknowledged military leader, president of the organization for two years, and a man who never feared risking failure or tired of waiting for tomorrow. Sweeny resigned after 1866; Devoy never led men into battle; and Collins left the Fenians to form the Clan na Gael and forge his own stellar reputation. Each of the others surpassed O'Neill in political understanding, planning, and longevity, and none were as arrogant, ego-driven, or immature as the general.

One hundred and fifty years after the Battle of Ridgeway, the 150th Ridgeway Anniversary History Conference was held on June 2–3, 2016, to commemorate the attack from Buffalo. More than two dozen academics lectured and discussed the attack at Ridgeway from both the Canadian and American perspectives with much fanfare. Not a single lecture had the seminal topic of John O'Neill, the hero of Ridgeway. Two speakers from the conference said that O'Neill was often mentioned, but still considered him a mystery unsolved, yet he was and is the pivotal figure of the invasion.[5]

There can be no argument that the Fenian Brotherhood's military campaigns ended disastrously for Irish Americans by 1871, though Canadian historians have, for one hundred and fifty years, pointed to the three O'Neill incursions, even the last in Manitoba, as one of several reasons Canada advanced its cause to Dominion status, as well as accelerated the ascent of John A. MacDonald as the George Washington of Canada. The late C.P. Stacey, renowned professor of history at the University of Toronto, time and again saw Fenianism as one of the most important and underappreciated developments in Canadian history.

Most Canadian historians have accepted that the Brotherhood raids "gave the necessary impetus to the federation of the provinces into one dominion."[6] Prior to the June 1866 attacks, there was little enthusiasm by the Canadian public for any unification, a population as arbitrary as the original thirteen American colonies had been; Canadian nationalism arose only after O'Neill and friends attacked at Ridgeway. It was certainly not an accident that Prime Minister John MacDonald used the Irish invasions to consolidate all the opposing factions in the Canadian provinces and saw Canada in full Dominion status almost a year to the day after the attack on Ridgeway. Even the bizarre third attempt by O'Neill helped galvanize the west of Canada into a firmer union.

Fenianism was a historical force in both America and Ireland, though Great Britain has rather successfully done the most these last one hundred and fifty years to define the Brotherhood's history as a farce, and it was certainly accelerated by the Great Famine of 1845–50. The Famine came close to destroying the Irish language, music, and educational system, and the concept of Irish nationalism was close to a collapse. With all its faults, the Fenian movement in America brought back from embers the concept of Irish freedom. Though the Fenian movement short-circuited due to internal squabbling and British spies, its effect on two continents was pervasive.

Carl Wittke, a much-respected American historian, has claimed, "The Fenian organization was the only one in United States history to arm and drill in public for the invasion of a country with which the United States was at peace, and whose plans were public knowledge before the invasion began and the attack on Canada was the most amazing example of group activity by an immigrant element in United States history."[7]

Even the Canadians, who were attacked, have been fair. But British historians have called the Fenian Brotherhood, in couched vocabulary, a bunch of misfits and clowns unable to get anything right. The Fenians, they have argued assiduously, were run by military nonentities with no specific purpose, and blamed their failure on a flaw of the Irish character, which they have done for centuries. Yet from Tom Sweeny on down, every soldier selected as a brigadier or colonel in the Fenian Brotherhood Army had a distinguished career in the Civil War. Thirty-five held ranks of captain, major, colonel, and general in the Civil War. At least four Medal of Honor recipients were involved in the Brotherhood invasion: Mike Murphy, John Lonergan, Patrick Murphy, and Edmund Rice.

"The Fenians had over 50,000 actual members, many of them trained, and hundreds of thousands of ardent supporters; in just seven years, and despite clerical condemnation, Fenianism had become the most popular and powerful ethnic organization in Irish-American history."[8] Yet many cartoons still appeared showing Fenians running away from battle, throwing their arms away in fright, with comic features and monkey tails. However, the British press never created ridiculous features or blamed the Irish character when more than five thousand Irish Ulstermen were killed in less than six hours at the Somme while fighting for Great Britain in World War I, or when ten thousand Aussies and New Zealanders, many of Irish descent, were killed at Gallipoli. But the Fenians and Irish Americans were fair game in the nineteenth century. One modern Irish historian, Patrick O'Sullivan, has argued persuasively that the British and Irish revisionist historians have written the Fenian Brotherhood "out of history."[9]

One example from the O'Neill era is the total falsification of the attack in Vermont in 1870. Even though the attempt by O'Neill at Eccles Hill was plagued by self-imposed political decisions, spies, and arrogance, the British press turned it into an Irish character assassination.

We will admit that the Fenians were at any rate not deficient in courage. They were ill-disciplined, ill-armed, badly officered, a mass of incoherent units, without knowledge of the country on which they were to levy war, or of the forces opposed to them.

General O'Neill approached the head of 200 men. Seeing the red coats of the enemy's skirmishers in front, he called a halt and addressed his soldiers in the Napoleonic style— "You are the advance guard of the Irish American army and are now about to enter the enemy's country. The eyes of your countrymen are on you. Forward March!"

A conservative Dublin paper unleashed their ire on O'Neill and fellow officers and was copied throughout Ireland. "The Fenians broke and fled. The General all this time was out of harm's way. Instead of being at the head of his men he saw the battle from inside a bedroom window! ... When arrested he stepped into a carriage amid the jeers or curses of the men he betrayed. They denounced him not only as a traitor or an ass.... Where General Starr came from or what his qualifications are no one seemed to know. The appointment was O'Neill's, and Starr was a general of the O'Neill stamp.... The leaders seemed to be little more than idiots. Heartlessness and deceit, ignorance and cowardice were the distinguished qualities of the Fenian leaders.... General Donnelly, another O'Neill stamp, died the next day."[10]

Though every single statement is factually untrue except the spelling of the Fenians mentioned, it must be said that J.J. Donnelly did not die until 1889. Critics and historians cannot ignore one important item—Ridgeway and the short invasion of Canada in 1866, however minor, was the only armed victory for the cause of Irish independence between 1798 and 1919.

When John O'Mahony died a pauper in 1877, even his enemies generally recognized his legacy as that of a proud, honest scholar with lifelong definitive nationalist convictions. But the *New York Times,* generally recognized as anti–Fenian if not anti–Irish, while admitting O'Mahony was "a sober and honest man," added, "He died like all Irish patriots of the sword—alone, friendless, wretched, and forgotten."[11] His funeral saw ten thousand in attendance at the New York service at St. Francis's Xavier Church on 16th Street and tens of thousands more when he was laid to rest in Glasnevin Cemetery in Dublin.

John Rutherford's book, *The Fenian Conspiracy,* described by Dennis Dowling Mulcahy, a doctor and Irish rebel, as "ten lies in twenty lines," had been accepted more or less as the gospel of Fenianism from the British point of view.[12] It took eighty years for a fair and objective history of the Fenian movement to appear. The tide began to turn in 1947 when Father William D'Arcy published his seminal work, *The Fenian Movement in the United States, 1858–1886.* In a June 1963 visit to Dublin, just months before his assassination, President John F. Kennedy laid a wreath at the Fenian memorial, to the chagrin of many on the other side of the Irish Sea. In recent years the memory of the Fenians has been kept alive by another Irish nationalist, historian, and balladeer, Derek Warfield. Warfield's band, The Young Wolfe Tones, have performed Irish rebel tunes worldwide for over thirty years, especially in America. He is equally renowned as a historian and lecturer, and has published a biography of the Irish martyr Robert Emmet. One of his favorite stops is O'Neill, where he has played the ballad, "John O'Neill, Nebraska," to thrilled audiences, though he would be upset to learn the general's removal to O'Neill has been twice denied. Canadian historians especially have taken to the Fenians with gusto in the last two decades. Canadian authority Peter Vronsky has become an expert on the Battle of Ridgeway, while David A. Wilson, Brian P. Clarke, and Shane Lynn have established Toronto as the leading base of complete Fenian studies in North America. Most recently, Eva O'Cathaoir has produced *Soldiers of Liberty: A Study of Fenianism, 1858–1908*, covering this "underestimated" history of the movement both in Ireland and America.

The Fenian dream of Irish freedom continued to crop up now and again, proving the fiery ideals of the general were difficult to extinguish. The respected *Minneapolis Journal* ran the following on January 6, 1900, twenty-two years after the death of the ex–Fenian Brotherhood president:

GENERAL JOHN O'NEILL
Soldier of Liberty, Promoter of the Fenian Raids, and colonizer of His Adopted State

From Omaha—Special to the Journal.

Are the Fenians of the United States about to strike another blow at the hated British government? Certain it is that Irish-Americans of Omaha, Lincoln, and other American cities are secretly considering plans not only to aid the struggling Boers, but to put every possible obstacle in the way of the British in the prosecution of the war upon the Dutch republics. Sunday, Dec. 31, the Irish-Americans of Omaha will hold a secret meeting, it is said, in consonance with a concerted movement upon the part of Fenians in other cities. It is the purpose of these men, in case Canada shall propose to send any more soldiers to South Africa, to make a demonstration on the Canadian frontier, thus to convince the Dominion government that it will need all its soldiers at home. Prominence has doubtless been given to Omaha and Nebraska in this movement because of the fact that the bones of the most prominent of the leaders of the invasion over thirty-three years ago rest in an Omaha cemetery. His memory was not forgotten.[13]

The remainder of the long piece rewound the history of the general, but left no doubt that his memory and dream struck a chord three decades after Ridgeway. The raid to South Africa never occurred, though two volunteer Irish brigades, including fifty Irish Americans, fought valiantly against British forces. Then there is the legacy of John O'Neill the colonizer. In the beginning of his last career, he was desperate and financially strapped, but for six years he zealously promoted Irish independence culturally in the west, at that time a mysterious and perilous place for the Irish, or anyone, from the east coast. He lay down the sword figuratively, and in a rash moment may have hocked his own sword literally, and put money he had and didn't have where his mouth was. O'Neill never gave up on his two countries. He made enemies, but had great and loyal friends nationwide even when down on his luck. He was never involved in scandal. It would be fair to say that in twelve years, John O'Neill was invited to speak, and spoke, to more people in more states about Irish nationalism, freedom, and the American dream than any Irish American in the nineteenth century. Since 1872, there is some evidence the general abused alcohol, which may have contributed to his death, but there is no proof except from the words of Le Caron, which has since been copied as gospel. When O'Neill died in 1878, there was a multitude of Nebraskans who believed he was a messiah, and just as many who thought he was a charlatan. Few doubted that John Charles O'Neill possessed a great Irish soul.

Even in death, O'Neill remained controversial, sometimes beyond reason. Nine years after the general died, and with the economy in the United States back on firmer footing, J.J. McCafferty, who had arrived with the second O'Neill colony in 1875 and was now a judge, brought up the idea of bringing O'Neill back home from his unmarked grave and purchasing a monument to the man who founded the city. O'Neill City was then a sturdy, blooming Midwestern town with a population of 1,000 and the timing seemed appropriate, at least to McCafferty. He contributed the first $10, and twenty-three-year-old son John Hugh promised $35. The *Omaha Bee* reported the idea as a fait accompli. "The citizens have at last taken hold of a too long neglected object—that of erecting a monument to the memory of General John O'Neill, the noted Canadian raider and leader of the Fenians, who founded the town and devoted the last years of his life to the settlement of Holt County. Four hundred dollars [$12,000 in 2016] have already been subscribed."

Judge McCafferty promptly chaired a public meeting and was more than a little surprised when many of the townspeople expressed not simply little interest, but definite determination not to allow the reburial, much less a monument. A spokesman for those against the move, never identified, stood and said to much approval, "Leave him in Omaha! He led the Irish astray, and was the cause of their suffering."[14] Shockingly, General John O'Neill stayed in Holy Sepulchre Cemetery, 180 miles away. The O'Neill Irish, it seemed, forgot nothing.

The move to deny the general was payback for Patrick Fahy, and perhaps even orchestrated by him. After O'Neill had eviscerated and exposed the fraud and non-compliance in the founding of O'Neill City, Fahy was not seen until he moved conveniently into the town in 1880, two years after the death of O'Neill. Oral history says Fahy, who left O'Neill for Idaho a year after the vote, denigrated the general for a decade. Some tangible proof can be found in *Andreas' History of Holt County*, published in 1882. One chapter includes biographical sketches of town leaders, taken by interviews. Fahy, for the first time, said he "employed O'Neill to go east and bring back at least twenty-five families" for his salary, and that is why he delayed paying him, because only fourteen (or eighteen) arrived. Fahy then said he nonetheless gave the general a "$100 present" when he discharged him.[15] He never mentioned that John J. O'Neill platted the town, lying when he said it was a Thomas Atwood. After boasting about how much money he donated to improving the life in O'Neill, he made the ridiculous statement that he was an "admirer of the great Irish warrior, Hugh O'Neill, and thus he named O'Neill City in his honor."[16] John O'Neill, were he able, would have regretted calling Fahy "an astonishingly intelligent Irishman," and Mary Ann Coughlin and the three O'Neill children had to hear his lies repeated for almost ten years in a small town. Fahy eventually abandoned O'Neill City, ending his nondescript days in North Dakota, but the damage to John O'Neill's memory lasted for decades.

But the memory of John O'Neill and his quest for Irish freedom had not been lost in the rest of America. On Saturday, February 11, 1893, the *Irish World*, still the most widely read Irish newspaper in the country, ran a front-page story with a penciled drawing of the general:

In Memory of General O'Neill

In the cemetery of Holy Sepulchre, on a beautiful eminence overlooking a large section of the City of Omaha, Nebraska, sleeps the sleep of the soldier, hero of Ridgeway, and the benefactor of his race, General John O'Neill. Surrounded by monumental tributes to private worth and evidence of public bereavement, the grave of the hero alone remains unmarked, as if indeed, the soldier having gone to his rest, his memory had been confined to oblivion. Whatever the circumstances that may have contributed to this seeming neglect, the fact is not one pleasant to contemplate nor credible to the patriotism of a people or the supporters of a cause to which he devoted his life. Gallant as a soldier upon the fields of his adopted country, enthusiastic and daring in the cause of his native land, and self-sacrificing in his labors for the amelioration of the condition of his countrymen, the name and memory of General John O'Neill should be inscribed upon the roll of Irish and Irish-American patriots whose name shall never die.

The Irish-American citizens of Omaha propose to raise upon the General's last resting place a monument which shall perpetuate alike the heroism of the patriot and the devotion of the public benefactor.... The organization proposes to raise the necessary funds as speedily as possible and to erect a suitable monument to the memory of our dead hero. Feeling however, that the duty and honor of commemorating our deceased countryman and brother belong not entirely to the Irish-Americans of Omaha and Nebraska, but that all of their race share in the admiration of the life and service of General O'Neill, they ask their countrymen throughout the United States to contribute, and all contributions will be promptly acknowledged.[17]

In less than a year, more than $1,500 had been raised and in August 1895, seventeen years after his death, a grand monument was installed. A magnificent fifteen-foot structure was dedicated to the memory of John Charles O'Neill of Drumgallan, and hopefully, some citizens of O'Neill City played a part. The O'Neill paper, at least, reprinted an article from the *Omaha Bee* on the occasion. The *Frontier* of August 15 reported:

Gen. O'Neill Monument
Tribute of Numerous Friends

For over seventeen years the grave of General John O'Neill in Holy Sepulchre cemetery in Omaha remained unmarked. By many this was regarded as a reflection on the patriotism of surviving friends, admirers, and associates in the movement for the betterment of his countrymen. But his memory was not forgotten nor was his grave neglected. Some time ago friends of the deceased in Omaha inaugurated a fund to procure a monument in all respects of his memory, and with the assistance of outside admirers their efforts were crowned with success. The monument stands at the head of the grave on the northern crest of the cemetery hill, and is a square column of polished granite, fifteen feet high. On the four squares are emblematic designs—the open hand, the Irish harp, the American eagle and stars, around these shamrock twins. On the main base the name "O'Neill" is carved in raised letters, and on the front of the monument is the following inscription[18]:

General John O'Neill
Hero of Ridgeway
Born in Ireland March 9, 1834
Died at Omaha, January 8, 1878
By nature a brave man, by principle a soldier of liberty.
He fought with distinction for his adopted country
and was ever ready to draw his sword for his native land.
to perpetuate his memory this monument was erected
by the Irish nationalists. God save Ireland.

The accompanying article summarized the general's life in great detail from the Civil War through the Fenian campaigns, and ended with his time in Nebraska.

General O'Neill is best remembered in Nebraska for his efforts in colonizing the state. More enduring than granite is the prosperous and progressive city in Holt County that he founded and bears his name. The best efforts of his later years were in the interest of the peace and prosperity of his countrymen. He labored zealously to draw them from the crowded cities to fertile lands, then to be had for the asking. Many acted on his advice and struggled through the hardships incident to pioneer farming. Scores of those pioneers are today rich in the world's goods, the ripened fruit of their energies directed by General John O'Neill.

In 1896, the general's status had even reached polite society. The Irish National Alliance was formed in Omaha, and membership was comprised of only the finest Irish Americans in the city and surrounding area. The name chosen was "The General John O'Neill Council." But anti–O'Neill feelings were still strong in O'Neill. John Hugh, the general's only surviving son, well respected both personally and professionally, married Catherine Donahue, a popular schoolteacher and daughter of a thriving Irish farmer. In 1895, seventeen years after O'Neill's early death, the *Frontier* reported announcement of the happy couple's wedding: "Young John O'Neill has bravely taken his father's place in supporting the family. He is a worthy son of a noble sire, and possesses a select library and is a great student of history. Spalding is proud to possess such a distinguished name." A wonderful public start for John Hugh and Margaret, but old grudges apparently couldn't be held back. The announcement cruelly added, "He is of course the son of General John O'Neill who did more for Ireland than he did for his family."[19]

Twenty-four years later, in October 1919, the Irish of Nebraska would see the future president of Ireland, Eamon De Valera, who was on a fundraising trek across the United States. De Valera had come to the U.S. in June, and stayed in America for a year and a half. He arrived in Omaha the evening of October 27, and gave a rousing speech at the new Creighton University gym. Four thousand enthusiastic Irish Americans cheered him on when he asked, "Do you accept the principle of self-determination?" After a loud agreement he continued, "Then how can you deny it to Ireland?" At the end of his lecture, he sounded like a young John O'Neill, telling his audience, "If England's empire were not the rotten thing it is at heart, it would not control the world."[20] Fifty-three years after Ridgeway the message remained similar to the general's, with only a new Irish herald.

Éamon de Valera, the future president of Ireland, unveiled the new dedication to the John O'Neill monument in October 1919 (Library of Congress).

The next morning the man known in Ireland as "The Long Fellow," toured a school and shook hands at the stockyards before going to Holy Sepulchre Cemetery, where for the second time in over twenty years, the monument to General John O'Neill was unveiled before two hundred beaming Irish Americans. Over the next eighteen months, De Valera would surpass only one other Irishman in American cities visited by train and audiences spoken to.

This rededication featured just one speech. Edward H. Whelan was now an Omaha lawyer, but one whose family lived in O'Neill City during the first decade of the twentieth century. Whelan would of course have heard both the praise and acrimony of local citizens regarding the town's founder. Whelan concluded his sincerest half hour oration with a key question, perhaps taking a verbal shot at the citizens of O'Neill, especially Fahy, who had rejected the general in 1889:

> Why is he here, and not in the town of O'Neill, which bears his name? Because I believe he would prefer to be here; for he lies among comrades and kindred spirits of the IRB men like Major McMahon, Thomas Tallant, Jeremiah Riordan and that noble Protestant Irish patriot, John Groves. I am sure that they are fit and congenial company for the gallant hero that lies among them. They it was who stood by him when a friend was a friend indeed. They cared for him in his last illness, interred him with honors as a soldier of the Republican army, and erected this magnificent token to his memory.
>
> The name of O'Neill will be long remembered in Nebraska as the name of a small town, but it will be only a name suggesting some indefinite Irish origin. The men who will remember General John O'Neill the longest will not think of him as a man who founded a colony. Any average man could do that. But only heroes do what O'Neill did on June 2, 1866, at Ridgeway. Only heroes lead forlorn hopes—heroes like Pearse, Plunkett, McDonough, McBride, Ashe—men who freely offer up their lives just to make the world think about the wrong of their country.[21]

Five years later in 1924 the town of O'Neill celebrated its 50th anniversary. In keeping with tradition, festivities were planned throughout the town. Track races, dances, and parades, including a stopover from the general's granddaughter, Ruth (O'Neill) Martin of San Diego, the last of the O'Neill family name in America. In early June, a visit by Jerry Howard, a prominent Omaha Irish American, resulted in the formation of another organization to move the general's body again back to O'Neill. The *Frontier* of June 13, 1924, ran headlines and a story:

> **The Burial Site Selected**
> **Many Prominent Irish Leaders To Be Here**
> **at Rededication on September 20th**
>
> The General John O'Neill association is the name of an organization perfected at O'Neill Sunday evening by prominent citizens for the purpose of removing from Omaha to O'Neill the remains of General O'Neill and the monument that marks his present resting place in Holy Sepulchre cemetery at Omaha. T.V. is president.... Neil Brennan is financial secretary. Brennan is the son of Gen. Neil P. Brennan, companion of General O'Neill in the colonizing of Holt County and the founding of O'Neill City.[22]

Golden, a past mayor of O'Neill City, was the owner of the town's largest hotel, the Golden House. Ironically, his future daughter-in-law, Lois Golden, was a direct descendant of Wilfred Francis Gaudrie, a French Canadian who fought in the Army of the British Commonwealth at Ridgeway, and as a reward was granted 160 acres in Ontario. The plan was to re-dedicate the monument in O'Neill on September 20, at the culmination of the town's 50th anniversary and the anniversary of Robert Emmett, the Irish martyr hanged by the British in 1803. Prominent Irish leaders from the entire country, including the Irish ambassador to the United States, were expected to attend.

The O'Neill memorial was to be erected in the center of the park that divided the Catholic Calvary Cemetery and the Protestant Prospect Hill Cemetery. The *Frontier* concluded the story, "The Grand Army of the Republic and the Loyal Legion will be invited to assist in the movement and the necessary funds will be raised by regular subscriptions of small amounts, that all may have a part. Jerry Howard of Omaha, was the first contributor with ten dollars."

The timing was serendipitous, as the *Frontier*, in the same June 13 issue, began running a huge six-part series on the founding of O'Neill from the general's pamphlet of 1876. The following week, Jerry Howard wrote a glowing review of his visit to O'Neill, which was printed in the *Frontier*: "I told my friends I never met with a more genial class of people than the 'present' residents of O'Neill; that my sojourn there was the most delightful and in every way satisfactory." After mentioning three dozen more citizens by name, Howard proclaimed the project "glorious," and said everyone connected with the organization were no doubt sterling Irish nationalists and that the entire population of O'Neill regardless of birth, race, or creed were in hearty accord with the movement. He ended the letter with an exaggeration all old Fenians would appreciate. "The re-dedication of the O'Neill monument to the memory of the hero of the Battle of Ridgeway will be the most historic event in the annals of Irish-American history."[23]

By early July Howard had written to the committee in O'Neill that if the project was ready by September 12, "there will be Irish men and women galore in O'Neill that day from eastern cities, also there will be delegations from Denver and Los Angeles."[24] But within a week, Howard received a letter in Omaha from the president of the committee, T.V. Golden, whose father had purchased a lot in O'Neill City from the General in 1876. He informed Howard that "all the members of the organization, including myself, feel there will be opposition to transferring the remains and monument of General John O'Neill,"[25] apparently asking Howard, at the very least, to postpone the project. In 1952, twenty-five years after that meeting, senior citizen J.B. Donahue of O'Neill remembered "some of the Irish people here saying, they wouldn't give a dime."[26] The committee soon disbanded, and from July until the date of the expected relocation expired in September, Howard wrote a series of letters to the O'Neill *Frontier* castigating the decision to once again leave O'Neill in Omaha, ending his last missive with "whoever is obstructing this national project ... will be known and held up to public ridicule and scorn of the entire Irish Race." John O'Neill still rests in Omaha, with his son Eugene and grandson John Francis O'Neill, who died in 1929 at age thirty-three. Fifty years later, it seems, the Irish in O'Neill hadn't forgotten or forgiven. In 1969, Governor Norbert Tiemann of Nebraska flew into O'Neill, stayed at the Golden Hotel, and, after a parade, proclaimed the city of O'Neill to be the Irish capital of Nebraska, a title it still claims.

Epilogue

He had his credit for it; not much money, for he was a bad man at business; not much worldly comfort, beyond the fragrance of poteen punch, or the beauty of rivers and mountains and green fields, or the love and contentment around his own hearth. But he had praise from great men who were many, and from some he had blame and bitter words.—Anonymous

The story of any emigrant running from famine, genocide, or war can never be told alone. There were no singular life stories emanating from Armenia in 1915; there are no isolated memories from Kosovo in 1999; and there are certainly few individual histories evolving from the Great Hunger in Ireland. Layers upon layers infect us all, and so the story of John Charles O'Neill cannot end with his life and death alone. No one person owns history, and thus any discussion of John O'Neill must involve that of his wife, Mary Ann Crow. After the general's burial the widow Mary Ann O'Neill was left alone in O'Neill with three young children, eerily similar to Catherine O'Neill's abandonment forty-four years before in Ireland. She was alone and living in the midst of settlers who either "excessively worshipped" or, "through indifference, [were] vehement in their dislike" of her late husband.[1] Mary Ann, whose personal life began in tragedy in San Francisco, had followed her lover back and forth across the United States. Her only remaining relations, the Macklins and O'Neills, were now 1,400 miles away in Elizabeth, New Jersey. Neither widow O'Neill nor the children would never see them again. Less than a year after his uncle's death, John J. O'Neill left Omaha and returned to a private practice as an engineer in New Jersey, never to return to Nebraska. Nonetheless the story of the O'Neills in northern Nebraska had just begun.

There is little doubt that the general was broke when he met Fahy in 1873, and the arrangement O'Neill made with him helped set the foundation to generate cash on his own developments, which had much potential. But along came grasshoppers (even to his son's own garden) and negative press from the understandably disillusioned early settlers that made his job very difficult.

The first two years the general barely broke even in his occupation as a realtor, traveling, lecturing, and cajoling Irish all over the country without gaining a dime for his efforts from the colonists. Then in 1876, he apparently learned that it was better to buy cheap farm or railroad land, survey it himself (through his nephew John J. O'Neill), and avoid running all over the country to drum up sales, saving travel and hotel costs from Michigan to Maine.

Though John O'Neill spent his Nebraska years just above the poverty line, at the time of his early death recent research has discovered that, approaching age forty, O'Neill was indeed cash poor, but land rich. In four years, the general had acquired, through purchase, gifts, and promises, more than 236 lots throughout Holt and Greeley counties.[2]

Following the abandonment of many of the third group of colonists in 1876 after the first major grasshopper scourge, O'Neill found himself in need of cash. His friend storekeeper Patrick Haggerty allowed him to run a monthly tab for the family, but he was usually five months in arrears. He held on to most of his land, selling little until October 1877. O'Neill was beginning to understand the West and how to make a living from it while at the same time keeping his promise to his beloved Irish. He had a fine development plan but was getting them done on a shoestring budget.

Just when prospects were looking up, in May 1877 the general became sick with asthma as well as pleurisy, both of which kept him housebound and incapacitated for almost five months. Finally unable to hold on to his growing land purchases, he was forced to conduct a fire sale in October, and in November 1877 he was stricken with a stroke. The combination of creditors banging at the door and illness once again set the O'Neills back excessively, almost to the point of bankruptcy. Compounding matters, the general had kept Mary Ann completely in the dark about business matters, and with the general incapacitated in the hospital at Omaha, the O'Neill finances were at a crucial crossroads.

It is even more admirable that O'Neill was able to sell as many lots as he did at decent prices. But when he became sick, he was forced to sacrifice properties in O'Neill City and Greeley County (Spalding) at far below market value just to survive. In October 1877, there was more or less a last, sad desperation sale, either because of creditors or the possibility that John knew his time on earth was limited, and thus he cleaned things up financially for Mary Ann and the children.

Either way, when O'Neill died in January 1878, Mary Ann suddenly discovered her husband had made John Nightengale his legal administrator. She was still left with 124 lots spread across two counties, but Nightengale handled it all. Nightengale was a capable colonist who helped plat the town of Atkinson and was trusted by the general to handle his financial matters.

Mary Ann would remarry, by all accounts, a nice, gentle farmer and Civil War veteran named James Coughlin, and they remained in O'Neill City until he died in 1895. The week before Mary Ann married Coughlin, there was notice of a benefit in Omaha. The *Columbus Journal* reported: "A raffle for a very handsome silver mounted revolver for the benefit of General John O'Neill will take place Thanksgiving Day in Omaha. Ticket will be 50 cents."[3]

Executor Nightengale lived in Atkinson twenty miles away, a difficult commute in nineteenth-century Nebraska. In addition to being Mary Ann's administrator, Nightengale primarily was a farmer, and his work with the O'Neill estate would drag on for more than a decade, made more difficult by the distance between them. Nightengale was a friend of O'Neill's and educated, but not an attorney. The O'Neill estate was a mess, and the choice of Nightengale as executor compounded the situation. Since Mary Ann had no sense of what the general was involved with, there was nobody for Nightengale to confer with about debts, ownership, or deals John may have been preparing for the future. Mary Ann was frustrated and from 1879 to 1889 the complications dragged on interminably. Mary Ann and James Coughlin needed money, but selling land during the decade of 1880 was a buyer's market, and in addition to the three O'Neill children, Mary Ann and James had three of their own. Genevieve, Grace, and Frank would be born in O'Neill and, though Frank would not survive his father, it still left Mary Ann with five children. In the end, Mary Ann was nickeled and dimed, money occasionally appearing, but never enough, and she eventually blamed Nightengale. She sued and won $600 ($12,000 today) in 1889, but it was too little too late.

What then, do we remember of John C. O'Neill, the little boy left in Drumgallan without a father in 1836? Certainly his irrepressible fighting spirit in the Civil War, and his courageous and extreme willingness to fight for the freedom of his native land. His hatred of England, which accompanied him to Elizabeth in 1848, was demonstrative. After a brilliant career in the Civil War, O'Neill became the face of Irish nationalism in America, the most visible, admired, and popular leader whose life mirrored the rise and fall of the very organization he managed.

O'Neill possessed a civilized military code of conduct generally unknown to the majority of recognized Irish American nationalists, which even his most outspoken critics have admired. He decried acts of violence perpetrated against civilians and was against bombing campaigns and assassinations, which were vigorously propagated by historical figures like O'Donovan Rossa, John Mitchel, Jerome J. Collins, and Alexander Sullivan of Chicago.

There is little doubt that O'Neill at times behaved immaturely during his Fenian career, which can be traced at least indirectly to misrepresenting his age upon enlistment in the army at nineteen, not twenty-three. For the remainder of his meteoric rise, the general was always considered young, but was unable to admit for political reasons his true age. This caused serious miscalculations following Ridgeway. When the Brotherhood made John the organization president, O'Neill was just thirty, and the executives who pushed him into leadership believed he was a very youthful thirty-four. O'Neill was without question vigorously obsessive and the energy he showed from the time he landed in Elizabeth in 1848 never wavered. The general was a natural leader and "born soldier," but upon accepting the mantle of the Brotherhood presidency, he became obstinate and unbending, demanding total loyalty, all signs of unseasoned maturity.[4] O'Neill showed time after time he was utterly fearless, but his dissociative personality from being left in Ireland at age two left him easily angered, impulsive, and often affectionless. Had he been blessed with a few more years of experience before his instant celebrity, General John O'Neill may be remembered today as more than just a cult figure of nineteenth century Irish nationalism.

O'Neill's intellect was superb, and is stunning when considering his background. He arrived in America at age eleven. In rural Monaghan, his grandfather would not let him attend the fledgling national schools, as he considered them pro–English, and though there are rumors he was tutored, his primary education also coincided with the Famine, always an impediment. In Elizabeth, O'Neill, by his own admission, attended school for one year. The handsome youngster's penmanship, grammar, and sentence structure would make a current college graduate blush, and he published long tracts on everything from tracking Indian cattle rustlers, sea voyages through Panama, and Irish history. Professing to be a poor speaker, O'Neill captivated crowds for over a decade throughout the country, both in Irish and English. He operated a bookstore before he was eighteen, and his first job after the Civil War saw him as a very successful national claims agent and military attorney at age twenty-eight.

The general was a man of action and had many friendships, but apparently few true friends. He trusted people too easily and was often disappointed or betrayed by them—Henri Le Caron with the Fenians, O'Donoghue in Pembina, and Patrick Fahy in Nebraska to name just three. O'Neill was a risk taker, a salesman, and a gambler—of war, Fenianism, politics, colonization. John was always a big-picture leader, seeing long-term potential; he was very focused but had no patience for detail. He was willing to take losses in the short run—in the army, the Brotherhood, Pembina, Nebraska—without becoming discouraged.

Was O'Neill rash, stubborn, a poor businessman, and prone to a drink? No doubt. But the issue of General John O'Neill as an alcoholic has plagued his memory unfairly. In the nineteenth century, it was a daily part of life, but certainly not as much as the eighteenth century when people drank in the morning, during the day, and at night. All the players in the O'Neill history had a history of imbibing. President U.S. Grant had a well-established problem, as did General Thomas F. Meagher, which may have killed him when he disappeared off a boat into the Missouri River. Andrew Johnson was drunk at his swearing as Vice President in 1864, when Lincoln, thoroughly embarrassed, forgave him, saying, "It has been a severe lesson for Andy, but I don't think he will do it again."[5] He did, of course. John A. MacDonald of Canada, the brilliant architect of Canadian nationalism during the Fenian period, was the most notorious alcoholic in Canadian political history. MacDonald, as Prime Minister, once failed to appear in public for ten days, a bender that shocked even Canadians, who were all aware of his weakness. For decades, when MacDonald was not well, he was referred to as "off again."[6] One of MacDonald's favorite drinking pals was the Irish poet, politician, and legitimate Irish legend Thomas D'Arcy McGee, who was found one morning curled up under his desk at the *Ottawa Citizen*. MacDonald chastised his friend, saying, "Look here McGee, this Cabinet can't afford two drunkards, and I'm not quitting."[7] There is, however, too much subliminal mention to suggest that O'Neill was a teetotaler, but he was not in the class of any of the above mentioned national figures, and his memory should not be lessened by the charge he was. There certainly has been a well-documented history of dislike of the General in O'Neill City, but not one person in fifty years that twice denied him a reburial in the town ever mentioned his abuse of *usice beatha*, the Irish "water of life."

But it is difficult to judge O'Neill. All leading Irish nationalists and Fenians were dedicated beyond reason, ruthless and tough, especially with each other. Most bankrupted themselves in search of their idealistic dreams. The general died in poverty, but so too did John O'Mahony, John Devoy, William Randall Roberts, Michael Davitt, and James Stephens. Nonetheless, separating myth from reality is often difficult. The American sometimes regarded as the epitome of a legendary tough cowboy, Irish American John Wayne, is often misrepresented as a national icon. Like O'Neill, Wayne was idolized because of his perceived military persona, and his toughness as the great westerner on the Hollywood screen. Bestselling author William Manchester, an ex–Marine, wrote of meeting Wayne in the Aiea Heights Naval Hospital in Hawaii after Okinawa, the longest battle of World War II. Wayne appeared dressed as a cowboy and was met first with total silence by the most gravely wounded Marines, followed by unanimous booing, before finally being escorted out.[8] Pete Hamill, one of America's greatest chroniclers, wrote in his obituary of the star, "John Wayne was not a hero. John Wayne was an actor who played heroes."[9] The Marines understood, while much of America still does not.

All nations suffer similar complications. O'Neill would fit the following description of a certified and recognized Irish hero. "He had the opportunity to construct his own movement, and become something bigger than a nationalist leader. Instead he was to face disappointment and humiliation, betrayed by a personality that left him endemically quarrelsome, and violently averse to criticism."[10] Only this wasn't John O'Neill, but James Larkin (1876–1947). "Big Jim," who has had hundreds of studies and books written about him, is one of the greatest figures in Irish labor history, and still a deserved central figure in Irish history. But his most important biographer, Donal Nevin, could not have painted a better picture if his subject was General John O'Neill.

Padraig Pearse was deep in debt when he died, his passing mourned by few but respected by many, and considered a sentimental egoist who was convinced of the necessity of blood sacrifice, very arrogant, and impatient for rebellion—again a description that could be of John Charles O'Neill. But Pearse was seen by many to be the embodiment of the 1916 Easter Rebellion. Pearse, a scholar chosen to be the spokesman for the rising, saw his fame spread like wildfire after 1920, four years after his execution by the British Army. Pearse's popularity spread rapidly following the civil war, especially by teachers searching for role models for Irish youngsters. Legends are often created afterwards, not just in Nebraska.[11]

John O'Neill was an intractably gifted man with an indomitable spirit whose life force has been felt across the North American continent, but a paradox, it is true. There are few stranger figures in the history of Irish nationalism in America. He invaded Canada—or tried to—three times, at least a minor reason Canada became a free land. He preached Nebraska colonization, but spent little precious time there, and came close, much too often, to abandonment of his wife and children. He may have drunk too much at the end, but he preached temperance to the colonizers. All agreed the general was ego driven, but none doubted his sincerity. He was a devout Catholic, though the Church condemned the organization he led. O'Neill loved his family and at least two of his young nephews, who accompanied their uncle a thousand miles away from home. Yet he was at serious odds with his only brother and uncle, and perhaps others in Elizabeth. Like so many other Irish nationalists in America, O'Neill had no family connections or wealth, and was under immense pressure to provide strong leadership.

The general was a traveling book salesman at sixteen, the owner of his own bookstore at eighteen, and a copious writer his whole life, yet there remains only three surviving letters (just one of which is to his family) despite the fact that his descendants have lovingly saved every scrap of material available for more than a hundred years. O'Neill's life intertwined like a pretzel with three presidents who knew him personally in the short space of five years. Andrew Johnson from Tennessee was a friend before his presidency but later a political enemy; Ulysses S. Grant had him arrested at Ridgeway before his election as president yet pardoned the general in a Vermont jail while president in 1870; and Grover Cleveland, a two-term president after O'Neill's death, served as the general's defense mentor for Fenians in Buffalo and by proxy for O'Neill in Eccles Hill.

The O'Neill legacy is of course the town he founded, now known as the Irish Capital of Nebraska.[12] Much is still made locally of General John O'Neill, with some past and current citizens referring to him in almost worshipful tones. Others, not so much. The town today might even consider its own past on St. Patrick's Day, perhaps with a third vote to bring its founder back home.

O'Neill was, in short, enigmatic to the core, but he was never mediocre, and he surely was not the first Irish patriot to fail. The inscrutable Irishman who has been relegated to the shadows of Irish and American history may best be summed up by historian Gerald Noonan: "O'Neill's mistakes were big ones; his accomplishments not less. The man O'Neill also grew, and much of what he was and became should not only be admired, but also imitated."[13] In the case of Irish American John C. O'Neill, maybe the rest should be acknowledged both in America and Ireland, and forgiven as well.

The story of General John O'Neill is incomplete, however, as was so often the case with first generation immigrant families, until the story of his second boat family became known. Argument may be made as to the greatest legacy of John O'Neill—Fenian revolutionary nationalist or Irish American colonizer—but his most enduring gift may indeed rest elsewhere. Leaving Mary Ann a widow at thirty-six with three young children, the history of the general's family is one of survival, loss, and eventual peace, prosperity, and honor far away from frontier Nebraska. Just short of two years after John died Mary Ann, with three young children, married Irishman James Coughlin in her home in O'Neill in 1879. The thirty-eight-year-old James was also a Civil War veteran who found his way to Nebraska from New York. Mary Ann and James would raise two daughters of their own, Genevieve and Grace, along with a son Frank. For ten years Mary Ann struggled to settle the estate of the general with a decent but overmatched executor, John Nightengale. Finally in 1890 the decade-long battle was settled and Mary Ann moved on to her next fight, the U.S. Pension Bureau. Like the conflict with Nightengale, it would go on for years.

In 1891 Mary Ann filed a petition as the widow of John C. O'Neill of the 5th Indiana Cavalry. In 1890 the Dependent Pension Amendment was passed, allowing any veteran of the war who had served honorably (or their widows) to qualify for a pension if at some time he had been disabled from manual labor, even if it was not war related. Mary Ann filed for a monthly lifetime check, saying that John O'Neill had contracted asthma as a result of his years with the cavalry, which is accurate, and been wounded twice.[14]

Filing a first petition more than twenty-five years after the war ended created a massive federal bureaucracy, as each case had to prove injuries, illnesses, and family histories, and it obviously was more difficult for a widow to gather and prove records over a quarter century time period.

Mary Ann began the process as Mary Ann Coughlin, and had to show proof of her first marriage. She sent to St. Mary's Church in Elizabeth, New Jersey, for records, and also asked young John J. O'Neill, then living in East Orange, New Jersey, and the general's sister Mary O'Neill in Elizabeth for letters as witnesses to the 1864 marriage, evidence that the O'Neills of Nebraska and Elizabeth had stayed in written contact after the general's death.

In this first petition, Mary Ann listed her daughters as Kate instead of Katherine and Mary instead of Mary Ella. This caused confusion in Washington and she was forced to explain these discrepancies by obtaining the children's birth records in Omaha, Nashville, and Washington, all of which went back years and took much time to procure. Mary Ann even tracked down the physician who had attended the general when he died in Omaha, as well as two former friends from the war. After some seven years, her pension request was denied.

James Coughlin and son Frank died in O'Neill in 1894, leaving Mary Ann the mother of five, with John Hugh (31) and Mary Ellen (Mamie) both recently married. Katherine (21) was living with Mary Ann and her two-step sisters, Genevieve (13) and Grace Coughlin (11). During this entire decade Mary Ann had fought the U.S. Pension Bureau and John Nightengale, the administrator of the general's estate, both of which had her interests at heart, but produced little or no results. When James died, Mary Ann, now forty-nine, moved to Spalding, where several of the children had relocated. In February 1895, Mary Ann married a third time to Henry Hads, another Civil War veteran who had homesteaded in Nebraska. Mary Ann and Henry lived comfortably in Elgin, Wheeler County, fifty miles southeast of O'Neill. Mary Ann, who had sacrificed so much, died in 1902 surrounded by her family after thirty years in Nebraska. and became the first Catholic buried in the new St. Boniface Cemetery in Elgin, Nebraska. The *Neligh Leader* ran her obituary:

> Mrs. H.J. Hads of Elgin, died at her home last Thursday morning, of cancer of the stomach, from which she had been a constant sufferer for several months past. The funeral was held at Elgin at ten o'clock am, on Friday. Her children were all at her bedside before she departed including J.H. O'Neill, Mrs. Mamie Steele, and Miss Eva Coughlin of Spalding, Miss Grace Coughlin of Elgin, and Mrs. R.J. Dwyer of Butte, Montana. The life of the deceased has been an eventful one. She was born in Australia, came to California early in childhood, and has traveled extensively since that time. Soon after the war she married General John O'Neill, who became distinguished as a leader of the Fenian raids into Canada, and who now has a monument erected in his honor at Omaha, and also a town named after him in the northern part of the state. Some time after Mr. O'Neill's death she was again married to Mr. James Coughlin of O'Neill. After the latter's

death she moved with her family from O'Neill to Fullerton, and later to Spalding. Here she was married to Henry Hads, who now survives her, and the two made their home at Elgin for the past five years. The deceased leaves many friends, and the sympathy of our people is especially directed toward the bereaved children who live in our midst.[15]

Mary Ann was fifty-eight years old, and every bit as heroic as her late husband. She is living proof of the enigmatic and emblematic Irish diaspora, whose unfortunate story is today often unknown, forgotten even among her own remaining family. The Irish Americans today stand upon her shoulders every bit as much as they do her more famous, youthful husband, John Charles O'Neill.

Mary Ann's children, raised by their stepfather James Coughlin, fared better, a brutal fact of most immigrants nationwide. John Hugh O'Neill, the only son of General John O'Neill, married Margaret Donahue in 1895. John Hugh was everything his father was and wasn't—smart, energetic, and quietly ambitious with very little ego. John Hugh played the piano, cultivated a large library, and was a very honest and sharp businessman, running an apothecary shop. It helped, like so many second-generation immigrants, that economics improved along with the attitude toward the second boat Irish. John Hugh conducted a thriving business while hundreds of other similar merchants failed. "He was conservative, honest and straightforward, and a good neighbor, warm friend, and model citizen."[16]

After his mother died in 1902, John and wife Margaret were well enough off to consider becoming third boat Irish. John took his son John F. O'Neill on a month-long journey to New York, Ireland, and London, while Margaret toured the west coast in Washington, Oregon, and California.

It had been thirty years since any of the general's family had been east of the Mississippi. John Hugh and son traveled to New York by train before the two-week ocean voyage to Ireland. There is no record that John reached out to visit any Macklin or O'Neill cousins in Elizabeth, though it would be surprising if his Uncle John J. O'Neill, living just miles away, was unaware of the trip.

John Hugh's trip to Ireland was, sadly, close but no cigar. He did all the touristy things many still do today, kissing the Blarney Stone, circling the Ring of Kerry, and observing the churches in Dublin. To his everlasting O'Neill credit, he took a jaunting car from Dublin to Monaghan, but he believed the O'Neills were from Drumgallon in County Armagh, not nearby Drumgallan in County Monaghan. John Hugh thus missed his home place by just a few miles, and then continued on to Belfast before going to London. He never got to meet any true relations that remained and the Irish census of 1901 showed Macklins and O'Neills that were indeed in Clontibret parish. John Hugh had become, like the O'Neills in New Jersey, an American in waiting, while his father, the general, had always remained Irish.

After his return to Nebraska, John Hugh received a letter from an Irish cousin, Edward Macklin, who had discovered too late that John Hugh was in Monaghan. Edward, in his sixties, still resided on what was once O'Neill family property in Fintully townland. Edward said, "There are still to be seen in Drumgallan parts of your father's birthplace, so if you come again I know you would be delighted to see what remains to be seen of your old house." The site Edward referred to is now just a tillage field. Whether John Hugh replied is unknown, but once back from Ireland, the last male O'Neill family packed their bags and relocated to San Diego, California.

John Hugh and Margaret also had one son, John Francis O'Neill, and three daughters, Helen, Grace, and Martha Ruth, known as Ruth. John Hugh became even more successful in San Diego, and like the O'Neills of Elizabeth, he and his family would never leave their adopted city. Ruth, the only O'Neill not born in Nebraska, never married, but all three sisters and their families became parishioners of Our Lady of Angels in downtown San Diego. In truth, these O'Neills helped establish that Catholic Church in San Diego, much as John's mother and uncle had done in Elizabeth, New Jersey.

Early death, however, could never fully escape the O'Neills, especially the general's three grandsons. In 1900 Mamie had become the widow Mary Steele, and was living with her brother John's family in Spalding, along with her two sons, Kennedy Donald, age five, and Sam O'Neill Steele, age four. When John moved his family to San Diego in 1905, only ten-year-old Donald went with them. After Mamie O'Neill Steele's death of peritonitis in 1907 at age thirty-six, a local Spalding family named Naughton adopted young Sam at age nine but he didn't stay long. In 1917, this grandson of General O'Neill's roamed the Midwest like his grandfather, working railroad construction in St. Paul, Minnesota; in 1920, he was still single and working in Memphis; and in 1930, Sam was constructing railroad ties in Colbert County, Alabama. He would die alone in Pittsburg in 1951 from fumes of an overloaded hotplate, an enigmatic figure much like his grandfather.

Kitty O'Neill married Richard Dwyer of O'Neill, and had two sons, Jerald and Harold. Kitty and Richard divorced, and she traveled north to Butte, Montana, leaving the boys with Richard. She married Frank Tipton in Montana before dying a widow in the O'Neill compound of San Diego in 1943 at age sixty-eight.

John Francis O'Neill, the third and last O'Neill west of New Jersey, inherited his grandfather's nomadic genes like his cousin Sam Steele, and by the age of nineteen left San Diego and was in Arizona working as a miner in 1917. He even looked like the general, tall and slender, with dark black hair and brown hazel eyes. In 1918, John joined the U.S. Army, married, and settled in Texas. His grandfather would no doubt have mixed feelings, loving the young man's desire to fight for his country, while more than a little upset that he would be fighting to protect England. If the young Lieutenant O'Neill were truly like his grandfather, he wouldn't have paid the general any mind. After the war John F. O'Neill died at thirty-three in Kansas City in 1929, and was appropriately buried in Omaha with his grandfather. John Hugh, the general's only son, born in Nashville just months before Ridgeway, died in San Diego in 1947 at seventy-three, having established his own wonderful O'Neill legacy in Southern California. John Hugh was the last of the Drumgallan O'Neills in the United States.

Though John Hugh's only son died young, his three daughters, the grand-daughters of the general, have created a marvelous Irish American birthright of their own. The oldest, Helen, married Nicholas Martin in San Diego and had five extremely successful children, including a lawyer, a nun, a teacher, and two respected businessmen. Both Helen and her husband Nicholas were recipients of Papal awards in 1943. Though Helen would die at ninety-four in 1991, her spirit, humanitarianism, and faith live on through her large extended family.

Helen's sister Grace was no less a success, and definitely possessed some of the general's nomadic genes. In 1925 Grace married Hans Nansen in Oslo, Norway, whom she met in California when he was visiting relatives. During World War II Mr. Nansen became a spokesman for the International Red Cross but when the Germans invaded Norway Grace and Hans became fugitives before finally escaping to San Diego.

After the war Grace O'Neill Nansen built the most extensive library based on the life and accomplishments of her husband's uncle, noted polar explorer Freidjet Nansen, who received the Nobel Peace Prize in 1922 for his work in repatriating World War I prisoners of war and creating a relief program for Russians. The foundation, the Nansen International Office of Refugees, was named after him and received the Nobel Peace Prize as well in 1938. Like Helen, Grace's courage and civic responsibility is still seen in the San Diego area, long after her death in San Diego in 1988 at age eighty-nine.

Ironically, the memory of the Clontibret-born freedom fighter John O'Neill was kept alive best by the only O'Neill born in California, where John and Mary Ann first met. Martha Ruth, always known as Ruth, collected, preserved, and spread the story of the general her whole unmarried life. She traveled over several decades to O'Neill, Nebraska, and was even found in Monaghan, Ireland, at the head of a parade honoring her grandfather late in her life before dying in 1993 at age ninety. She was the keeper of the flame of John Charles O'Neill. The story of O'Neill and the girl he met in a candy store had come full circle twice. General John O'Neill attempted to fill the west with Irish, only to see his children push it all the way to the sea and fulfill the dream of Irish migration, becoming a great American family.

Appendix A:
1876 O'Neill Manifesto

Philadelphia, Pa.
December 8, 1876

Fellow Countrymen:

It is now a little over eleven years since I first joined the Fenian Brotherhood. I then believed and have had no reason to change my opinion that there was a splendid opportunity for the Irish people in America to strike a fatal blow at our ancient enemy England. With an army of trained and disciplined soldiers of our own race fresh from the battlefields of the recent war not only willing but anxious to embark in the movement, with thousands of Americans and men of other nationalities ready to join us, with some of the ablest generals of America who had offered their services to command, with the greater portion of the American people both north and south in sympathy with and willing to assist us, with the government at Washington disposed to wink at the movement, with nothing but an imaginary line between us and that hated red flag which represents the English Government, I confidentially believed that one of the best opportunities ever presented to an oppressed people to strike for their freedom had been placed within our reach. But unfortunately for Ireland the ancient curse of our race, disunion, which it has ever been the policy of England to encourage, followed us across the Atlantic, and the opportunity which should have found us organized, united and determined upon a common platform found us quarrelling amongst ourselves, and fritting away our strength on non-essentials until the opportunity had passed. While a fragment of the Irish race were willing to risk their lives in striking a blow for the old land and the great bulk of our people were not ready, and some of them I fear will never be ready. They can talk patriotically enough but when it comes to practical work they prefer to talk a little more. The first attempt upon Canada in 1866 failed because the

Irish people in America were not ready or willing to take advantage of the splendid opportunity, which then presented itself.

After the failure of the first movement some of those who had been engaged in it were willing to abandon the cause and thereby virtually acknowledge that they were whipped. Such men should never have embarked in a revolutionary movement or induced others to do so. They are not made of the stuff out of which patriots are molded. Marching up Broadway in New York or any other city in the United States on St. Patrick's Day would suit them much better than marching to meet the enemy in hostile array and drawing the corks of champagne bottles at St. Patrick's night suppers would be more congenial work than drawing the fire of the red coats on the battle field. There were others, however, who believed in making another effort— men who were not willing to acknowledge defeat, they who thought that the cause for which so many martyrs had perished (and which had been transmitted to us by our forefathers) was worthy of greater sacrifices than any of us had yet made. (And here let me say that although we professed to be following in the footsteps of the patriots who had gone before us, yet our sacrifices and sufferings were but little indeed when compared with theirs.) I was one of those who believed in making another effort and under the most solemn pledges and assurances of assistance and cooperation was induced to accept the Presidency of the organization, and for nearly two years and a half with others I worked incessantly night and day to prepare for a second attempt. Finally the time arrived when I was satisfied that our arrangements were as complete as we could expect to make them and at the same time to keep up the morale of the organization, for after various disappointments the members, particularly the military men, were becoming impatient.

Demoralization began to set in and I am convinced that the longer we waited the weaker we would become and the better prepared the Enemy would be to meet us. I therefore insisted upon carrying out the pledges which we had repeatedly made to the people to commence the fight. I was well aware that our preparations were not such as would enable us unsupported to continue the struggle with the enemy for any length of time but all I expected of the Fenian organization was to furnish the nucleus of an army with which to commence the work, take up a position in the enemy's country, no matter where, and hold it for a short time. This being done I had no doubt but that millions of our race in the United States would come to our assistance promptly and with enthusiasm. A few thousand men properly handled were all that was necessary for the start and to convince the world that we were in earnest.

It is not my intention at present to enter into the details of the cause of the trouble between myself and the Senate of the Fenian organization, for this would require a good sized volume which has yet to be written. The reason given by the Senate for opposing the movement upon Canada was that we were not prepared for it. Of course they assumed that they were more competent to judge of this matter than I was but the true cause of the trouble was that I believed, and I had good reason for the belief, that the Senate or at least the controlling power in that body had no intention of fighting at all. It was not until I was fully satisfied on this point that I decided to act on my own judgment and independently of the Senate. I saw that many of the members of that body were much more concerned about advancing their own interests politically than they were about the freedom of Ireland and were using myself and the organization over which I presided, so far as they could do so, simply to serve their own personal ends and aims. They could well afford to wait for an indefinitive [sic] period but the honest earnest men of the organization who had everything to lose and nothing to gain by delay were differently situated. Very few of the Senators were of an earthly account in building up or keeping the organization together. Many of them indeed were dead weights to carry. In nearly every place I visited where one of them resided I found the organization completely demoralized and the members loud in their complaints against them, yet as an engine for tearing them down and destroying they were all powerful, and the fact that I had been associated with them so long gave them the power to seriously injure me when it suited their purpose to do so.

Previous to ordering the men to the front for the second attempt upon Canada in 1870 I had every assurance and as full promises as any man can ever have that I would be supported, but the actions of the Senate and their false statements by letters, circulars, and personal appeals had the desired effect and the members of the organization were thrown into confusion and hesitated and delayed until it was too late. The Senators and their friends had proclaimed that the movement would be a failure and in order to make their word good did everything in their power to make it so. If one fourth of the men who had previously pledged themselves to obey my orders had only done so and had been on the border in time to meet me—no man can say that I ordered him to the front and stayed behind myself, for I was there with the first—then we could have taken up a position on the other side of the line and got our arms and ammunition across and there held our own until a sufficient number had joined us to justify an advance on the enemy. But the men did not come up in time and the movement failed and I had to bear the blame. Now, so far as I am personally concerned I have never admitted and don't now admit that I failed in anything I undertook in connection with the Fenian organization. I did not undertake to do all the work myself and it is unjust for others to blame me for their own failures. I did all that any man had a right to expect of me.

Immediately, after getting out of prison in the fall of 1870, in conjunction with others, I commenced making arrangements for yet another movement against England, which was inaugurated in the fall of 1871 in the Red River Country of British North America north of the state of Minnesota and the Territory of Dakota. I have always believed in striking at England wherever we could reach her, and wherever the English flag floats and the English government is recognized and there are English soldiers in arms to defend the flag and maintain the government I hold that the Irish people, particularly the Irish exiles whom her oppressive laws have driven from their native land, have a right to go there and make war on England. No doubt she would much prefer having them make the attempt nearer home where she could more readily concentrate her forces and crush them out, but it is high time that Irish patriots who claim to be revolutionists should learn to act not as England desired but in the way best calculated to serve their own purpose. If we could meet England at a disadvantage at the North Pole, that in my judgment would be the best place to strike her. There is no spot of earth on the habitable globe where I would rather fight England than on Irish soil but if it is not practicable to fight her there than I am in favor of fighting her wherever we can reach her.

There is a long line of British frontier between Nova Scotia and Vancouver's Island, with the Atlantic and Pacific oceans as an outlet, and there are millions of the Irish race in the United States from whom to recruit an army and man privateers to prey on British commerce. I imagine that if Hugh O'Neill or Owen Roe, Patrick Sarsfield, Wolfe Tone, Lord Edward Fitzgerald or Robert Emmet were living in America today it would not be long before an Irish army would be encamped on British soil with the green flag floating over it. Fellow countrymen, there is not one of you, I know, who does not feel a pride in the achievements of these heroes of the past, but are you on whom devolves the responsibility of defending the cause for which these patriots fought and bled and died ready to perform your duty to Mother Ireland as they performed theirs? If so, England can soon be made to tremble for her North American possessions and her commerce on the high seas.

The failure of the movement in the Red River Country was caused by a mere accident. The boundary line between the United States and British North America as originally surveyed was supposed to be on the 49th parallel, and directly north of this line the British Custom House and the Hudson Bay Company's Fort are located. But subsequent observations made by a United States Engineer officer while stationed at Fort Pembina led to the discovery that the boundary line had not been correctly located and that the British Custom House and Hudson Bay Company's Fort were on American soil. This fact, however, was not generally known and I was not aware of it until too late.

We took possession of the Custom House and the Fort and had occupied them as a vantage ground but a short time when Colonel Wheaton of the United States Army with his command crossed over after us. The Colonel, who was in command at Fort Pembina, a frontier outpost of this government located a short distance from where we crossed the line, being in sympathy with the British government and willing to do England's dirty work, took advantage of the information which he possessed in reference to the boundary line to interfere with us and in doing so acted without authority either from his Department Commander or from the Government of Washington. He is not likely to receive a gold medal from Congress for his exploit on that occasion. We either had to fight or surrender and while we were unwilling to surrender, for we felt that Colonel Wheaton had no right to interfere with us, yet so long as there was any doubt about the boundary line we did not wish to offer resistance, which we could have done successfully as we had more men than he had and besides had the advantage of being inside a stockade.

The correct boundary line has since been established by a joint commission appointed by both governments, the United States and Great Britain, and hereafter no Irish revolutionary body need mistake the territory of the United States for that of Ireland's enemy. I could not without compromising others and exposing my future plans enter into any explanations of the many advantages of this movement. Suffice it to say that I regard it as the most practical and easy of accomplishment of any of the movements in which I have been engaged, and the ultimate result equally as certain.

Perhaps it ought not to be thought strange if, after participating in three different failures inside of five years and after being vilified and slandered with a persistent villainy by men who very unjustly blamed me for their own shortcomings, and feeling keenly the injustice done me, I had abandoned the cause, but no such thought ever entered my mind. I did not join the Fenian organization for the purpose of gaining the applause of men, but simply to discharge a duty which I felt incumbent upon me in common with all other Irishmen who desired to see their native land free and who were willing to assist in accomplishing that much desired result.

It is true that for more than six and a half years I have taken no active part with any Irish national organization, but it by no means follows that I have ceased working or abandoned the cause. I have studiously avoided active or public work for two reasons—first, to recruit my health and to replenish my exchequer, both of which were seriously impaired by my connection with the Fenian organization, secondly because I desired to leave the field clear for those everlasting growlers, so called patriots, who were so loud in their denunciations of my every act while I was officially connected with the organization, and to give them a chance of showing to the Irish people how much more competent they were and how well they could manage the affairs of the Brotherhood when left to themselves. I don't know whether they are yet satisfied with themselves or not, but judging them not by their professions or their own estimate of themselves or not, but by their deeds and by the estimation in which they are held by the public, who have had an opportunity of seeing the hollowness of their pretensions, I don't think it is necessary for me to hold back any longer.

I now come before the Irish people of America to say I am prepared to continue the work commenced on the 2nd of June 1866 at Ridgeway, Canada West, where a few hundred Irish soldiers met the English enemy on his own territory and whipped him. 'England's difficulty is Ireland's opportunity' was the favorite maxim of O'Connell, but whether the present complications in Europe will afford us the long sought for opportunity or not if we are only true to ourselves, either with or without the aid of the Czar of Russia, in the name of God and Ireland I now ask you, fellow countrymen, to stand by me and assist me in striking another blow for Mother Ireland.

You should certainly know me by this time. You know I have never deceived you. You know I have never made a pledge of a promise to the Irish people which I have not tried to redeem, and if I have not been successful it was because they listened to the voice of the Slanderer who misrepresented me and did not sustain me as they had promised. You know that on more than one occasion I risked my life in defense of the cause which you love so dearly, and I am now ready to risk it again. Yes, and sacrifice it if necessary, on the altar of Irish liberty.

Some of the men who were prominently connected with the Fenian organization have already passed away and have appeared before Him who judges of the motives and the acts of men, not by the misrepresentations of their enemies but by the light of truth and justice. In a few years hence we will all have passed away. Robert Emmett says, "The man dies but his memory lives." We fellow countrymen who claim to be patriots and who desire to follow in the footsteps of Robert Emmett what have we done that our memories should live? Remember that when the future historian comes to write the glorious deeds of the past it is not the number of wounds which we have inflicted upon one another or the number of homes we have made unhappy by our unjust and uncharitable accusations that are going to count in our favor but the number of wounds we have inflicted upon the enemy of our name and race, England.

I believed that the next best thing to giving the Irish people their freedom at home is to encourage and assist such of them as come here of their own volition in procuring homes for themselves in this free land. And immediately after the failure in the Red River Country, knowing that some time must necessarily lapse before I could undertake another movement, I commenced just five years ago to travel through the western states with a view to seeing the country and selecting suitable places for colonies.

I spent two years in examining the country and for the last three years have devoted most of my time to organizing and locating colonies in Nebraska. This of itself I regard as a noble work, and worthy of the most serious consideration and support from every true Irishman. The thousands whom I have recently met in this and other cities, begging for the privilege of working for the means to keep them from starving, fully confirms me in this opinion. But I had a double object in encouraging our people to emigrate from the overcrowded cities and states of the east to settle upon the cheap and free lands of the west. The first was that they might better their own condition and that of their families and the second that they might be in a position, from their improved circumstances and their nearness to the contemplated field of future operations, to assist the cause of Irish liberty. I think I can safely promise from the colonies which I have already established at least some of the young men to assist us on the battlefield while the older ones are raising corn, flour, potatoes to help sustain them. And I know that there are many other settlements in the western states and territories ready and willing to do their share of the work. One correspondent writes to me from the Black Hills that he has enough of men there ready to inaugurate the movement whenever ordered to do so. Although the grasshoppers, who have been our most formidable enemies so far, have seriously interfered with my immigration scheme, yet I have every reason to be thankful for the success which I have met with up to the present.

Some of those who have migrated to the west may think that they have had a hard time of it because everything is new and strange to them and for the present they are deprived of many of the conveniences and comforts which older settlements afford, but I can assure all such that there are thousands of their countrymen and countrywomen in the East, now out of employment, who would willingly change places with them. In a few years these same parties who are now dissatisfied will bless the day on which they started for the west and commenced working for themselves on their own farms instead of depending on others for their daily bread and often begging for the privileges of working to enrich their neighbor. I shall continue to furnish information on the subject of immigration and organized colonies, and for this purpose have established an office in this city and have secured the services of a competent Secretary, Colonel William McWilliams, a well known Irish Nationalist, who will attend to all correspondence in my absence. I travel through the country myself, devoting the next few months to this state, and attend meetings and deliver lectures on Irish immigration and Irish Revolution, for I propose to have both these noble objects go hand in hand. A circular of instructions for organizing immigration committees will accompany this address.

In conclusion, fellow countrymen, I beg of you to lend me your assistance in this movement. Give me one more chance untrammelled and my word for it, you will never regret it. The governing passion of my life, apart from my duty to my God, is to be at the head of an Irish army battling against England for Ireland's rights; for this I live and for this, if necessary, I am willing to die."

Appendix B:
Timeline

1800—John O'Neill, Sr., born about this date in County Monaghan, Clontibret Parish, Drumgallan townland.

1805—Catherine Macklin, born about this date in County Monaghan, Clontibret Parish, father George Macklin, mother Mary Macklin.

1813—Catherine's brother John Macklin born in County Monaghan, Ireland.

1828—Approximate marriage, John O'Neill and Catherine Macklin, Clontibert Parish, County Monaghan.

1830—Birth of Bernard O'Neill, first child of John and Catherine O'Neill, Clontibret Parish, County Monaghan.

1832—Birth of Mary O'Neill, second child of John and Catherine O'Neill, Clontibret Parish, County Monaghan.

1838—Birth of John Charles O'Neill, March 9, Clontibret Parish. Father died five weeks before, in February, during outbreak of cholera.

1839—Catherine O'Neill and brother John Macklin leave Ireland for Elizabeth, New Jersey. Start grocery store on Elizabeth Avenue.

1843—Bernard (age 13) and Mary (age 11) O'Neill arrive in Elizabeth. John Charles O'Neill (age 7) left with grandparents in Drumgallan, County Monaghan. Patrick Walsh marries Bridget Walsh in Parramatta, New South Wales.

1844—John O'Neill's first cousin George Macklin born in Elizabeth, first Macklin/O'Neill born in U.S.

1844—Mary Ann Crow born in Parramatta, Australia.

1848—John O'Neill arrives in Elizabeth (age 11) on June 23 aboard the ship *Gertrude*.

1849—Patrick, Bridget, and Mary Ann Crow leave Melbourne, Australia, for the Gold Rush in San Francisco.

1852—Bernard O'Neill, brother of John, age 22, marries Ann Gaffney at St. Mary's Church in Elizabeth on October 31. Approximate date of Patrick Crow returning to Australia, abandoning wife and daughter.

1854—Bridget Crow dies in San Francisco. Mary Ann placed in Catholic orphanage.

1855—John O'Neill opens Catholic bookstore in Richmond, Virginia.

1856—John O'Neill joins the Emmett Monument Association in Richmond.

1857—John O'Neill's bookstore folds and he joins the U.S. Army as a dragoon in Baltimore, May 30.

1858—John O'Neill deserts U.S. Army at Camp Floyd, Utah, on August 7, and arrives in San Francisco in October. The Fenian Brotherhood begins in New York City.

1860—O'Neill meets Mary Ann Crow in a San Francisco candy store. O'Neill rejoins the army in Red Bluff, California, July 8.

1860—Mary Ann Crow joins household of G.W.P. Bissell as teacher in San Francisco, age 16.

1861—John O'Neill leaves San Francisco for Washington, D.C., and the Civil War.

1862—O'Neill involved in Peninsula Campaign in Virginia, afterwards appointed 2nd Lieutenant and sent to 5th Indiana Cavalry.

1862—Mary Ann Crow reunites with father Patrick via letter from Sydney while she is working as a domestic in San Francisco, age 18.

1863—O'Neill appointed 1st Lieutenant, involved in much action in Western Theatre. Wounded at Walker's Ford, Clinch River. Mary Ann Crow leaves California by way of Panama, arrives in Elizabeth in December, sees snow for the first time.

1864—O'Neill promised, and then denied, promotion. Resigns from army in protest. Is offered and accepted as Captain of 17th U.S. Colored Regiment. Marries Mary Ann Crow in Elizabeth in November at St. Mary's Church. O'Neill resigns from army a second time. They move to Nashville, Tennessee, and O'Neill joins the Fenian Brotherhood.

1865—O'Neill opens a claims office in Nashville. O'Neill appointed Colonel of 13th Fenian Regiment.

1866—John Hugh O'Neill born in Nashville, March 2. John O'Neill leaves Nashville for Buffalo, May 27. He attacks June 2. Battle of Ridgeway and Fort Erie.

1868—O'Neill named President of the Fenian Brotherhood. Mary Ella (Mamie) O'Neill born in Washington, D.C. O'Neill appoints his friend, Henri Le Caron (British spy), his chief aide.

1870—O'Neill invades Canada a second time at Eccles Hill, Vermont. Arrested, tried, convicted. Pardoned by President Grant in October. Stays in Vermont for six more months. Eugene O'Neill born December 25 in Burlington, Vermont.

1871—Family returns to Elizabeth, then moves to East St. Louis. O'Neill joins Bernard O'Donoghue in attack in Dakota Territory. Arrested and released, returns to family in East St. Louis.

1872—O'Neill begins lecture series around the country.

1873—Depression hits America. John O'Neill meets Patrick Fahy, signs contract. Mary Ann O'Neill receives last letter from her father Patrick, then in Melbourne, Australia, aged 57.

1874—Katherine (Kitty) O'Neill born in Omaha in July. Eugene O'Neill dies and is buried in Omaha. First of four groups of colonists arrive in O'Neill City.

1875—Second group of colonists arrive in O'Neill. They are joined by Mary Ann and three children, as well as John Joseph and Tom O'Neill, nephews from Elizabeth and two oldest sons of brother Bernard O'Neill.

1876—Third group of colonists arrive in O'Neill. The general writes his final manifesto of Irish independence in Philadelphia. John Rutherford publishes "The Fenian Conspiracy" and hurts O'Neill deeply. Catherine (Macklin) O'Neill dies December 26 in Elizabeth.

1877—Fourth and last group of colonists arrive in O'Neill and Atkinson. John O'Neill sick most of the year. In November suffers stroke and taken to Omaha.

1878—John O'Neill dies in Omaha in January, age 39, and is buried in unmarked grave with deceased son Eugene.

1879—Mary Ann O'Neill remarries Civil War veteran James Coughlin in O'Neill City in October. John Macklin dies in Elizabeth, age 57. Very successful grocer and city leader.

1880—Tom O'Neill leaves O'Neill City, spends a year in Plattsmouth, Nebraska. Nephew of General John O'Neill. Frank Coughlin born to Mary Ann and James Coughlin in O'Neill.

1881—Tom O'Neill dies in Fort Wayne, Indiana, in factory accident at Bass Foundry and Machine Works, age 25. Bernard O'Neill, brother of General John O'Neill, dies in Elizabeth, age 51. Francis Coughlin born to Mary Ann and James Coughlin in O'Neill City, October.

1883—Genevieve (Eva) Coughlin born in O'Neill City, October.

1886—Grace Coughlin born to Mary Ann and James Coughlin in O'Neill in February. Grace is the seventh child to Mary Ann, five of whom survive to adulthood. She is now forty years old.

1889—Fund begun for reburial of John O'Neill in O'Neill City. Public outcry ends proposal.

1892—Mary O'Neill, unmarried sister of General John O'Neill, dies in Elizabeth. Last of the family born in Ireland.

1893—Monument raised at unmarked grave of General John O'Neill in Omaha, Nebraska.

1891—James Coughlin dies in O'Neill City, August 1. Mary Ann files widow pension claim for General John O'Neill with federal government. After eight-year fight, she is denied.

1895—Mary Ann marries Henry Hads in Greeley County, Nebraska. John Hugh O'Neill marries Margaret Donoghue in Spalding, Nebraska.

1902—Mary Ann (Crow, O'Neill, Coughlin) Hads dies in Elgin, Nebraska, February 6, age 58.

1905—John Hugh O'Neill leaves Nebraska for San Diego with family.

1907—Mary Ella (Mamie) Steele dies at 37 in Spalding, Nebraska. Oldest daughter of John and Mary Ann O'Neill.

1919—Eamon De Valera unveils monument to General O'Neill in Holy Sepulchre Cemetery, Omaha, Nebraska.

1924—Fiftieth anniversary of the founding of O'Neill City. Idea develops to relocate John O'Neill remains and monument to O'Neill from Omaha. For second time, proposal is dropped by the public.

1942—Katherine (Kitty) Tipton dies at 68. Youngest child of John and Mary Ann O'Neill. Kitty had two sons she left in Nebraska, and after divorcing husband, remarried Robert Tipton in Lewiston, Idaho. Died in California.

1965—Genevieve (Eva) Coughlin dies at 92 in Payette County, Idaho.

1969—Governor Tiemann proclaims O'Neill City "Irish Capital of Nebraska." John Hugh O'Neill, only surviving son of General John O'Neill, dies in San Diego, California, age 73. His four children leave a great legacy of success.

Appendix C:
The O'Neills/Macklins
in New Jersey

John O'Neill's death began a marked demise in the fortunes of both the O'Neill and Macklin families, coincidence or not. One year after the general's death in 1878, John Macklin, the patriarch, died in Elizabeth at age 57. Macklin had been the male leader of the family since 1840 when he and his sister Catherine O'Neill had emigrated to New Jersey. For almost forty years John Macklin had been a successful businessman and father, and his funeral was attended by every major figure in Elizabeth. John and his wife Jane (Murphy) had twelve children, ten of whom reached adulthood. Only the youngest, Charles, had sons, as six of the other ten remained unmarried or had no children. This Macklin name died out in America by 1950.

George J. Macklin, the eldest son, was the only Macklin cousin close to John O'Neill. George was the best man at O'Neill's wedding in 1864 and the godfather of his only son in 1866. George left Nashville for Texas before returning to Elizabeth, where he worked with his father as a clerk in the uptown grocery business until 1876. At age 32 he left New Jersey again, but did not go far. In 1900 the 56-year-old George was still single and living alone in the Bowery in Manhattan, not a good place. After 1885 all surviving Macklins were found in different boroughs of New York City, their record of sixty years as a leading family in Elizabeth a thoroughly forgotten memory. The earlier Macklins are buried in the family plot at St. Mary's Cemetery, while those after 1900 are scattered throughout New York. None of the large Macklin family followed the general into war or colonization.

John's brother Bernard, as noted, remained his entire life in Elizabeth after arriving in 1843 at age thirteen. He and his wife Ann (Gaffney) raised a family of eight—six boys—each of whom survived childhood. There is ample circumstantial evidence that Bernard and his famous younger brother were not particularly close, but that did not extend to all Bernard's children.

The two oldest, John Joseph and Tom, worked with and followed their uncle John to Nebraska. John J. returned to New Jersey after the general's death and led a very successful life as an engineer throughout the East. He was the closest of all the O'Neills to the general, and as an older man gave further evidence of the split between brothers John and Bernard, with John J. siding with the general.

When John J. O'Neill died on St Patrick's Day in 1914 at his home in Jersey City, New Jersey, at 61, he was a well-known civil engineer and architect. His obituary stated that he was "one of the founders of O'Neill City, the county seat of Holt County, Nebraska." John J. had spent much of his adult life as the city engineer of East Orange, New Jersey, an affluent suburb ten miles north of Elizabeth. In late 1892, still a young man, he purchased a family plot at Holy Sepulchre Cemetery in East Orange, where his Iowa-born wife Imogene and only son William would one day be buried. But John's first act after the purchase was to remove his grandmother Catherine O'Neill, his aunt Mary O'Neill, and sister Mary from the O'Neill family plot at St. Mary's in Elizabeth and have them interred in East Orange. He left his mother and father at Saint Mary's, a silent but defining act.

Tom O'Neill went with his older brother to Nebraska in 1874 as a seventeen-year-old teenage colonist, and there is no way to know if Bernard and Ann approved. Tom, like so many of the early settlers, left quickly after the sudden death of his uncle, though he did not go home to New Jersey. This was not uncommon with early settlers, as James Cutler wrote in *The History of Holt County*, in 1882. "Most men prefer to endure the privations of a new country than subject themselves to the ridicule of their acquaintances, which would have been lavished upon them, upon a return to the conveniences, comforts, and delights of home." Tom bounced around the Midwest for seven years, but on January 9, 1881, just three weeks after his 25th birthday, he was killed in an accident while working as a laborer at the Bass Foundry and Machine Works in Fort Wayne, Indiana.[7] Bernard brought his young son's body home immediately and he was buried in the O'Neill family plot at St. Mary's. Three years previously, Bernard's famous brother, General John O'Neill, had died alone, but Bernard and John Macklin, both of whom could afford it, left the general in Omaha.

Bernard must have been crushed by Tom's death, and it may be no coincidence that he died of a heart attack three months later at 51. The death of the popular downtown grocer was reported in the *Elizabeth Daily Journal*, and it is just as revealing for whom it does not mention.

Mr. Bernard O'Neill died last night at his residence, 805 Elizabeth Avenue, in the 52 year of his age. He was moderately well yesterday afternoon, was about his store, and seemed to be suffering only from a little cold. He ate his supper and afterwards went upstairs. He was taken sick and though physicians were summoned, he died at 11 p.m.

Mr. O'Neill was born in County Monaghan, Ireland, in 1830 and came to this country in 1843. He has lived in this city, a respected citizen, for thirty-eight years, for twenty-six years of which time he has been engaged in business for himself. He has been honored in being elected year after year as assessor in the Third Ward in which he lived, and he filled the office acceptably and well for many years. He leaves a wife and six children. About three months ago he lost a son, who died very suddenly out West.

Of the eight O'Neill children, only one son, Bernard Jr., would raise another generation of Irish Americans in Elizabeth. Bernard Jr. married local girl Sarah Murphy and raised eight more O'Neills. One son, John O'Neill, would eventually move to Danbury, Connecticut, with his only daughter; another Tom O'Neill died even younger than his namesake; and Bernard III and George O'Neill, who both carried into the 1970s names of long ago Macklins and O'Neills, stayed unmarried, living together at Lowden Avenue in Elizabeth with their spinster sister Irene.

Bernard was the first to go, dying at 78, the last perhaps to carry on the fighting O'Neill spirit. Bernard was for many years well known as a bantamweight and featherweight professional boxer, whose reputation spread throughout the East. George and Irene died in 1982, the last of the very popular and respected O'Neills in New Jersey, 142 years after arriving to begin a new life from County Monaghan. But the Macklins and O'Neills in Elizabeth unfortunately cannot be mourned. The small St. Mary's Cemetery, where most of the two families are buried, was closed soon after John Macklin's son William was interred at age 30 after dying in New York in 1891. All headstones were knocked down in the 1950s and have now sunk into the earth, leaving the grounds looking like a fenced in suburban lawn of inner city Elizabeth. Though still well kept, the gates are locked, no visitors are allowed, and no locations are known in the two-acre setting, leaving us to mourn collectively the 1,500 or so Irish buried there who came to Elizabeth for a new life. The hurt and the pain of the Famine can never be fully understood.

Chapter Notes

Chapter 1

1. Henri Le Caron, *25 Years in the Secret Service* (London: William Heinemann, 1892), 40.

2. William Carleton, *The Black Prophet* (New York: P.F. Collier, 1881).

3. The breakdown of Irish land can be found in *Irish Names and Places*, by P.W. Joyce (Dublin: DeBurca, 1995). Notes on Catherine O'Neill and Edward Macklin and their time in Elizabeth, New Jersey, were found in U.S. Federal census records, 1840–1880, O'Neill interviews with John Savage, and John Hugh O'Neill's Notebook (1936).

4. Most details on the early life of O'Neill are from an 1868 interview with the *Irish-American* newspaper, soon copied by John Savage in his *Fenian Heroes and Martyrs* (New York: P. Donahue, 1868), and accepted as gospel to the present. Also, Dumas Malone, ed., *Dictionary of American Biography* (1934), 44–45. Similar information found in *Ridgeway* by Scian Dubh (James McCarroll) (Miami: Hard Press Books, 2011). With exception of Le Caron, all O'Neill biographical information was supplied in 1868 by O'Neill himself to McCarroll, Savage, and the *Irish-American*. McCarroll's book in particular is a historical fiction, but there is little doubt that only O'Neill could have provided such exact documentation about his Civil War material.

5. O'Neill consistently said he was raised by his grandparents rather than a nationalist—Protestant—school. There was only one such school in Clontibret in the early 1840s, run by a Protestant schoolteacher. It had sixteen Protestant students, fourteen Presbyterian students, and twelve Catholics. O'Neill's version makes much sense, at least based on his statement and feelings on America. For more than a century and a half, O'Neill's birthplace has been misguided. The well-meaning Irish Rev. L. Marron of Castleblayney Parish in Monaghan told the general's daughter Ruth in 1960 that the O'Neill home place, though not recorded, was at "Beth's Lane," since the O'Neills were always under the impression that the general's mother was named Elizabeth. The O'Neills, however, were not from Castleblayney Parish, but nearby Clontibret, and O'Neill's mother was named Catherine. Though an honest mistake, it has been picked up as gospel by many.

6. The early history of Elizabeth and the Irish is found in *Historical Elizabethtown, 1664–1932*, and Nicholas Murray's *Notes, History, and Biographies Concerning Elizabethtown* (1844). The Know-Nothing episode is treated in *The Catholic Church in New Jersey* by J.M. Flynn (1904), 9, and *The Hidden History of the Irish in New Jersey* by Tom Fox (Charleston: History Press, 2012).

7. The issue of O'Neill's age has perplexed authors and researchers for years, with only O'Neill's interviews in 1868 claiming his birth year as 1834, which has been repeated to the present day. All have tried to fit the history of O'Neill based on his claim of an 1834 birth, a claim he only made in 1857 when enlisting in the Army underage, which he then stuck to

for the rest of his life. In "Passenger Lists of Arrivals in New York Harbor" no John O'Neill born between 1832 and 1836 arrived in New York, which was the only port near Elizabeth, just nine miles away. Only one John O'Neill, age 11, arrived between 1847 and 1850, on the *Gertrude* in June 1848. A more accurate record is found in the Hall of Records in Elizabeth, New Jersey, where it is recorded that on a marriage certificate in November 1864, a 26-year-old John O'Neill married 20-year-old Mary Ann Crow, meaning he was born in 1838, not 1834. There is no reason O'Neill would lie in front of family or clergy. They of all people would know his age. Mary Ann's age is also accurate. O'Neill and family members signed the record. A birth record of 1838 fits every bit of the rest of O'Neill's history.

　　8.　The history, past and present, of County Monaghan is explained explicitly in Darach MacDonald's *Hard Border* (Dublin: New Island, 2018), *The Atlas of the Great Irish Famine* (New York University Press, 2017), *The Monaghan Story* by Peadar Livingstone (Monaghan: Clogher Historical Society, 1980), and *The Atlas of the Rural Irish Landscape* (Cork University Press, 2011), among others.

　　9.　*Punch Magazine*, 1847.

　　10.　Colm Toibin, *Walking Along the Border* (London: Queen Anne's Press, 1987), 134.

　　11.　Macdonald, *Hard Border*, 186.

　　12.　*Nashville Press and Advertiser*, July 14, 1866, 1.

　　13.　John Crowley, ed., *Atlas of the Great Irish Famine* (New York University Press, 2012), 442–44.

　　14.　Kirby Miller, *Exiles and Emigrants* (New York: Oxford University Press, 1985), 3–8, 127.

　　15.　Genealogy of the Macklin/O'Neill family was conducted by the author and personal interviews, 2012–2018.

　　16.　Anonymous, *The City of Elizabeth, New Jersey, Illustrated* (New Jersey: *Elizabeth Daily Journal*, 1889), 10–20.

　　17.　*Newark Advertiser*, 1854.

　　18.　Joseph Flynn, *The Catholic Church in New Jersey* (Morristown: 1904), 10.

　　19.　*The Jersey Journal*, April 4, 1854.

　　20.　O'Neill's time in Richmond by visits to the Richmond Public Library. Directory on file with author. His army enlistment from Baltimore to his time in Utah by visits to the National Archives in Washington, D.C. O'Neill's enlistment copy (May 1857) on file with author.

　　21.　Eva O'Cathaoir, *Soldiers of Liberty: A Study of Fenianism* (Dublin: Lilliput Press, 2018), 12.

　　22.　Michael Funchion, *Irish American Voluntary Organizations* (Westport, CT: Greenwood Press, 1983), 101–105.

　　23.　O'Neill in the *Irish-American* interview in 1866 said his mother did not want him to serve in the military, and thus the lie about his age began. *Irish-American*, January 15, 1878, and Savage, *Fenian Heroes and Martyrs*.

　　24.　Captain John Adams's early career is covered in Bryan Lane's "The Familiar Road: The Life of Confederate Brigadier General John Adams" in *Civil War Times*, October 1996, 40–46, as well as National Archive records.

　　25.　*Wild West Magazine*, June 12, 2006, as well as *The Mormon Rebellion: America's First Civil War* (Norman: University of Oklahoma Press, 2011) by David Bigler and Will Bagley and *To Utah with the Dragoons and Glimpses of Life in Arizona and California, 1858–1859* (Salt Lake City: University of Utah Press, 1974), edited by Harold D. Langley.

　　26.　U.S. Army records, National Archives, Washington, D.C.

Chapter 2

　　1.　Patrick Crow's arrest and transportation is found in the National Archives of Ireland, County Wexford, 1791–1853. Confirmation is found in the "New South Wales State Records for Convicts, 1788–1842" and "Irish Convicts to NSW" by Peter Mayberry, www.pcug.org.au.

2. Bridget Walsh's (Welsh) arrival is shown in the "State Records of NSW" reel 1318. She was an "assisted immigrant" whose passage was either subsidized or paid by another person.

3. Marriage of Bridget and Patrick Crow is found in the "NSW Registry of Births, Deaths, and Marriages" certificate number V18432063 93/1843. Though married in Parramatta, the couple lived in Concord, a suburb of Sydney ten miles away.

4. Record of the Crow family's trip to San Francisco and the life of Australians in that city is found in Jay Monaghan's *Australians in the Gold Rush: California and Down Under, 1849–1854* (Los Angeles: University of California Press, 1966), 48, and from Ann Copeland at the State Library of Victoria Genealogy Team. Ship records of the *William Watson*, June 27, 1849, on file with author.

5. Monaghan, 48.

6. Violence during the gold rush in San Francisco is described in *Vigilantes in the Gold Rush, San Francisco* by Robert Sienkewicz (1985), 75–80.

7. A copy of the death and burial register, in addition to Bridget's local address, San Francisco History Center. A letter from John Hugh O'Neill to the Idaho Historical Society, March 1936, on file with author.

8. The history of the Sisters of Charity (later the Daughters of Charity) and their journey from Maryland to start an orphanage and school in San Francisco is found on www.daughtersofcharity.com.

9. *The San Francisco Irish, 1848–1880* by R.A. Burchell (Manchester: Manchester University Press, 1979) and *California: The Irish Dream* by Patrick Dowling (San Francisco: Golden Gate Publishers, 1989) cover the early years of the Irish in the city, as does David Emmons, *Beyond the American Pale: The Irish in the West, 1845–1910* (Norman: University of Oklahoma Press, 2010), 258.

10. John Hugh O'Neill's Notebook, unpublished, 1936, 2–3. Hereafter referred to as JHON.

11. Le Caron, *25 Years*, 38–40.

12. The meeting of Adams and O'Neill in San Francisco is from the *Irish-American* (February 15, 1868) and oral history of the O'Neills, as well as the National Archives records of O'Neill's desertion, on file with author.

13. History of Fort Crook is from John C. O'Neill's Notebook (1862) and United States Army records, National Archives, both on file with author, and at www.militarymuseum.org/cpcrook.html.

14. The progress and movement of Fort Crook personnel to war on the East Coast is found in JHON and National Archives, on file.

15. Lane, *Civil War Times*, Vol. 35, October 1966.

Chapter 3

1. Journey and arrival of O'Neill and Fort Crook troops from JHON, 1861.

2. Peninsula campaign from *To the Gates of Richmond* by Stephen Sears (New York: Ticknor & Fields, 1992), 67–78, and *A Pitiless Rain: The Battle of Williamsburg* by Earl C. Hastings, Jr., and David Hastings (Shippensburg, PA: White Mane Publishing, 1997), 114–121.

3. JHON, 1862.

4. Stoneman, March 8, 1864, *Official Records of the War of the Rebellion.*

5. O'Neill family records, on file with author.

6. Dubh, *Ridgeway*, 48.

7. *Ibid.*

8. *Official Records*, Series 1, Vol. 23, Part One, 367–69.

9. Indiana 5th Cavalry records of engagements, www.civilwararchive.com. Fifth Indiana Cavalry in Frederick Dyer's *A Compendium of the War of the Rebellion* (1908) and *The Union Army*, Vol. 3 (Federal Publishing Co., 1908), 45. Judah report of Morgan's Raid. *O.R.* Series 1, Vol. 23, Part 1, 657.

10. C.P. Stacey, *The Fenian Paladin: The Story of John O'Neill*, unpublished notes, (University of Toronto Library), 8.

11. Dubh, *Ridgeway*, 49.

12. Savage, 48. Three years later the Archbishop lashed out strongly against the Fenians. Brian Jenkins, *Irish Nationalism and the British State* (Montreal: McGill-Queen's University Press, 2006), 296.

13. U.S. National Archives, Lt. John O'Neill, 5th Indiana file.

14. Patrick Crow, 1862 letter to Mary Ann Crow from O'Neill/Martin family records, copy with author.

15. JHON, 3.

16. *O.R.* Series 1, Vol. 21, Part 1, December 5, 1863.

17. Dubh, 50.

18. *Indianapolis Daily Journal*, January 30, 1864.

19. Dubh, 52.

20. O'Neill family papers and Dubh, 51.

21. Stacey, 7.

22. Dubh, 51.

23. *Ibid.*, 52.

24. *Ibid.*, 53.

25. *Ibid.*

26. *Ibid.*

27. Ron Chernow, *Grant* (Penguin Press, 2017), 130 and 131.

Chapter 4

1. Marriage record of O'Neill and Mary Ann Crow from Hall of Records in Elizabeth and in Civil War pension request No. 575.926, 1898.

2. Battle of Franklin discussed in Wiley Sword's *Embrace the Angry Wind: The Confederacy's Last Hurrah* (New York: HarperCollins, 1992), 263–227. In addition, see *Cleburne and His Command* by Irving Buck (Jackson, TN: McCowat-Mercer Press, 1959).

3. Nashville City Directory, 1866.

4. The move to Nashville found in Nashville directory, 1864–65, Nashville Public Library, *Nashville Morning Times* (1865), and JHON, 5.

5. Nashville Fenians from DeeGee Lester, "Tennessee's Bold Fenian Men," *Tennessee Historical Quarterly*, Winter (1997), 262–277. Also Mike Ruddy, *Fenians-L Archives*, March 31, 2008. Information on Tom Sweeny from *Through American and Irish Wars: The Life and Times of General Thomas W. Sweeny* by Jack Morgan (Dublin: Irish Academic Press, 2006), 104, 108, 116, 125, and Tom Kelly, *Dictionary of Irish Biography* (2009).

6. O'Neill's claim of losing fortune in Dubh, *Ridgeway* (1868), 54, and JHON, 6. An 1864 Nashville newspaper article gives some credence to the success of O'Neill's agency saying that the "present prospect" planned to bring in more than a million dollars' worth of claims.

7. Miller, 7.

8. Histories of the early origins of the Fenians abound. In particular, *Irish-American Nationalism* by Thomas Brown (Philadelphia: Lippincott, 1966); *The Fenian Movement* by Mabel Gregory Walker (Colorado Springs: Ralph Myles Publisher, 1969); *The Fenian Movement in the United States, 1858–1886* by William Darcy (New York: Russell & Russell, 1947); and, most recently, *Soldiers of Liberty: A Study of Fenianism* by Eva O'Cathaoir (Dublin: Lilliput Press, 2018). From a British point of view was John Rutherford's *The Fenian Conspiracy* (London: C. Keegan & Paul, 1876).

9. The reported meeting of Sweeny and Cleburne is found in Irving Buck, *Cleburne and His Command* (Jackson, TN: McCowat-Mercer Press, 1959), 213.

10. Early Fenian finances are especially discussed in Walker, 64–66, and O'Cathaoir, 112–115. Report of the purchase of the Moffat House from www.ansionnachfionn.wordpress.com, 2016, 1–9.

11. U.S. relations with Canada following the Civil War from *Blood and Daring: How Canada Fought the American Civil War and Forged a Nation* by John Boyko (Canada: Vintage Canada Press, 2014), 237–47, and O'Cathaoir, 56–57.

12. Desmond Ryan, *The Fenian Chief: A Biography of James Stevens* (Coral Gables: University of Miami Press, 1967), 200.

13. D'Arcy, 36–37.

14. Sweeny from Morgan, 3–6.

15. *Ibid.*, 7.

16. Walker, 53.

17. The scarcity of U.S. troops along the border found in Vronsky, 28.

18. P.B. Ellis, "Ridgeway, the Fenian Raids and the Making of Canada," in *The Untold Story: The Irish in Canada*, Vol. 1 (Toronto: Celtic Arts of Canada, 1988), 537–553.

19. Vronsky, 24–30.

20. C.W. pension request, 1898, and JHON, 3.

21. Carl Wittke, *Irish in America* (Baton Rouge: Louisiana State University Press, 1956), 150.

22. Peter Edwards, *Delusion: The True Story of Victorian Superspy Henri Le Caron* (Toronto: Key Porter Books, 2008), 46–47.

Chapter 5

1. *Sun-Sentinel*, November 9, 2012.

2. Steven V. Ash, *A Massacre in Memphis: The Race Riot That Shook the Nation One Year After the Civil War* (New York: Hill and Wang, 2013), 4.

3. Military plans for the invasion found in Vronsky, 34–5; Walker, 90–92; O'Cathaoir, 155–6; David A. Wilson, *The Fenians in Canada* (Toronto: Library and Archives, 2014), 1–2; and W.S. Neidhardt, *Fenians in North America* (University Park: Penn State University Press, 1975), 55.

4. James Gibbons to Fenian Brotherhood membership, May 9, 1866.

5. Tevis to O'Neill, May 10, 1866. Author copy from O'Neill family records.

6. Ryan, 197.

7. O'Cathaoir, 158.

8. Tevis being dismissed for cowardice in *The Journal of the American-Irish Historical Society*, Vol. XXII (1922), 203.

9. Walker, 23.

10. Vronsky, 44.

11. Morgan, 133.

12. Vronsky, 152–3.

13. *New York Herald*, June 1, 1866.

14. *Irish Canadian*, June 4, 1866.

15. O'Neill telegram to Sweeny; Walker, 96; and Morgan, 133. Sweeny's response to fallback found in *The Journal of the American-Irish Historical Society*, Vol. XXII (1922), 200.

16. Vronsky, 162–3.

17. Stacey, 5.

18. Vronsky, 161–2.

19. Robert O'Driscoll, *The Untold Story: The Irish in Canada*, Vol. 1 (Toronto: Celtic Arts of Canada, 1988), 551.

20. Vronsky, 162.

Chapter 6

1. *New York Herald*, June 1, 1866.

2. Walker, 98.

3. O'Neill to Gallagher, June 2, 1866, from USS *Michigan*.
4. *New York Times*, June 3, 1866.
5. *Ibid.*, June 5, 1866.
6. *New York World*, June 5, 1866.
7. *New York Post*, June 4, 1866.
8. Walker, 127–8.
9. *Nashville Press and Times*, July 9, 1866, and 1866 Fenian Convention in Pittsburgh.
10. Stacey, 8.
11. *The Buffalo Commercial*, June 7, 1866, 1.
12. *Ibid.*, 1.
13. *Nashville Press and Times*, July 14, 1866.
14. *Ibid.*, July 15, 1866. Under headline "General John O'Neill—Welcome Back to Tennessee." Also found in Walker, *The Fenian Movement*, 116.
15. George Macklin absconding with funds found in JHON, 6. O'Neill claimed for decades he lost $30,000 when he abandoned his agency, *Irish-American Weekly*, September 28, 1867. How much was lost to George is unknown.
16. *Memphis Daily Appeal*, August 10, 1866; *Irish-American*, September 8, 1866; and *Nashville Morning Times*, November 1866.
17. *Nashville Daily Union*, September 14, 1866.
18. *Irish-American*, September 15, 1866.
19. "Sweeny's Official Report to the Convention," September 4, 1866, in *The Journal of the American-Irish Historical Society*, Vol. XIII (1924), 195–8.
20. *The Buffalo Commercial*, June 5, 1866.
21. *Cincinnati Enquirer*, December 15, 1866. O'Neill avoided the same situation, Walker, 130.
22. Neidhardt, 75.

Chapter 7

1. *New York Times*, June 10, 1866.
2. *Ibid.*, June 2, 1866.
3. *Official Report of Gen. John O'Neill on the Attempt to Invade Canada, May 25, 1870—Also a Report on the Battle of Ridgeway, Canada West, June 2, 1866* (New York: John Foster Publisher, 1870), 4.
4. JHON, 7.
5. Steward, 122, and D'Arcy, 145.
6. Corcoran, Cleburne, and Sheridan from Michael Glazier's *The Encyclopedia of the Irish in America* (Indiana: University of Notre Dame Press, 1999), 153–15. Corcoran also from Thomas Caughwell's *The Greatest Brigade: How the Irish Brigade Cleared the Way to Victory in the American Civil War* (Beverley, MA: Fair Winds Press, 2011), 36–38. Cleburne from Muriel Phillips Joslyn's *A Meteor Shining Brightly: Essays on Major General Patrick Cleburne* (Milledgeville, GA: Terrell House Publishing, 1999). Roy Morris best handles Sheridan in *The Life and Wars of General Phil Sheridan* (New York: Crown Publisher, 1992).
7. Timothy Egan, *The Immortal Irishman* (Boston: Houghton Mifflin Harcourt, 2016), 257.
8. The controversial Meagher discussed in John M. Hearne's *Thomas Francis Meagher: The Making of an Irish American* (Dublin: Irish Academic Press, 2005), Paul R. Wylie's *The Irish General: Thomas Francis Meagher* (Norman: University of Oklahoma Press, 2007), and, most recently, Tim Egan's *The Immortal Irishman: The Irish Revolutionary Who Became an American Hero* (New York: Houghton Mifflin Harcourt, 2016). His death described in David Emmons's *Beyond the American Pale: The Irish in the West* (Norman: University of Oklahoma Press, 2010), 205.
9. O'Neill, *1870 Report*, 7.

10. Clerkenwell bombing in Manchester from O'Cathaoir, 214–224.

11. *Address to the Officers and Members of the Fenian Brotherhood*, John O'Neill, February 27, 1868, 17.

12. *Ibid.*, 16.

13. *Ibid.*, 4.

14. *Irish-American Weekly*, May 9, 1868, 1.

15. *Ibid.*

16. Walker, 101.

17. Thomas D'Arcy McGee murder and aftermath from David Wilson's *Thomas D'Arcy McGee*, Vol. 2, Part Four (Montreal: McGill-Queen's University Press, 2011), 341–368.

18. *Ibid.*, 230.

19. Edwards, 78, and Wilson, 355–373.

20. Edwards, 63.

21. *Ibid.*

22. Walker, 169.

23. Edwards, *Delusion*, 66.

24. Patrick Roche calling Le Caron a spy found in Hereward Senior, *The Last Invasion of Canada: The Fenian Raids, 1866–1870* (Toronto: Dundurn Press, 1991), 136.

25. Edwards, 290.

26. JHON, 10.

27. Records from C.W. Pension request, 1898, and JHON, 8.

28. "A Look Back in History," *Philadelphia Inquirer*, March 30, 2018, The Historical Society of Pennsylvania.

29. "O'Neill appears to be thoroughly earnest in his intentions," Neidhardt, 112.

30. *Ibid.*

31. *Ibid.*, 113.

32. Proceedings of the Senate and House of Representatives of the Fenian Joint Convention, Philadelphia, November 24–29, 1868, 14.

33. *Elizabeth Daily Journal*, August 18, 1880, 1.

34. JHON, 8.

35. Fitzpatrick as double agent in O'Cathaoir, 187.

36. O'Neill's speaking tour in the Midwest and East found in the *Irish American Weekly*, February 6, 1869. O'Neill's southern tour reported in the *Irish-American, New Orleans Republican, Mobile Register*, and *Louisville Journal*, among others, from May through June.

37. The shooting of Meehan led to national news, the majority of which came from *The United Irishman* on March 12, 1870, and *The Irish-American* on March 19, 1870, continuing for weeks. O'Neill's response was also in the March 19 *Irish-American*. The *New York Herald* also provided complete coverage each week in March 1870. The news was reported and read as far away as *The San Francisco Chronicle, The Cleveland Plain Dealer*, and the *Mobile Register*.

38. Walker, 184.

39. Steward, 200.

Chapter 8

1. A.M. Sullivan, ed., *American-Irish Historical Society* (1965), 15.

2. Le Caron, 79.

3. D'Arcy, 344.

4. Le Caron, 78–9.

5. "Men of Ireland, I am ashamed of you. You have acted disgracefully today, but will have another chance," Neidhardt, 121.

6. Foster putting a gun to the head of O'Neill from Capt. John MacDonald, *Troublous Times in Canada: A History of the Fenian Raids* (Toronto: W.S. Johnston, 1910), 161.

7. *Ottawa Citizen*, May 28, 1870, 1.

8. "The men who framed and executed this last abortion of war-making," Ian Kenneally, *From the Earth, A Cry: The Story of John Boyle O'Reilly* (Cork: Collins Press, 2012), 121.

9. *South Carolina Phoenix*, July 24, 1870, 1.

10. O'Neill interview in jail, *Burlington Weekly Free Press*, July 12, 1870, 1.

11. *Ibid.*, 2.

12. John O'Neill, *Official Report of General John O'Neill on the Attempt to Invade Canada, May 25, 1870—Also a Report on the Battle of Ridgeway, Canada West, June 2, 1866* (New York: John Foster Publisher, 1870), 58.

13. Richard Gwynn, *Nation Maker: Sir John MacDonald: His Life, Our Times*, Vol. 2, 1869–1891 (Toronto: Random House Canada, 2011).

14. O'Neill, *O.R.*, 61.

15. *Elizabeth Daily Journal*, June 5, 1870.

16. O'Neill, *O.R.*, 7.

17. *Ibid.*, 6.

18. *Ibid.*, 9.

19. *Boston Herald*, August 4, 1870.

20. Record of St. Mary R.C. Fundraiser displayed in Rectory office, author copy.

21. Edwards, 95.

22. Brian Jenkins, *Fenians and Anglo-American Relations During Reconstruction* (Ithaca: Cornell University, 1969), 315.

23. O'Neill, *O.R.*, 60.

24. JHON, 9–10.

Chapter 9

1. Agreement with Savage Wing in letter from Windsor Prison, Sept. 7, 1870. Archive of the Catholic University, Washington, D.C.

2. "Any further attempt would be criminal," *O.R.*, 60.

3. O'Donoghue, the Metis, and the raid on Pembina from Joseph Kinsey Howard, *Strange Empire: The Story of Louis Riel, the Metis People, and Their Struggle for a Homeland on the Plains of the United States* (St. Paul: Minnesota Historical Press, 1994), 216–222; Patrick Steward and Bryan McGovern, *The Fenians: Irish Rebellion in the North Atlantic World, 1858–1876* (Knoxville: University of Tennessee Press, 2013), 208–211; Thomas Flanagan, *Louis Riel: Prophet of the New World* (Toronto: University of Toronto Press, 1979), 32–33; and Roy Johnson, *The Fenian "Invasion" of 1871* (Winnipeg: Historical and Scientific Society of Manitoba, 1952), 30–37.

4. Johnson, 33.

5. John J. Pritchett, "The Origins of the So-Called Fenian Raid on Manitoba," *Canadian Historical Review*, Vol. 10, No. 1 (March 1929), 37.

6. *Ibid.*, 39.

7. *Ibid.*

8. The O'Neill family move to East St. Louis from JHON, 12–13.

9. Johnson, 33.

10. Le Caron, 97–99, and Edwards, 101–102.

11. O'Neill "army" of men from Steward, 208–9.

12. Howard, 220.

13. Hereward Senior, 179.

14. Walker, 191, and *Chicago Tribune*, October 16, 1871.

15. *St. Paul Press*, October 23, 1871, 1.

16. Tom Curley from www.revolvy.com/thomascurley(wisconsin).

17. J.J. Donnelly from www.fortbenton.blogspot.com.

18. John Savage, "The Irish Cause on the Pacific Containing an Account of the Visit of

the Chief Executive of the Fenian Brotherhood on the Pacific Coast" (New York: American News Company, 1870), 35.

    19. Le Caron, 40.

Chapter 10

    1. *Middlebury Register* and *New York Star*, October 24, 1871.

    2. Edwards, 24.

    3. Walker, 185.

    4. Kilpatrick and O'Neill shared much. Both were New Jersey ex-cavalry officers, egotistical, and poor businessmen always looking for better finances. Kilpatrick allowed the Fenians' use of his farm in New Jersey as an arms cache, and O'Neill spent at least some time there in Sussex county writing letters to his constituents. See Le Caron, 79.

    5. W.H. Whelan, Omaha, Nebraska, October 28, 1919, at gravesite dedication.

    6. *Irish-American*, February 1878.

    7. Langan, 23.

    8. Lecture title from *St. Joseph Daily Gazette*, June 11, 1872, but was the same as many.

    9. Samuel Martin, *Kill-Cavalry: The Life of Union General Judson Kilpatrick* (Mechanicsburg, PA: Stackpole Books, 2000), 250–259.

    10. *St. Joseph Daily Gazette*, June 11, 1872.

    11. 1873 Great Depression found in Edwin Burrows and Mike Wallace, *Gotham: A History of New York City to 1898* (New York: Oxford University Press, 1998), 1021.

    12. *Iowa Evening Press*, June 21, 1872.

    13. *Missouri Democrat*, September 12, 1872.

    14. Letter from Patrick Crow to Mary Ann O'Neill, from O'Neill/Martin family records, author copy. A search for Patrick Crow after January 3 was inconclusive, despite a search by Grant Hamston of the State Library of Victoria. In 1873 Patrick would have been 57 and miners in particular were notorious for prospecting alone, often never heard from again in the Australian bush. Such was most likely his fate.

    15. William J. Hynes's history, O'Cathaoir, 337.

    16. O'Neill 1875 letter to William Joseph Hynes from O'Neill/Martin family, copy with author.

    17. *O'Neill Frontier*, July 1924.

Chapter 11

    1. The move to Omaha in JHON, 15–16.

    2. Patrick Fahy history in William Cutler, ed., "Andreas History of Nebraska, Holt County," Part 2, 5, www.kancoll.org.

    3. O'Neill and Fahy contract in *O'Neill Frontier*, July 4, 1924.

    4. *St. Joseph Daily Gazette*, November 25, 1873.

    5. *O'Neill Frontier*, July 4, 1924, 6.

    6. Le Caron, 40.

    7. *West Point Republican*, September 10, 1874.

    8. Bishop John Ireland and western immigration found in Marvin J. O'Connell, *John Ireland and the American Catholic Church* (St. Paul: Minnesota Historical Society, 1988), 136–145. Less charitably, Ireland's efforts found in Bridget Connelly's *Forgetting Ireland* (St. Paul: Borealis Books, 2003), 110–120.

    9. O'Connell, 138, and James P. Shannon, *Catholic Colonization on the Western Frontier* (New Haven: Yale University Press, 1957), 39.

    10. O'Connell, 143.

    11. Langan, 25, and *Omaha Herald*, April 1877.

12. Langan, 24.

13. Gerald Noonan, "A Characterization of General John O'Neill in the Light of His Colonizing Efforts in the State of Nebraska," unpublished thesis, St. Paul Seminary (1961), 27.

14. Original settlers found in Henry Casper, *History of the Catholic Church in Nebraska*, Vol. 3 (Milwaukee: Bruce Publishing, 1966), 12.

15. Gregory R. Passewitz, unpublished thesis, University of Nebraska (1973), 1.

16. "Some high ground is not worth taking," from *North and South of the River*, co-written by Christy Moore, Bono, and the Edge, 1995.

17. *O'Neill Frontier*, July 26, 1924.

18. Pension request, 1898, and JHON, 16.

19. JHON, 19.

20. "The land around the Elkhorn River is conceded to be as rich in fertility as any land in the state," Noonan, *Clogher Record*, 295, and Langan, 28.

21. Henry Casper, *History of the Catholic Church in Nebraska*, Vol. 3 (Milwaukee: Bruce Publishing Company, 1966), 26.

22. *Irish World* editorial, August 1874, 1.

23. Patrick Ford found in Aidan Clarke, *Dictionary of Irish Biography*, Vol. 3 (Cambridge University Press, 2009), 1054–56, and James Paul Rodechko, *Patrick Ford and His Search for America* (New York: Arno Press, 1976), 58–61.

24. John Atkinson found in Charles Chadman, *Cyclopedia of Law*, and *Detroit Free Press*, August 18, 1898.

25. O'Neill second group arrival found in *O'Neill Frontier*, June 26, 1924, and Sister Aquinta Martin, "The Catholic Colonization in the Diocese of Omaha, 1856–1890," unpublished thesis (1932), 23.

26. J.B. Donahue, *Omaha Bee*, February 24, 1952.

27. Noonan, *Clogher Record*, 33.

28. JHON, 21–22.

29. Noonan, *Clogher Record*, 24, and John O'Neill, "The Founding of O'Neill," *O'Neill Frontier*, August 28, 1924. Also, *The Irish World*, March 22, 1876.

30. Noonan, *Clogher Record*, 34.

31. O'Neill wooden frame home, JHON, 23.

32. *Daily Inter Ocean*, Vol. 4, Issue 9, 6.

33. *West Point Republican*, 1875.

34. O'Neill to E. Johnson, from Omaha, September 17, 1877.

35. JHON, 21.

36. O'Neill second letter to Johnson, December 30, 1875, from Burke's Hotel, Chicago.

37. O'Neill to Johnson, January 1876.

38. *Detroit Tribune*, March 1876.

39. *Omaha Herald*, May 12, 1876.

40. Noonan, *Clogher Record*, 42.

41. *Neligh Journal*, January 4, 1877.

42. *Ibid.*, January 11, 1877.

43. *Daily Morning Herald*, June 1876.

44. *O'Neill Frontier*, July 3, 1924.

45. O'Neill Manifesto, Philadelphia, December 8, 1876, 1.

46. *Ibid.*, 5.

47. *Ibid.*, 8.

48. *Ibid.*

49. *Ibid.*, 10.

50. *Ibid.*, 11.

51. *Ibid.*

52. *Ibid.*, 12.

53. John Rutherford's *The Fenian Conspiracy* (London: C. Keegan & Co., 1876), 310.

54. *Ibid.*, 307.
55. John O'Neill, "Address to the Officers and Members of the Fenian Brotherhood," February 27, 1868, 18.
56. *Catholic Benevolent Union Journal*, 1877.
57. Death of Catherine O'Neill from New Jersey Death Records, Trenton, NJ, and *Elizabeth Daily Journal*, December 27, 1876, 3.
58. *Scranton Sunday Free Press*, January 28, 1877.
59. *Ibid.*
60. The difficulty of recruiting in eastern PA in 1877 found in Thomas Brown, *Irish-American Nationalism*, 46–8.
61. JHON, 21.
62. *Ibid.*, 22.
63. John O'Neill letter to his son, March 11, 1877.
64. John O'Neill letter to Edward Johnson, April 24, 1877, from Burke's Hotel, Chicago.
65. Casper, 23.

Chapter 12

1. O'Neill letter to Johnson, September 17, 1877.
2. O'Neill sick in Little Rock on November 14, Casper, 32. It took him five days to travel the 800 miles to O'Neill, when he became sick again. Mary Ann then took him 180 miles to Omaha, where he was admitted.
3. Casper, 33, and *Irish-American*, January 8, 1878, 1.
4. Mary Ann O'Neill letter to young John Hugh from Omaha, November 24, 1877.
5. John Joseph O'Neill letter to his Aunt Mary Ann, January 7, 1878.
6. Le Caron, 99.
7. Edwards, 251.
8. D'Arcy, 285.
9. Captain John MacDonald, *Troublous Times in Canada* (Toronto: W.S. Johnston, 1910), 182.
10. Cutler, 6. www.kancoll.org.
11. Obituary of John O'Neill, *Nebraska Tribune*, January 12, 1878, 1.
12. Obituary of John O'Neill, *Chicago Irish Tribune*, January 8, 1878, 2.
13. John O'Neill obituary from the *Irish-American*, January 8, 1878, and February 15, 1878.

Chapter 13

1. *Des Moines Register*, May 15, 1878.
2. 3,665 deaths in Northern Ireland found in David McKittrick, ed., *Lost Lives: The Stories of the Men and Women and Children who died as a result of the Northern Irish Troubles* (Manchester, UK: Main Street Publishing, 1999).
3. Morgan, 149–152.
4. Mike Ruddy, *America's Irish Nationalists* published (2016), 18.
5. 150th Battle of Ridgeway History conference program in Buffalo, New York, June 2–3, 2016.
6. Neidhardt, 134–5.
7. Carl Wittke, *The Irish in America* (Baton Rouge: Louisiana State University, 1952), 158–9.
8. Miller, 336.
9. Patrick O'Sullivan, *The Creative Migrant* (New York: St. Martin's Press, 1994), 133.
10. *Tralee Chronicle* and *Killarney Echo*, June 14, 1870.

11. *New York Times*, February 9, 1877.

12. O'Sullivan, 137.

13. *Minneapolis Journal* editorial, January 6, 1900, 1.

14. Gerald Noonan, "A Character of General John O'Neill in the Light of His Colonizing Efforts in the State of Nebraska," unpublished thesis (1961), iii.

15. William Cutler, ed., "Andreas History of the State of Nebraska, Holt County," Part Two (1888). www.kancoll.org/books/andreas.

16. *Ibid.*, 4.

17. *Irish World*, February 11, 1893.

18. *O'Neill Frontier*, August 15, 1919.

19. *Ibid.*, May 9, 1895.

20. De Valera visit to Creighton University, Omaha, "Out of Old Nebraska," *The Columbus Journal*, February 16, 1971.

21. Edward Whelan speech at O'Neill monument, October 28, 1919. www.historicomaha.com/whelan.htlm.

22. "The General John O'Neill Association," *O'Neill Frontier*, June 13, 1924.

23. Jerry Howard, *O'Neill Frontier*, June 18, 1924.

24. Jerry Howard letter to editor, *O'Neill Frontier*, July 12, 1924.

25. T.V. Golden, *O'Neill Frontier*, August 28, 1924.

26. Mr. J.B. Donahue, "Second attempt to remove O'Neill body to O'Neill City, June 1924," *Omaha Bee*, February 21 and 24, 1952. Donahue also said the town was named in honor of the general only after a dispute.

Epilogue

1. "Either excessively worshipped, through indifference, to a vehement dislike," Noonan, iv.

2. The history of O'Neill's finances, land dealings, and property ownership undertaken by genealogist and retired Nebraskan forensic accountant, Linda Berney, over a three-month period in 2016 in Holt County, Greeley County, and Omaha.

3. *The Columbus Journal*, October 20, 1879.

4. "Born soldier," C.P. Stacey, 3.

5. John Boyko, *Blood and Daring: How Canada Fought the American Civil War and Forged A Nation* (Canada: Vintage Canada Edition, 2013), 242.

6. *Ibid.*, 256.

7. *Ibid.*, 247.

8. William Manchester about John Wayne found in *New York Times*, July 17, 1987.

9. *New York Daily News*, June 12, 1979, 5.

10. Emmet O'Connor's *Big Jim Larkin: Hero or Wrecker?* (Dublin: University College Dublin Press, 2015), 241. Similar comparisons also found in Donal Nevin, ed., *James Larkin: Lion of the Fold* (Dublin: Gill & MacMillan, 1998).

11. Comparison of O'Neill to Pearse can be found in Ruth Dudley Edwards, *Patrick Pearse: The Triumph of Failure*, 334–337.

12. *O'Neill Frontier*, March 20, 1969.

13. Noonan, *A Character of John O'Neill*, 53.

14. Civil War Pension request No. 575.926, 1898, filed by widow Mary Ann (O'Neill) Coughlin.

15. *Neligh Leader*, February 12, 1902.

16. The story of the O'Neill family following the general's death, a genealogical study by the author and confirmed by the O'Neill family of California, as well as letters over a fifty-year period by Ruth O'Neill, the general's youngest granddaughter, copies with the author.

Bibliography

Books

Aalen, F.H.A, Kevin Whelan, and Matthew Stout. *Atlas of the Irish Rural Landscape*. Toronto: University of Toronto Press, 1997. Volumes 1 and 2.

Akenson, Don. *An Irish History of Civilization*, Vols. 1 and 2. London: Granta Books, 2005.

Akenson, Donald. *The Irish in Ontario*. Canada: McGill-Queen's University Press, 1984.

Akenson, Donald Harman. *Being Had: Historians, Evidence, and the Irish in North America*. Ontario, P.D. Meany, 1985.

_____. *Small Differences: Irish Catholics and Irish Protestants, 1815–1922*. Montreal: McGill-Queen's University Press, 1988.

_____. *The United States and Ireland*. Cambridge: Harvard University Press, 1973.

Ambrose, Joe. *The Fenian Anthology*. Cork: Mercier Press, 2008.

Amos, Keith. *The Fenians in Australia, 1865–1880*. New South Wales: University of New South Wales Press, 1988.

Anonymous. *The City of Elizabeth, New Jersey, Illustrated*. Published by the *Elizabeth Daily Journal*, 1889.

Ash, Stephen V. *A Massacre in Memphis: The Race Riot that Shook the Nation One Year After the Civil War*. New York: Hill and Wang, 2013.

Axelrod, Alan. *The Battle of the Somme*. Connecticut: Rowman & Littlefield, 2016.

Baylor, Ronald H., ed. *The New York Irish*. Baltimore: Johns Hopkins Press, 1996.

Beatie, Russel H. *Army of the Potomac: McClellan Takes Command, September 1861–February 1862*, Vols. 1 and 2. Cambridge: Da Capo Press, 2004.

Berkeley, G.F.H. *The Irish Battalion in the Papal Army of 1860*. Dublin: Talbot Press, 1929.

Bigler, David L. and Will Bagley. *The Mormon Rebellion: America's First Civil War, 1858*. Norman: University of Oklahoma Press, 2011.

Blessing, Patrick. *The Irish in America: A Guide to the Literature and the Manuscript Collections*. Washington, D.C.: Catholic University Press, 1992.

Bourne, Kenneth. *Britain and the Balance of Power in North America, 1815–1908*. Berkley: University of California Press, 1967.

Boyce, David George. *Nationalism in Ireland*. Baltimore: Johns Hopkins University, 1982.

Boyko, John. *Blood and Daring: How Canada Fought the American Civil War and Forged a Nation*. Canada: Vintage Canada Edition, 2013.

Brown, Thomas N. *Irish-American Nationalism*. Philadelphia: J.B. Lippincott, 1966.

Buck, Capt. Irving J. *Cleburne and His Command*. Jackson, TN: McCowat-Mercer Press, 1959.

Burchell, R.A. *The San Francisco Irish, 1848–1880*. Manchester, U.K.: Manchester University Press, 1979.

Campbell, Christy. *Fenian Fire: The British Government Plot to Assassinate Queen Victoria*. London: HarperCollins, 2002.

Carleton, William. *The Black Prophet*. New York: P.F. Collier, 1881.

Casey, Daniel J. and Robert Rhodes. *Views of the Irish Peasantry, 1800–1916*. Hamden, CT: Archon Books, 1977.

Casper, Henry W. J. *History of the Catholic Church in Nebraska*, Vol. 3. Milwaukee: Bruce Publishing Company, 1966.

Chernow, Ron, *Grant*. Penguin Press, 2017.

Clark, Brian P. *Piety and Nationalism: Lay Voluntary Associations and the Creation of an Irish-Catholic Community in Toronto, 1850–1895*.

Clark, Dennis. *Hibernia America: The Irish and Regional Cultures*. Connecticut: Greenwood Press, 1986.

_____. *The Irish in Philadelphia: Ten Generations of Urban Experience*. Philadelphia: Temple University Press, 1973.

Clarke, Aidan, ed. *The Dictionary of Irish Biography*. Cambridge University Press, 2009.

Cole, J.A. *Prince of Spies: Henri Le Caron*. London: Faber & Faber, 1984.

Coleman, Terry. *Going to America*. New York: Random House, 1972.

Comerford, R.V. *The Fenians in Context: Irish Politics and Society, 1848–1882*. Dublin: Irish Academic Press, 1998.

Connelly, Bridget. *Forgetting Ireland*. St. Paul: Borealis Books, 2003.

Coogan, Tim Pat. *Wherever Green Is Worn: The Story of the Irish Diaspora*. New York: Palgrave, 2000.

Creighton, Donald. *John MacDonald: The Old Chieftain*. Boston: Houghton-Mifflin, 1956.

Crowley, John, ed. *Atlas of the Great Irish Famine*. New York University Press, 2012.

D'Arcy, William. *The Fenian Movement in the United States*. New York: Russell & Russell, 1947.

Devoy, John. *Recollections of an Irish Rebel: A Personal Narrative*. New York: Chas. Young Company, 1929.

Dooley, Terence. *The Irish Revolution in Monaghan, 1912–23*. Dublin: Four Courts Press, 2017.

Dowling, Patrick. *California: the Irish Dream*. San Francisco: Golden Gate Publishers, 1989.

Drudy, P.J. *The Irish in America: Emigration, Assimilation and Impact*. Cambridge University Press, 1985.

Dubh, Scian (James McCarroll). *Ridgeway: An Historical Romance of the Fenian Invasion of Canada*. Miami: Hard Press Books, 2011.

Dungan, Myles. *How the Irish Won the West*. Dublin: New Island, 2006.

Dunn, J.F. *Recollections of the Battle of Ridgeway*. Ontario: Welland County Historical Society, 1926.

Edwards, Peter. *Delusion: The True Story of Victorian Superspy Henri Le Caron*. Toronto: Key Porter Books, 2005.

Edwards, Ruth Dudley. *Patrick Pearse: The Triumph of Failure*. Dublin: Irish Academic Press, 2006.

_____. *The Seven: The Lives and Legacies of the Founding Fathers of the Irish Republic*. London: One World Press, 2016.

Egan, Timothy. *The Immortal Irishman: The Irish Revolutionary Who Became an American Hero*. New York: Houghton Mifflin Harcourt, 2016.

Elliot, Bruce S. *Irish Migrants in the Canadas: A New Approach*. Montreal: McGill-Queen's University Press, 1988.

Emmons, David M. *Beyond the American Pale: The Irish in the West, 1845–1910*. Norman: University of Oklahoma Press, 2010.

English, Richard. *Irish Freedom: The History of Nationalism in Ireland*. London: Macmillan, 2007.

Ferriter, Diarmaid. *A Nation and Not a Rabble: The Irish Revolution, 1913–1923*. New York: Overlook Press, 2015.

Fitzgerald, Margaret E. and Joseph King. *The Uncounted Irish in Canada and the United States*. Toronto: P.D. Meany, 1991.

Flanagan, Thomas. *Louis David Riel: Prophet of the New World*. Toronto: University of Toronto Press, 1979.

Flood, Nicholas Davin. *The Irishman in Canada*. Ireland: Irish University Press, 1969.

Flynn, Joseph. *The Catholic Church in New Jersey*. Morristown, NJ: 1904.

Fox, Tom. *Hidden History of the Irish in New Jersey*. Charleston: History Press, 2011.

Funchion, Michael F. *Irish American Voluntary Organizations*. Westport, CT: Greenwood Press, 1983.

Gibson, Florence E. *The Attitudes of the New York Irish Toward State and National Affairs, 1848–1892*. New York: Columbia University Press, 1951.

Glazier, Michael, ed. *The Encyclopedia of the Irish in America*. Indiana: University of Notre Dame Press, 1999.

Golway, Terry. *Irish Rebel: John Devoy and America's Fight for Ireland's Freedom*. New York: St. Martin's Press, 1998.

Groh, George W. *Gold Fever*. New York: William Morrow & Co., 1966.

Gwyn, Richard. *John A: The Man Who Made Us*. Toronto: Vintage Books, 2007.

_____. *Nation Maker: Sir John A. MacDonald: His Life, Our Times, 1867–1891*, Vol. 2. Toronto: Random House Canada, 2011.

Hanigan, Dave. *De Valera in America: The Rebel President and the Making of Irish Independence*. New York: Palgrave, 2010.

Harmon, Maurice. *Fenians and Fenianism*. Seattle: University of Washington Press, 1970.

Hastings, Earl C., Jr. *A Pitiless Rain: The Battle of Williamsburg, 1862*. Shippensburg, PA: White Mane Publishing, 1997.

Heaney, Seamus. *New Selected Poems, 1966–1987*. London: Faber & Faber, 1990.

Hearne, John M., ed. *Thomas Francis Meagher: The Making of an Irish American*. Dublin: Irish Academic Press, 2005.

Howard, Joseph Kinsey. *Strange Empire: The Story of Louis Riel, the Metis People, and Their Struggle for a Homeland on the Plains of the United States-Canada Border*. St. Paul: Minnesota Historical Society Press, 1994.

Jenkins, Brian. *Fenians and Anglo-American Relations During Reconstruction*. Ithaca, NY: Cornell University Press, 1969.

_____. *Irish Nationalism and the British State*. Montreal: McGill-Queen's University Press, 2006.

Joslyn, Muriel Phillips, ed. *A Meteor Shining Brightly: Essays on Major General Patrick R. Cleburne*. Milledgeville, GA: Terrell House Publishing, 1999.

Joyce, P.W. *Irish Names of Places*, Vols. 1, 2, and 3. Dublin: DeBurca Publishing, 1995.

Kavanagh, Patrick. *Collected Poems*. New York: W.W. Norton, 2007.

Kelley, Frank Bergen. *Historic Elizabeth, 1664–1914*. Published by the *Elizabeth Daily Journal*, 1914.

Kenneally, Ian. *From the Earth, a Cry: The Story of John Boyle O'Reilly*. Cork, Ireland: Collins Press, 2009.

Kenny, Kevin. *The American Irish: A History*. New York: Pearson Education Press, 2000.

Kerrigan, Gene. *The Scrap: A True Story from the 1916 Rising*. Dublin: Transworld Ireland Publishing, 2015.

Langley, Harold D. *To Utah with the Dragoons and Glimpses of Life in Arizona and California, 1858–1859*. Salt Lake City: University of Utah Press, 1974.

Le Caron, Henri. *Twenty-Five Years in the Secret Service: The Recollections of a Spy*. London: William Heinemann, 1892.

Livingstone, Peadar. *The Monaghan Story*. Monaghan: Clogher Historical Society, 1980.

Loughery, John. *Dagger John: Archbishop John Hughes and the Making of Irish America*. Ithaca, NY: Cornell University Press, 2018.

MacDonagh, Oliver and W.F. Mandle. *Ireland and Irish-Australia: Studies in Cultural and Political History*. London: Croom Held, 1986.

MacDonald, Capt. John A. *Troublous Times in Canada: A History of the Fenian Raids of 1866 and 1870*. Toronto: W.S. Johnston, 1910.

MacDonald, Darach. *Hard Border: Walking Through a Century of Irish Partition*. Dublin: New Island, 2018.

MacDonald, Helen G. *Canadian Public Opinion on the American Civil War*. New York: Columbia University Press, 1925.

Martin, Samuel J. *Kill-Cavalry: The Life of Union General Hugh Judson Kilpatrick*. Mechanicsburg, PA: Stackpole Books, 2000.

McCafferty, Lawrence J. *Textures of Irish America*. Syracuse, NY: Syracuse University Press, 1992.

McGoogan, Ken. *Celtic Lightning: How the Scots and Irish Created a Canadian Nation*. Toronto: HarperCollins, 2015.

McGuire, James and James Quinn, eds. *Dictionary of Irish Biography: From the Earliest Times to the Year 2002*, Vol. 7. Cambridge: Royal Irish Academy, 2009.

McKittrick, David, ed. *Lost Lives: The Stories of the Men, Women, and Children Who Died as a Result of the Northern Irish Troubles*. Manchester, UK: Main Street Publishing, 1999.

Metress, Seamus. *The Irish in North America: A Regional Bibliography*. Toronto: P.D. Meany.

Miller, Kirby. *Emigrants and Exiles: Ireland and the Irish Exiles to North America*. New York: Oxford University Press, 1985.

Monaghan, Jay. *Australians and the Gold Rush: California and Down Under, 1849–1854*. Los Angeles: University of California Press, 1966.

Morgan, Jack. *Through American and Irish Wars: The Life and Times of General Thomas W. Sweeny, 1820–1892*. Dublin: Irish Academic Press, 2005.

Morris, Roy, Jr. *Sheridan: The Life and Wars of General Phil Sheridan*. New York: Crown Publishers, 1992.

Murray, Nicholas. *Notes, Historical and Biographical, Concerning Elizabeth-Town, Its Eminent Men, Churches and Ministers*. Elizabeth, NJ: E. Sanderson, 1844.

Neidhardt, W.S. *Fenianism in North America*. University Park: Penn State University Press, 1975.

Nevin, Donal. *James Connolly: A Full Life*. Dublin: Gill & Macmillan, 2005.

_____. *James Larkin: Lion of the Fold*. Dublin: Gill & Macmillan, 1998.

Newark, Tim. *The Fighting Irish*. New York: Thomas Dunne Books, 2012.

O'Brien, Gillian. *Blood Runs Green: The Murder That Transfixed Gilded Age Chicago*. Chicago: University of Chicago Press, 2015.

O'Broin, Leon. *Fenian Fever: An Anglo-American Dilemma*. New York University Press, 1971.

O'Cathaoir, Eva. *Soldiers of Liberty: A Study of Fenianism, 1858–1908*. Dublin: Lilliput Press, 2018.

O'Concubhair, Padraig. *"The Fenians Were Dreadful Men": The 1867 Rising*. Cork, Ireland: Mercier Press, 2011.

O'Connell, Marvin R. *John Ireland and the American Catholic Church*. St. Paul: Minnesota Historical Society Press, 1988.

O'Driscoll, Robert and Lorna Reynolds, eds. *The Untold Story: The Irish in Canada*, Vols. 1 and 2. Toronto: Celtic Arts of Canada, 1988.

O'Farrell, Patrick. *The Irish in Australia*. Kensington, New South Wales: University of New South Wales Press, 1987.

O'Grady, Joseph P. *How the Irish Became Americans*. New York: Twayne Publishers, 1973.

O'Neill, Joseph. *The Manchester Martyrs*. Cork, Ireland: Mercier Press, 2012.

O'Sullivan, Patrick. *The Creative Migrant*. London: Leicester University Press, 1994.

Oursler, Fulton and Will Oursler. *Father Flanagan of Boys Town*. Garden City, NY: Doubleday, 1949.

Rodechko, James Paul. *Patrick Ford and His Search for America: A Case Study of Irish-American Journalism*. New York: Arno Press, 1976.

Rose, Paul. *The Manchester Martyrs: The Story of a Fenian Tragedy*. London: Lawrence & Wishart, 1970.

Ruddy, Michael. *The Collapse of the Fenian Brotherhood and the Rise of the Clan-na-Gael*. Pittsburgh: Self Published, 2018.

Rutherford, John. *The Secret History of the Fenian Conspiracy*. London: C. Kegan & Co., 1877.

Ryan, Desmond. *The Fenian Chief: A Biography of James Stephens*. Coral Gables: University of Miami Press, 1967.

Savage, John. *Fenian Heroes and Martyrs*. New York: P. Donahue, 1868.

Sears, Stephen W. *George B. McClellan: The Young Napoleon*. New York: Ticknor & Fields, 1988.

_____. *To the Gates of Richmond: The Peninsula Campaign*. New York: Ticknor & Fields, 1992.

Senior, Hereward. *The Last Invasion of Canada: The Fenian Raids, 1866–1870*. Toronto: Dundurn Press, 1991.

Shannon, James P. *Catholic Colonization on the Western Frontier*. New Haven: Yale University Press, 1957.

Shaw, A.G.L. *Convicts and the Colonies: A Study of Penal Transportation from Great Britain and Ireland to Australia*. London: Faber & Faber, 1966.

Senkewicz, Robert M. *Vigilantes in Gold Rush San Francisco*. Stanford: Stanford University Press, 1985.

Slattery, T.P. *The Assassination of Thomas D'Arcy McGee*. Toronto: Oxford University Press, 1920.

_____. *"They Got to Find Mee Guilty Yet."* Toronto: Doubleday Canada, 1972.

Snay, Michael. *Fenians, Freedmen and Southern Whites*. Baton Rouge: Louisiana State University Press, 2007.

Stanley, George. *The Birth of Western Canada*. Toronto: University of Toronto Press, 1992.

Steward, Patrick and Bryan McGovern. *The Fenians: Irish Rebellion in the North Atlantic World, 1858–1876*. Knoxville: University of Tennessee, 2013.

Stewart, A.T.Q. *The Shape of Irish History*. Montreal: McGill-Queen's University Press, 2001.

Sword, Wiley. *Embrace an Angry Wind: The Confederacy's Last Hurrah: Spring Hill, Franklin, and Nashville*. New York: HarperCollins, 1992.

Tansill, Charles Callan. *America and the Fight for Irish Freedom, 1866–1922*. New York: Devin-Adair Co., 1957.

Toibin, Colm. *Walking Along the Border*. London: Queen Anne's Press, 1987.

United States War Department. *The War of Rebellion: A Compilation of the Official Records of the Union and Confederate Armies*. Washington, D.C.: U.S. Government Printing Office.

Vronsky, Peter. *Ridgeway: The American Fenian Invasion and the 1866 Battle That Made Canada*. Toronto: Allen Lane Canada, 2011.

Walker, Mabel Gregory. *The Fenian Movement*. Colorado Springs: Ralph Myles, 1969.

Warner, M.M. *Warner's History of Dakota County, Nebraska: From the Days of the First Pioneers and First Settlers*. Dakota City, NE: Lyons Mirror Job Office, 1893.

White, Lawrence William and James Quinn. *1916: Portraits and Lives*. Dublin: Royal Irish Academy, 2015.

Wilson, David A. *Irish Nationalism in Canada*. Montreal: McGill-Queen's University Press, 2009.

_____. *Thomas D'Arcy McGee*, Vols. 1 and 2. Montreal: McGill-Queen's University Press, 2008, 2011.

_____. *United Irishmen, United States: Immigrant Radicals in the Early Republic*. Ithaca, NY: Cornell University Press, 1998.

Wittke, Carl. *The Irish in America*. Baton Rouge: Louisiana State University Press, 1956.

Wylie, Paul R. *The Irish General: Thomas Francis Meagher*. Norman: University of Oklahoma Press, 2007.

Yost, Nellie Snyder. *Before Today: The History of Holt County, Nebraska*. O'Neill, NE: Miles Publishing Company, 1976.

Articles and Manuscripts

American Civil War Database. http://www.civilwardata.com.

Ancestry.com. "Census Records, 1840–1940." http://www.ancestry.com.

_____. "U.S. City Directories, 1822–1995." Provo, UT: 2011.

Brusher, Joseph S. "The Fenian Invasion of Canada" (unpublished thesis). St. Louis University, 1943.

Buckley, Benjamin Clyde. "The Fenians and Anglo-American Relations after the Civil War" (Master's thesis). Kansas State University, 1973.

Chorley, Jasmine. "The Green Ghost over the Red River." http://jasminechorley.wordpress.com. February 2, 2015.

Clark, Dennis. "Militants of the 1860s: The Philadelphia Fenians." *Pennsylvania Magazine of History and Biography*, 1971.

Colonial Office. Correspondence of the Governor-General of Canada, Series 537. Supplementary Correspondence: Canada. Public Record Office, London, 101.

D'Angelo, Anthony Tyler. "The 1866 Fenian Raid on Canada West: A Study of Colonial Perceptions and Reactions Towards the Fenians in the Confederation Era" (unpublished Master's thesis). Queen's University, 2009.

Dunn, J.F. "Recollections of the Battle of Ridgeway." *Welland County Historical Society*, Vol. 2 (1926), 50–56.

Gallagher, Francis. "The Francis Gallagher Papers." Wynnewood, PA: Philadelphia Archdiocesan Historical Research Center.

Gevinson, Alan. "What Happened to the Fenians after 1866?" http://teachinghistory.org.

Gibbons, James. "Address to the Centres and Circles of the F.B. of Penna." Philadelphia: 1866.

Harrison, Paul. "Record Group 94: Records of the Adjutant General's Office, Entry 91A: Series 1 Enlistment Papers (John O'Neill)." Washington, D.C.: National Archives, 2014.

"History and Growth of St. Boniface Parish, 1902–1977." Elgin, NE: 1978.

"John Boyle O'Reilly and the 1870 Fenian Invasion of Canada." *Irish History Online*. http:www.theirishstory.com

Johnson, Roy. "The Fenian 'Invasion' of 1871." Winnipeg: Historical and Scientific Society of Manitoba, 1952. 30–37.

King, Clyde L. "The Fenian Movement." *The University of Colorado Studies* (April 1909), 187–213.

Langan, Sister Mary M. "General John O'Neill: Soldier, Fenian, and Leader of Irish Catholic Colonization in America" (unpublished Master's thesis). Notre Dame University, 1937.

Lester, DeeGee. "Tennessee's Bold Fenian Men." *Tennessee Historical Quarterly* (Winter 1997), 262–277.

Lewis, J.G.W. "Who's Who 1940 Holt County." http://www.rootsweb.ancestry.com.

Lynn, Shane. "Before the Fenians: 1848 and the Irish Plot to Invade Canada." *Eire-Ireland*, Vol. 51 (Spring/Summer 2016), 61–91.

Martin, Sister Aquinta. "Irish Catholic Colonization in the Diocese of Omaha, 1856–1890" (unpublished Master's thesis). University of Notre Dame, 1932.

Civil War Pension Files, Regular Army Records, National Archives Records Administration, Washington, D.C.

Nebraska State Historical Society. "General John O'Neill." Lincoln, NE: 2000.

Noonan, Gerald. "A Chapter on General John O'Neill." *Clogher Record*, 1967.

_____. "A Character of General John O'Neill in the Light of His Colonizing Efforts in the State of Nebraska, 1872–1878" (unpublished thesis). Saint Paul Seminary, 1961.

O'Brien, Michael, ed. "General Tom Sweeny's Report to the Fenians 1866." *The Journal of the American Irish Historical Society*, Vol. XIII (1924).

O'Neill, John. "Address to the Officers and Members of the Fenian Brotherhood." February 27, 1868.

_____. "Northern Nebraska as a Home for Immigrants." *Sioux City Times*, 1875.

_____. "O'Neill's Personal Account of the Founding of O'Neill, Nebraska." Reproduced in the Semi-Centennial Edition of *The Frontier*, July 3–Aug. 28, 1924.

O'Neill, John C. "Official Report of Gen. John O'Neill on the Attempt to Invade Canada, May 25, 1870—Also a Report on the Battle of Ridgeway, Canada West, June 2, 1866." New York: John Foster, 1870.

_____. "1876 O'Neill Manifesto." December 8, 1876.

Passewitz, Gregory R. "O'Neill Nebraska, the First Century" (unpublished thesis). University of Nebraska at Omaha, 1973.

Peterman, Michael. "James McCarroll." October 10, 2011. http://thecanadianencyclopedia.com.
Pieper, Ezra Henry. "The Fenian Movement" (unpublished thesis). University of Illinois, 1931.
Pritchett, John Perry. "The Origins of the So-Called Fenian Revolt on Manitoba." *Canadian Historical Review*, No. 1, Vol. 10 (1929), 23–42.
Robson, Ken. "Larger Than Life Frontier Character, Colonel John J. Donnelly." Historical Fort Benton Blog, January 28, 2012. http://fortbentonblog.com.
Savage, John. "The Irish Cause on the Pacific; containing an account of the visit of the chief executive, F.B. to the Pacific Coast." *American News Company* (1870), 35.
Stacy, C.P. "Confederation: The Atmosphere of Crisis." Toronto: Ontario Historical Society, 1967.
_____. "The Fenian Paladin: The Story of John O'Neill" (unpublished biography). Toronto Library.
Sweeny, Thomas William. "Thomas William Sweeny Papers, 1865–1941." Manuscript and Archives Division, New York Public Library.
Sweeny, William M. "The Fenian Invasion of Canada, 1866." *American-Irish Historical Society Journal*, Vol. XXIII (1924), 193.
Warfield, Derek. "John O'Neill and the Fenian Invasion of Canada." *An Phoblacht*. Ferghal O'Hanlon Memorial Lecture, 2000.
Whelan, E.H. "Dedication of Monument at Gravesite of General John O'Neill." October 28, 1919. http://www.historyofomaha.com.
Wilson, David A. "The Fenians in Canada." Canada Library and Archives, University of Toronto.

Newspapers

Boston Evening Transcript
Boston Herald
Boston Pilot
Brooklyn Eagle
Buffalo Commercial
Buffalo Courier
Burlington Weekly Free Press
Chicago Daily Inter Ocean
Chicago Daily Tribune
Chicago Irish Republic
Chicago Irish Tribune
Cincinnati Enquirer
Cleveland Plain Dealer
Columbus (OH) Daily Telegram
Davenport (IA) Daily Gazette
Decatur Republican
Detroit Tribune
Dixon (IL) Telegraph
Dubuque Times
Elizabeth Daily Journal
Fort Wayne Sentinel
Green Bay Gazette
Holt County Frontier
Holt County (NE) Independent
Indianapolis News
Irish World
Irish (NY) Voice
Lincoln (NE) Journal

Louisville Courier-Journal
Memphis Daily Appeal
Middlebury (VT) Register
Missouri Daily Democrat
Mobile Register (AL)
Montreal Gazette
Montreal Herald
Nashville Morning Times
Nashville Press and Advertiser
Nebraska Tribune
Neligh (NE) Leader
New York Gaelic American
New York Herald
New York Irish-American
New York Star
New York Times
Newark Advertiser
Niobrara (NE) Tribune
Omaha Bee
Omaha World-Herald
Philadelphia Inquirer
St. Joseph (MO) Daily Gazette
St. Paul Daily Press
St. Paul Pioneer Press
San Diego Union Tribune
San Francisco Chronicle
Scranton Free Press
Sydney (Australia) Morning Herald
Toronto Leader
Washington Times
Washington (D.C.) Evening Star
Waterloo Daily Courier
West Point (NE) Republican

Index

Numbers in *bold italics* indicate pages with illustrations